D1446939

Studies in Sociology

Edited by

PROFESSOR W. M. WILLIAMS

University College, Swansea

4

THE FAMILY

STUDIES IN SOCIOLOGY

1 The Sociology of Industry
by S. R. Parker, R. K. Brown, J. Child, M. A. Smith

2 Urban Sociology
by Professor R. N. Morris

3 Demographic Analysis
by Bernard Benjamin

Social Stratification
by James Littlejohn

Social Statistics
by Bleddyn Davies

Community Studies
by Professor W. M. Williams

Political Sociology
by Philip Abrams

THE FAMILY

AN INTRODUCTION

C. C. Harris

University College, Swansea
Author 'The Family and Social Change'
(with Colin Rosser)

London
GEORGE ALLEN AND UNWIN LTD
RUSKIN HOUSE . MUSEUM STREET

FIRST PUBLISHED IN 1969
SECOND IMPRESSION 1970

SBN 04 301019 9 *cloth*
SBN 04 301020 2 *paper*

PRINTED IN GREAT BRITAIN
in 10 on 11 point Plantin type
BY WILLMER BROTHERS LIMITED
BIRKENHEAD

PREFACE

The task of the textbook writer is not an easy one. This book will be found by many to be profoundly unsatisfactory because it both omits discussion of certain issues and ignores certain bodies of material. In particular, I am aware of having failed to do justice to the richness of the vast range of American studies, and to much fascinating and important data on family behaviour throughout the non-European world. I have tried to focus on Britain and Europe in so far as the data are concerned, and to cover what I consider to be the central theoretical issues.

The task of textbook writers in sociology is made even more onerous by the large number of different theoretical approaches adopted by writers in any one field. Because I believe a textbook should be argumentative and stimulating, I have chosen one of these approaches and stuck to it throughout this book. This has, I believe, the advantage of giving the reader an overview of the field from a single stand-point. It has also the effect of making the text critical of certain authors and certain points of view. I have tried as far as possible to criticize arguments and not people; and where I have, in the course of discussion, criticized the work of one man, it is because I consider the work's importance and quality so great as to require treatment in detail.

I do not doubt that in pressing my point of view I have sometimes inadvertently misrepresented my 'antagonist'—and I beg both his pardon and that of the reader. I hope that the latter will find what I have written a useful guide to those authors whose work I discuss, and that he will make up his own mind about the quality and accuracy of my account after reading such authors for himself.

The time has not yet come, though it is rapidly approaching, when it will be possible for one author to do justice simultaneously to the approaches and materials of both sociology and anthropology. I fear that what I have written may infuriate both sociologists and anthropologists; the former because my account is 'too anthropological', and the latter because my necessarily summary treatment fails to do justice to the intricacies of anthropological thought. I have tried, however inadequately, to give the reader some notion of the range of variation in kinship behaviour, since I believe that it is only through an appreciation of this diversity that it is possible to arrive at any theoretical understanding of the Western family system.

I have been greatly assisted in this task by Robin Fox's excellent introduction to the anthropological study of kinship, and Chapter

Two in particular owes a great deal to his extraordinarily clear exposition of exceedingly complex matters.

I also wish to record my thanks to Dr Maurice Bloch, whose views on certain anthropological issues acted as a great stimulus to me at the time when I began the writing of this book; to Professor W. M. Williams for his delicate advice; to Mrs M. Stacey with whom I argued out some of the implications of bilateral kinship systems; to Dr Colin Rosser, under whom I served an apprenticeship in the study of the family; and to Dr J. B. Loudon for listening to my rantings about those with whom I disagreed. To all these, and to all those whose works are so inadequately reflected in the following pages, I offer my apologies that this book is no better than it is.

C.C.H.

CONTENTS

PRELIMINARIES

The purpose of this preliminary chapter is to say something about the nature of sociology as an academic discipline. Many readers of this book will not be students of sociology and it may be helpful to them if they have some notion of what sociological study involves in general. For others it will provide a guide to the theoretical viewpoint of the author and thus enable them to evaluate the strengths and weaknesses of his general sociological approach by locating it on the map of sociological theory. It is important that the reader should recognize that a work of this kind does represent an approach, and only one of many possible approaches, to a field of study. It should, therefore, be approached critically and its conclusions and the opinions expressed within it compared with those of other writers. The reader should recognize that if he chooses to cite and attribute an opinion expressed in this book, he is citing one informed opinion among other more or less informed opinions, and not an authority.

THE NATURE OF SOCIOLOGICAL STUDY

By the meaning of the word, sociology is concerned with the study of societies. This as a definition is not however very helpful since it is not very clear either to most people or even to most sociologists what is meant by, or how it is useful to define, 'a society'. What is obviously being referred to here is the fact that men everywhere and at all known times have lived in groups, lived 'in society'—that is in association with one another—and do not seem to be able to survive as men except in some form of association. To say that men live in social groups is to recognize that men share certain things with others over and above physical proximity and similar biological characteristics. The most distinctive and important element in this 'something more' is language. Language both distinguishes men from animals, and at the same time, is distinctively social. People belonging to the same language group share the same language by virtue of having been born into an already existent group whose members speak that language. They acquire the language by interacting with other people who speak it. Possession of the language makes it possible for them to think, that is to relate the concepts and ideas connoted by the words they use. So being a man—which involves being a thinking, talking animal—involves being a member of a social group which has certain ways of behaving which it teaches to new recruits (children), thus making them members of the group.

It is as true, however, that language makes it possible for men to form groups as it is that language, possessed by a group, makes it possible for men to be men. Without the possession of language any but the simplest interaction between men is impossible. Consequently, it is impossible to develop any but the most rudimentary common ways of acting together. For in order to co-act or co-operate with anyone it is necessary either to know what he is going to do, because he is following some sort of agreed procedure which must be expressed in words, or because continued communication between the parties is possible. When we speak of a SOCIAL GROUP we are usually referring to a plurality of people who share common ways of behaving other than speaking; but their sharing common ways of behaving will depend on their sharing a common language.

When we speak of 'a society' therefore, we are referring, amongst other things, to a collection of regularities in the way a group of people behave which derive from their following common rules of behaviour couched in their common language. Perhaps here it will be helpful to give an example. Any transport system involves the co-operation of a large number of people: different types of transport workers and the public. We, as members of the public, are enabled to use the transport system because we have learnt the rules which govern the behaviour of the transport workers. Hence we expect the bus to stop at some sorts of bus stop without any action on our part; we expect it to stop only if we hail it at others. We expect a bus conductor to ask for money when we board his bus and so on. But in order to use the system we have to be able to distinguish buses from other types of vehicles, and bus conductors from other passengers. There must also be consistency between what the bus conductor expects of a passenger and what a passenger expects of a bus conductor. But the distinction between bus conductor and passenger depends on the rules governing the use of these terms—that is the language—and upon both parties following the same rules.

Hence, in order to participate in the pattern of ordered activity which we call 'the transport system', we have to share the expectations and concepts of those others participating in the same system. We could not participate in, and people could not co-operate together to constitute, such a system unless they shared the same way of categorizing people and the same expectations as to the behaviour of people in those categories. We could say, therefore, that sociology is the study of the languages and rules which govern the behaviour of members of social groups.

This will not do, however. As I write this, the railway workers are 'going slow'.[1] That is, of course, to say that they are following one set of rules, which they usually break, and as a result breaking another set of rules they usually keep. Now without discussing this interesting case in detail, it is worth noting that sudden changes in regular behaviour of this kind are of great interest to sociologists, and constitute phenomena which the sociologist is rightly called upon to help explain. It is also worth pointing out that very often the situation is far more complicated than we have allowed so far, there being many sets of rules and values, by no means entirely consistent, which can be used as guides to action by individuals or subgroups within a group at any given time. Hence, simply to describe all these and trace their inter-relations with one another does not by itself necessarily enable us fully to understand why people act in the way they do.

Sociology is therefore concerned both with the beliefs and values and rules that groups of men share *and* the way in which the men act in the light of those beliefs, rules and values. This will not quite do either. In our concern for the social world, we have somehow left out of account the non-social world, the stage so to speak on which the social drama takes place. Men have to eat and drink and clothe themselves if they are to survive and they have to produce and rear children if the society or group is to survive. These are 'the facts of life' which apply to all men everywhere. However, the conditions under which they do these things will obviously vary. Hence the situation in which men are placed involves the need to satisfy certain basic needs under certain environmental conditions. The beliefs and values that men share will inevitably refer to these basic conditions of life. They are ways of making sense out of the situation in which they find themselves. There may be many different ways of making sense of the scame situation. However, the sense they make of it and the concepts they use will have to be such as to permit of social arrangements which are good enough to provide for the survival both of the individuals who make up the group and the group itself.

Sociology is, therefore, the study of the sense men make of their situation, and the way in which regularities in the way they behave to each other are related to that shared sense. If we want to explain

[1] To follow a rigid and extremely literal interpretation of the rules governing job performance in order to force the employer to accede to some request made to him by the workers.

why it is that a given group has available to it at a given time a particular set of ideas and values, we shall have to refer to the non-social conditions under which these ideas make the sort of sense that enables men to act together under those conditions. We shall also have to use some sort of historical explanation to explain how it has come about that they make sense of their situation in the way that they do and not in some other equally possible way.

If we want to explain why it is that a given group behaves in a given way at a given time, we shall have to refer to the ideas that happen to be available to the group at that time, which will in part determine what they *choose* to do. We shall also have to refer to the conditions which actually face them, and under which they act, which will determine what they *can* do.

To make this clearer a simple example may be helpful. Let us suppose we have a situation in which a number of people live close together in a part of a certain town. Apart from sharing their place of residence they also share the characteristic of being poor, and have therefore incomes which make it difficult for them to live lives which they consider decent and comfortable, without over-spending their income. To say this is to imply of course that they share something else besides common residence and poverty: they share also beliefs about what are minimum standards of comfort and decency. They are trying therefore to achieve certain things, which are defined by the ideas which they share, under certain material conditions. Because it is difficult to achieve the living standards they want, the households in the neighbourhood frequently spend their income before the next week's wages are due. Hence, in order to last out until the end of the week, they need to borrow. Now borrowing implies that someone else is willing to lend, and people will be willing to lend only if they know that they can borrow in return. Hence if people are to deal with the situation by borrowing, they will have to come to some agreement among themselves as to the *rightness* of borrowing in this situation. They will have to regard borrowing as *legitimate*.

Whether they will so regard borrowing will depend on other ideas and values which they have. If they believe that it is your *duty* to cut your coat according to your cloth, to manage on whatever you have; if they believe that those with higher incomes are in some way 'better' than those with lower incomes, then they may regard borrowing as a sign of extravagance, inefficiency and inferiority, and will therefore choose to do without rather than make a public admission of these faults by borrowing. If however they regard poverty as a curse inflicted by an inscrutable fate, and not related in any way to the merits of the individual; if they regard poverty as the illegitimate result of the exercise of power by other people, they may regard borrowing almost as a virtue—an affirmation that the borrower is one of 'us' rather than one of 'them', as a recognition of the need to stick together in the face of adverse circumstances.

In order to understand why a particular residential group practises and values borrowing between neighbours, one has to relate this both to the conditions under which they act and the values which determine the choice they make between different courses of action. But of course the values which make borrowing legitimate are themselves related to the conditions under which people act. Those who are not poor are less likely to regard poverty as an inevitable fact of life, while those who are poor and have consistently failed to improve their economic position are much more likely to regard poverty as inevitable rather than culpable.

Let us now take this example a little further. Suppose we found that, of two residential groups both of which were faced by the same economic conditions, and both of which had the same values, the members of one group borrowed from neighbours whereas the members of the other did not. How are we to explain this difference? Well, since the members of both are poor, and since both groups disvalue going without till the end of the week, it is reasonable to assume that the members of both borrow. If the members of one group do not borrow from neighbours, then they must borrow from someone else. From whom? The most likely answer is that they borrow from relatives who, though not neighbours, live near enough to be borrowed from. Here then we have two groups with the same values and acting under the same conditions of action, except for the presence of relatives in one case, the members of one of which borrow from neighbours whereas the members of the other do not.

Now it will not do to say that the differences between the two groups as regards borrowing from neighbours is due to the presence of relatives in one case. It will not do because it does not follow *by itself* that the presence of relatives will affect the pattern of borrowing from neighbours. To understand why the two groups differ, we have to add a further consideration: that people prefer to borrow from kin rather than neighbours. To say this is to recognize that people belong of course not to one but to many social groups, or to put it another way, society is composed of a large number of social groups, some of which overlap. The people who constitute the society share expectations, and frequently also values, concerning the way different groups do and should overlap, that is how memberships of different types of group are and should be combined and how members of different social groups do and should behave to each other. The actual overlap of any social group with other groups and the rules governing the behaviour of one group to another and regulating the membership of several groups or types of group are referred to by sociologists as the STRUCTURE of the society.

The position of any group or plurality of individuals within the structure of the society may be said to determine the social conditions of action of the individuals or group concerned. In our example there was no structural difference which produced the occurrence of a borrowing pattern. There was a difference in the non-social conditions of action; that is in the degree of geographical dispersal of kin. The effects of the variation in this condition are only understandable if we place the group in which we are interested in its structural context. Only if given certain social conditions, i.e. that members of the neighbourhood group have relationships with relatives, and that they think it right to borrow from relatives rather than neighbours, will a difference in the non-social conditions of action (the dispersal of relatives) produce a difference in borrowing from neighbours.

Sociology then is concerned not only with the sense that men make of their situation, and the way in which regularities in their behaviour are related to it, it is also concerned with the consequences of different types of behaviour for other types of behaviour, of the relation of one set of social rules to other sets of rules, and with the effect of the combination of different types of group membership. To come clean about this: sociology is concerned with both 'culture' and 'structure'. If these terms have been introduced rather late in this discussion this is not entirely for reasons of presentation. By avoiding referring too often to beliefs and values and stressing instead the sense that men make of a situation and the importance of language in the study of society, it is hoped that the reader has been prepared to recognize that explanations of why men behave as they do depend in large part on the way they categorize their experience.

If we ask 'what is that man doing?' and are told 'he is visiting a relative', then this 'explanation' of his behaviour implies that among all the individuals whom he knows, or knows of, he distinguishes a category or class of people whom he considers to be related to him, and that he visits such people because he so categorizes them. To understand this action we have to see that the man concerned *himself* categorizes his action as fulfilling one of a category of obligations which people have towards relatives; we also must relate his action to the idea which he has of 'being related to' somebody; to what he means by it. All social behaviour implies categorization of some kind: making distinctions between individuals which allow one to expect different things from them and to know which way one is expected to behave towards them. In our example there are not two distinct objects of study—an action (visiting relatives) and a set of beliefs and values about kinship, which can be considered independently of each other. If you do not understand the latter you do not know that he *is* 'visiting a relative'. The sense that he makes of his relatedness and the beliefs he has about it are inseparable from the actions he takes, whether or not they are in accordance with those beliefs.

Similarly one cannot talk about the structure of a society and its culture as if they were separate and distinct things. To recognize a relationship, to recognize a group membership, implies the ability to categorize and to make distinctions. It follows that the pattern of relationships in a society, the way in which the various groups which compose it overlap, is not a separate thing from the relations between the ideas and beliefs and values that members of that society share.

What sociology is about therefore is the ideas and beliefs and values and ways of acting which groups of men share; it is about the distinctions men draw between different categories of people; it is about the groups they form on the basis of these distinctions, and the relationships they enter into through the membership of groups. It is also about the conditions under which they act and the way those conditions affect their beliefs and actions and the consequences of those beliefs and actions for one another in those conditions.

The rest of this book, the reader will be relieved to be assured, is about the family (well, more or less) but it is to be hoped that the preceding discussion will have made it clear that it must concern the family in society. That is to say it must be concerned with the way in which the family is related to other categories and groups and to the processes which go on in society as a whole. Sociologically, at any rate, there is no other way in which the family can be understood.

PART I

1

Kinship

'I'VE just come back from visiting a relative in hospital.'

'What sort of relative?'

'Well, I'm not quite sure; she's connected with my parents, I know that. I think she's some sort of cousin. She used to come and visit Mum when we were kids; Auntie Florrie we used to call her. Of course she wasn't our auntie, that is not really. But she's definitely related—not close of course—but related.'

'Why did you go and see her?'

'Well, her being in hospital and that, you know, she could probably do with cheering up.'

'But you don't visit everyone who is in hospital? Why did you visit her?'

'Because she isn't just anyone, I suppose. I mean when I was over at Mum's on Tuesday—no wait a minute it was Wednesday, because that was the day the laundry came just as I was going out —Mum said, "You remember Auntie Florrie—she's in the General." "Well I never did," I said. "What's wrong with her?" "It's for the veins in her legs," she said. So seeing as how I had to pass so close, I more or less had to pop in and see her, didn't I? I mean, she is related isn't she?'[1]

We are all familiar with conversations of this type. They constitute expressions, not only of the feelings or sentiments of the individual concerned but also of beliefs as to what is socially demanded of people who stand in that relation to one another signified by the term 'related'. The last phrase 'she is related, isn't she?' is clearly not, in this context, a plea for confirmation that the

[1] Although this conversation was 'made up' it may well be based on the subliminal recall of an illustration given by Dr J. B. Loudon in his paper 'Kinship and Crisis in South Wales', *Brit. Jour. Sociol.* 12, 1961, p. 349.

speaker is in fact related to Auntie Florrie, but an appeal to a rule concerning the behaviour of persons categorized as related to one another, which the speaker expects her audience to share. She expects the other person to say, 'Ah, now I see why you went to see this person. She was a relative' (i.e. was a member of a socially recognized category of persons) 'and we all know that people ought to visit their relatives, especially when in trouble' (i.e. she therefore had to be treated in the way laid down by some rule specifying the behaviour of members of that category towards one another).

If we examine this conversation further it is possible to make certain inferences about the system of rules which govern the behaviour of persons belonging to the same group as the speaker.

In the first place, she is not at all clear how Florrie is related to her. Hence Florrie's exact relationship to her is of small importance compared with the fact of her relationship. Secondly, she does make the distinction between close relatives and others (placing Florrie among the 'others') even though she cannot be sure whether that relationship is through the mother or the father. Hence we might guess that relationships through each parent are probably of equal importance. We might infer also that it is how 'far away' a person is that matters rather than who they're related through. That is to say that there may be more important differences between the way one is expected to behave to one's brother as opposed to one's father's brother or one's father's brother's son than between, say, your mother's brother and your father's brother. Or to put it before technically, we might say that the degree of GENEALOGICAL DISTANCE is more important than differences in FILIATION (being the child of).

In the third place, we may note that she uses the term 'aunt' of someone who is not her aunt according to the normal definition. It seems likely that she was expected to behave towards Florrie in the same way as to an aunt, which is why she was of course called 'aunt'. Her feeling that she has niece-like duties towards her (visiting her in hospital) tend to confirm this view. But both her verbal statement ('she wasn't our "Auntie" ') and the fact that it is only because she is passing so close that makes her feel she has to visit, suggests that though using the title 'Aunt' for both 'real' and 'fictive' 'aunts', she is nevertheless very well aware of the difference.

Finally, it is quite clear from her account that she does not feel any particular feeling of affection for the person concerned, she has not been in frequent contact (she didn't know she was ill until her mother told her—her mother said 'you remember . . .') but that nevertheless she feels some sort of obligation to 'pop in': 'I *had* to pop in and see her.' But no-one was watching to see whether she went in (except God who is not referred to). No sanctions on her behaviour are mentioned—no rewards or punishments offered or threatened by other persons. This suggests that the sense of obligation she feels to visit the 'aunt' (though only when passing) comes (at the point of time the speaker is referring to) from 'inside' herself.

Nevertheless she assumes that others will understand and recognize this sense of obligation which sugests that it has a public rather than a private nature. This could be because all men everywhere feel the same sense of obligation. The obligation depends upon Florrie being categorized in a certain way and upon certain duties being accepted between members. But all men everywhere do not categorize people in the same way nor consider the same duties appropriate. Her assumption depends in part on her expectation that we too associate the same duties with membership of the same categories. This feeling of obligation is then something that she shares with other members of the group (to which she thinks we also belong), *because* she belongs to that group. It is a feeling that she has acquired by virtue of being born into and taught the values and ways of the group. It is not a sentiment attached to Florrie as a person.

SOCIAL RELATIONSHIPS AND BIOLOGICAL RELATIONS

The study of behaviour of this kind is what the study of kinship is about. But behaviour of exactly what kind? Well, it is the study of how people feel they ought to behave to people in different GENEALOGICAL categories, that is to say how they ought to behave to people who are related to them by ties of blood (CONSANGUINEAL ties: father's father or mother's father's sister's daughter's son, for example) or by ties of marriage (AFFINAL ties: wife, brother's wife, sister's husband, wife's sister's son, for example).

Taking a given individual as our starting point or EGO, we may distinguish relationships according to their DEGREE. Mother, father, brother, sister, child are FIRST DEGREE consanguineal relationships, father's father, father's brother or sister ('sib' is a useful shorthand for 'brother or sister'), mother's father, mother's sibs are second degree consanguineal relations and so on.

There is no standard way of classifying affines. Normally a distinction is made between spouses (husbands or wives) of Ego's consanguineal KIN ('kin' is often used as a shorter word for 'relations') on the one hand and the consanguineal kin of Ego's spouse on the other. Both types of affine can therefore be classified in the same way as consanguineal kin, that is as the spouses of Ego's first, second, third . . . degree kin or as the first, second, third . . . degree kin of Ego's spouse.

We can also distinguish between kin on the basis of the GENERATIONAL DISTANCE from Ego, Ego's father belonging to the FIRST ASCENDING generation and his children to the FIRST DESCENDING generation; his grandparents to the SECOND ASCENDING generation and his grandchildren to the SECOND DESCENDING generation and so on.

We can then combine both classification and refer, for example, to the Mo Bro as Ego's second degree consanguineal kin in the first ascending generation.

For some purposes it is sometimes useful to classify ascending kin through the parents of Ego. (All ascending kin must be related through Mo or Fa since these are the only first degree kin Ego has in the first ascending generation.) These are usually referred to as Ego's MATRILATERAL and PATRILATERAL kin, these simply being Latin-derived shorthand forms for 'blood relatives on his mother's and father's side' respectively.

Basically then we have two types of kin—consanguineal and affinal; that is people related by ties of blood and of marriage. These relations are basically biological. All that is meant by this statement is that they have reference to the biological activities of begetting and bearing children, being begotten by and born of the same person and so on. But to refer to a kinship tie is not to refer to a biological relation except indirectly. In the example with which we began this chapter we never discovered even what this relation was. What mattered was that, because a relation was *recognized,* this affected the behaviour to one another of the parties between whom the relation was recognized to exist. It affected it however because the group to which they belonged had rules which governed the behaviour between people recognized to be so related.

When two people or two categories of people share common expectations about the way they ought to behave to each other then we may say that a SOCIAL RELATIONSHIP exists between them. *A kin relationship is a social relationship and not a biological relation.* The term never refers except indirectly to such a relation. There are all sorts of problems which arise from this definition as we shall see later (see page 26) but this will do for the moment.

To say that a kinship relationship is a social relationship which refers to a biological relation is not to say that the one is always identical with the other. In our society the rights and duties of fatherhood are rights and duties towards a person which another person has usually by virtue of their being the biological father, i.e. the GENETIC FATHER, of that person. But an illegitimate child's genetic father has not, even where his identity is known, the rights of a 'father'. That is to say the child has no 'social father' or PATER. A father is not necessarily the genetic father of a child. A father is a man who is recognized by the society as a whole as having the responsibilities and rights of a 'father'. These rights and duties are usually acquired by prior marriage to the genetic mother of the child.

To say that children have to have genetic parents is of course a tautology.[2] The statement that in all societies children have to have social fathers is not self evident. The universal social recognition of the necessity of a pater has been expressed by the British social anthropologist, Malinowski, as the *principle of legitimacy*. This declares that 'in all societies a father' (we should now say 'pater') 'is regarded by law, custom and morals as an indispensable element of the procreative group. The woman has to be married before she is allowed legitimately to conceive, or else a subsequent marriage or an act of adoption gives the child full tribal or civil status.'[3]

This is not the place to discuss this principle in detail. Here we need only note four points which arise. In the first place, the importance of this principle depends on the distinction between 'pater' and 'genetic father'. In the second place, whenever we consider a kinship relationship we shall have to bring in other people than the parties actually involved, as Malinowski has to. The references to law, custom and morals and to tribal and civil STATUS (social position) imply the existence of shared expectations by others, who constitute the group which shares the agreement on the way people ought to behave which is expressed in legal, customary and moral rules. The fact that we have to bring in other people indicates that we are dealing with a SOCIAL INSTITUTION. A relationship or piece of behaviour can be said to be institutionalized when the relevant behaviour is known and expected throughout the group concerned. (Relationships or systems of relationships can only be institutionalized *within a group*. The statement that a piece of behaviour is 'institutionalized' is meaningless unless the group within which it is institutionalized is specified.)

In the third place, the reference to other people which is implied shows quite clearly that we are not dealing with the feelings of fathers:

[2] A statement which is true by virtue of the meaning of the terms in which it is expressed.

[3] Malinowski, B., 'Kinship', *Man* 30, 17, p. 24. For further discussion see Chapter 2.

the 'natural' affection and concern of a man for his offspring. Fatherhood has public and not merely private characteristics.

Lastly the fact that fatherhood is institutionalized suggests that it must be of importance not merely to the father and child but to the whole group, and entails that the rules governing the determination of fatherhood and the behaviour of fathers are supported by legal, customary and moral sanctions.

However, we may feel that to describe fatherhood simply in terms of rights and duties is not enough. In our society a man has no specific duty to make model boats for his son or to take him fishing or play cricket with him in the back garden. But having a father around makes these things possible and there are certainly expectations shared among us that these sorts of things will happen if the man is a 'good father'. This whole complex of social expectations as to what it is to be 'a good father' constitutes an example of what sociologists call a SOCIAL ROLE or just a ROLE. The word 'good' shows that these expectations involve some sort of moral evaluation and hence we can say that a role is a set of expectations which are *valued*. The role of father does not therefore only refer to the rights and duties, legal, customary or moral, which are attached to the social position or status of 'father', but enables us to consider the expectations which apply to those occupying that position which do not result from the knowledge of specific rules.

Now members of groups share not only expectations about the behaviour of other people; they also share expectations about the way in which such roles shall be allocated. In our society it is expected that the role of 'pater' will normally be played by the genetic father. This presupposes two things. First that we are able to ascertain who the genetic father is; secondly that we understand how children are generated. Hence biological or genetic relations enter the picture through the process of allocation of kinship roles which depends on *beliefs* of the group about the biological facts of life.

(You may say that you 'know' the way that children are generated. I beg to disagree. Most readers will be unable to produce the scientific evidence which shows that children are generated in the way we think. They claim they know because they have been told by persons in authority in their society. In other words they 'believe' what they have been told. This does not necessarily constitute a justification for making a claim to 'know'.)

Primitive societies have widely different beliefs concerning the relationship between copulation and birth and these beliefs are related to the *structure* of their kinship system, that is to say the pattern made by the types of relationship which constitute it.

For example some societies have been thought only to recognize that intercourse is necessary to 'open the way' for birth. Hence the child's filiation to the mother but not to the father is recognized. Alternatively the child may be thought of as being conceived by the father, the mother merely 'housing' the child. Here the child's filiation to the father and not the mother is recognized. These are extreme cases, but the beliefs mentioned may be seen to be consonant with the way that the societies concerned arrange the social relationships which are based on the recognition of kinship.

FILIATION AND DESCENT

Because the child is not considered related by blood to one or other parent, one parent is, in such a system, an affine and not a blood relative. Now all kinship systems use the links of filiation as a means of transferring rights from one generation to another, though societies vary as to whether all types of right—to office, property and membership of social groups—are inherited in this way. Now sometimes these rights are transmitted through males and sometimes through females. When ties of filiation are recognized for the purposes of the transmission of rights to *group membership,* then we may speak of the members of the society concerned tracing DESCENT through such ties. A descent system is a pattern of socially recognized relationships which are used for the transmission of such rights. Transmission may occur and descent may be traced through *males only* or through *females only*. In both cases we have a system of UNILINEAL transmission. If the male principle is used then rights will be transmitted through the father. If the female principle is used then rights will be transmitted through the mother. Hence we may speak of unilineal systems being either PATRILINEAL or MATRILINEAL, that is, transmitting rights through the male or female line. Of course it can be more complicated than this. We find systems where one type of group membership or property is inherited through one line, and another type through another line. These are sometimes called double unilineal systems (nothing comes down both lines, different things come down different single lines).

We have to consider yet another possibility, that is a BILATERAL or OMNILINEAL systems.[4] In such a system rights are transmitted to Ego on *both* sides. Now it may be thought that we have already dealt with this case. Is not Ego in a double unilineal system, a recipient of rights from both sides? He is not. Rights are transmitted through

[4] Bilateral is a term usually reserved for describing a system of *recognition* of relationships. Omnilineal is used for a system of *transmission,* e.g. inheritance.

both parents (as in bilateral systems). But rights descend not from his father's mother, only from his father's father.

In a bilateral system he inherits not merely from the males or females on one side; nor one thing from the males on one side and another from the females on another side; but the same things from *both* males *and* females on *both* sides: hence 'omnilineal'.

This brief exposition will, it is hoped, give the reader some idea of the variety of ways in which filiation can be used as the basis for transmission of rights and for tracing descent. *But the recognition of ties of filiation is not the same as the recognition of descent.* The study of descent systems is a study of the principles adopted by groups who use ties of filiation as the basis for the transferring of rights and the allocation of statuses. It is the study of what different societies use kinship for and how they do it. The rightness of what they do may be expressed in terms of the beliefs they have about the biological facts of existence. Our two extreme examples of societies who recognized respectively the facts of biological maternity and paternity *only,* had, it will surprise no-one to hear, systems of matrilineal and patrilineal descent.

In most societies, however, the facts of biological maternity and paternity are recognized if not understood, and even where this is not the case the activities associated with the roles of motherhood and fatherhood are found and constitute the basis of social relationships. This fact may be expressed by saying that *the recognition of filiation as opposed to descent is universally bilateral.* The range of the recognition of filiation will however be affected by its descent significance, and by the other uses to which it is put. Similarly, if a kinship relationship is also a relationship which is recognized for the purposes of descent, it may acquire a societal[5] or economic or political significance.

THE DEFINITION OF KINSHIP

We can now return to our problem of the definition of kinship. Kinship is a universal institution, hence the most likely place to find an explanation of its nature is not in other social institutions since their incidence and forms vary between societies, but in the conditions of action of all men everywhere. Whatever a society may be thought of as using kinship for, it is plain that what is being used is a set of ideas concerning the *biological* conditions of action of a society. This set of ideas—the sense which men make of their

[5] Related or appertaining to the society as a whole.

biological nature—must be such as to lead to social arrangements which make it possible for the members of the society to survive under these conditions. Hence the study of kinship always involves a consideration both of these conditions of action and the sense made of them and the way in which this sense is embodied in action.

This is the first sense in which it may be said that kinship is 'about' man's biological nature. Secondly, it can be argued that kinship relationships 'systematically overlap' biological relations. We have to say 'systematically overlap' because the people in the society concerned may not recognize biological relations that exist, and may recognize 'biological relations' that do not exist. Our interest in the non-recognition of actually existent biological relations may be justified in terms of our interest in the biological conditions of action. In the second case we may say that the social relationships which are intelligible only in terms of an erroneous belief about biological relationships are kinship relationships precisely because they *do* have a biological reference although it be erroneous.

The difficulty raised by the notion of overlap lies in the fact that not only do biological relations and the social relationships which we call kinship relationships sometimes fail to coincide, but even recognized *biological* relations do not always coincide with such social relationships. Societies where 'social paternity' is in no way dependent on genetic paternity are cases in point.

Let us pause and consider the implications of this argument. The question is 'can kinship relationships be said systematically to overlap biological relations?' The question implies that we already know what kinship relationships are. If we leave out the word 'kinship' then the question isn't worth asking. If we know what kinship relationships are *before we have decided whether they have anything to do with biological relations* then it would seem that their being kinship relationships cannot be dependent upon their having something to do with biological relations.

There are two possible answers to the question 'how do we know what kinship relationships are'. The first is that they are relationships which we, the observers, would describe as kinship on the basis of the notions of kinship which exist in our society. The second answer is to be found by turning not to *our* ideas, nor directly to the ideas of the members of a number of different societies, but to the conditions of action common to all societies. Men everywhere must make sense of such conditions. Hence all societies have a set of ideas about birth procreation and so on.

Social relationships are only possible because the people participating in them share common ideas which give the relationships meaning. *Those relationships which are intelligible only in terms of the ideas a society has about what we think of as its biological conditions of action may be regarded as constituting the class of relationships described as kinship relationships.*

By focusing on the conditions under which men everywhere act we have arrived not only at what is involved in the study of kinship, but also at a criterion for distinguishing a class of social relationships which is not determined by the ideas governing social relationships in one society.

We must conclude our consideration of this issue with a word of caution however. Any type of social relationship derives its meaning not merely from the set of ideas which are constitutive of it. It derives its meaning also from the relation it has to other types of social relationship. Hence any social relationship is not meaningful in terms of its constitutive ideas alone. Where relationships of two different types are regularly combined, it will not be possible to understand the meaning of the relationship to the actor without reference to the other type of relationship. Hence the definition given above should not be taken as restricting the members of the class of kinship relationships to those relationships which are uniquely meaningful in terms of the sense made of biological conditions.

THE IMPORTANCE OF KINSHIP TO THE INDIVIDUAL AND SOCIETY

This last consideration brings us back to the distinction between filiation and descent. Where ties of filiation are recognized for descent purposes they will be meaningful not merely in terms of beliefs held by the society about man's biological nature but also because they determine rights to property, patterns of political allegiance and so on. They will be of importance not merely to individuals but also to the group as a whole.

While no one would dispute this point, the distinction between filiation and descent has been a matter of some controversy among anthropologists. It is not disputed that individuals recognize kin ties through both parents however the relationship is reckoned for the purposes of descent. What is a matter of dispute is whether, for example in a society where descent is patrilineal, the relationship between a man and his mother's brother should be regarded as a relationship between a sister's son and a *mother's* brother (filiation) or whether it should be seen as a relationship between a father's son and a father's *wife's* brother (affinal).

Two quite distinct problems are involved here. They concern the way in which it is useful for the *observer* to look at the relationship and the way in which *the people themselves* actually look at it.

In societies with which anthropologists deal, unilineal descent is frequently associated with a rule of EXOGAMY. Such a rule requires that members of a DESCENT GROUP, recruited according to the rules of descent, should marry persons from outside the descent group. So we have a society which is composed of exclusive groups recruited on the basis of unilineal descent between whom exist ties of marriage. Competition between descent groups for political and economic power usually occurs and alliances between groups for such purposes are usually cemented by the creation of marriage ties between allied groups.

It follows from this that such ties are significant in two quite distinct ways. In the first place they are significant to the individual since the affinal ties of his father are consanguineal ties for himself. Within the descent group such ties differentiate individuals in terms of the different matrilateral filiations, which together with patrilateral ties serve to 'define and sanction a personal field of social relationships for the individual', as Fortes has put it. Ego's matrilateral ties are however of significance not only to the individual but also to the descent group, since they are the means of cementing alliances which are not of personal and individual significance but of political and economic significance to the group.

Now if we are concerned with political and economic groupings in the society and the relationships between them, clearly these ties should be regarded as affinal. If however we take the standpoint not of the group but of the individual, such ties may be regarded as ties of filiation. Two distinctions have been made here. One is between the individual and the group. The other is between relationships within the group and between groups. What makes the whole thing so confusing is that relations between groups are significant to the individual within groups. And relationships which constitute an important element in the personal field of individuals, who are members of a group, are of significance to the group because they extend outside it and thus affect the relationships between groups.

Relationships between groups are of political and economic significance in the *society*. Relationships for the individual are of personal significance whether they are within or between groups. It is precisely the personal significance of kinship relationships which makes it possible to use them to bind together otherwise hostile groups in some sort of political and economic alliance.

Now it might appear that we could solve this difficulty by saying that matrilateral ties should be regarded as affinal when we are considering the relationships between groups, but as ties of filiation when we are considering the individual's field of personal relationships. This will not do, however, since we started off this discussion by noting that the meaning of these ties to the individual will be affected by their economic and political significance. We could now put this another way and point out that inter-group ties are of significance to individuals because they are after all group members as well as individuals.

If therefore we are interested in inter-group relationships we can look at such ties as affinal and as having a primarily economic and political significance. If we are interested in the individual's field of personal relationships we may regard them as ties of filiation. But in each case we shall have to recognize that the actual behaviour we are studying is intelligible only in terms of its meaning to the people concerned and such meaning will depend both on its meaning to the individual as an individual and also to him as a member of the wider group or groups to which his affinal ties are of importance.

Descent we have seen is a set of institutions which use kinship relationships as the basis for the formation of political, economic and other types of group. Rules of descent therefore, because they link kinship relationships with other types of relationships, always have a significance both to the individual and to society as a whole. They insure a degree of fit between these different sets of relationships. This is particularly evident in primitive societies where kinship relationships form the basis for the allocation of other types of relationship as well. But the means of the transmission of rights, of which descent is a special case, are always of significance both to the individual and to the members of society as a whole. This is so even where, as in our own society, their influence on the allocation of roles of those relationships which constitute what Fortes has called the 'domestic domain' is less direct. By this phrase Fortes means those relationships which centre around 'begetting, bearing, and above all exercizing responsibility in rearing a child'. In this sphere the recognition of relationships is normally bilateral. It is the wider significance of such relationships, the wider social uses to which such relationships are put, that results in the 'distortion' or weighting of one side of this bilateral pattern of recognition.

Throughout this book therefore it will be necessary not merely to attempt to understand systems of kinship from the point of view of the individual but also to attempt to see that system from the point of view of social groupings to whose inter-relations we refer in part when we speak of society as a whole.

THE UNIVERSALITY OF KINSHIP

Why is it that kinship institutions are found in all known societies? This question could be put in two quite distinct ways. It could be rephrased to read 'Why *is* it that man's understanding of his biological nature *leads* him to use the biological relations which he thus recognizes as a basis for social relationships?' or 'Why *has* man *been led* to do this?'

As the different tenses used by the different questions imply, the first demands an explanation in terms of the conditions that apply universally at all times. The second demands some sort of historical explanation.

Questions of this kind are questions about how society or aspects of society came into being. They start from an *initial situation* in which there is no society. They therefore refer to non-social conditions under which society exists; and the mechanisms by which such patterns arise, and in whose terms their existence must be explained, must be *non*-social mechanisms of some kind. The most obvious mechanism which would do the job is some sort of psychological mechanism.

We have to distinguish this type of answer from a third type however. Instead of attempting a general historical explanation, or an explanation in terms of general conditions, we could try to explain the universality of kinship in terms of the characteristics which a society has to have for social life to be possible.

Now the second type of explanation we distinguished was, at one time, a very popular one. It has one enormous drawback. Since human society emerged long before the date of the earliest written records, it is not possible to provide any but purely conjectural historical explanations of the existence of kinship institutions or the way in which they work.

The first type may appear more attractive. At a time when the feelings that people had towards kin were regarded as defining the nature of kinship relationships, it was tempting to use psychological explanations. Even if we accept the public rather than private nature of social relationships it is still tempting to try and derive the recognition of kinship obligations from the psychological nature of man.

What is usually called the 'extension theory' of kinship was such an attempt. This theory, which has come to be associated with Malinowski and was at one time widely held, stated that kinship could be explained in terms of natural feelings of loyalty and affection which arose between members of the biological group of parents and offspring, which were 'extended' to more remote categories of related persons.

Now let us suppose that sentiments of loyalty and affection are generated by cohabitation and nurture, the activities which characterize the domestic domain. Can we go on to say that explanations of this type tell us anything about why men in the societies of which we have knowledge behave in the way they do? Well obviously they can. What they can explain is those regularities in behaviour which arise again in each generation as the same processes of cohabitation and nurture take place. Now this might be plausible if all societies had the same type of kinship system. But although kinship institutions may be said to be universal they are, as we have seen, of very different kinds. Malinowski thought of this difficulty however. He saw the generation of sentiments as being bilateral but this natural pattern being distorted by 'culture'. This however is exactly what we are trying to explain. If people in different societies behave in different ways in this matter of kinship it is because the societies concerned have different rules governing kinship behaviour, or to put it another way, have different systems of kinship relationships, which exist prior to the arrival of each new generation. These cannot be accounted for in terms of sentiments which are continually created afresh.

We have not done with this argument however. Even if kinship institutions were identical everywhere, the extension theory *still* would not do. It would not do because the argument which has just been put forward applies with equal force in this situation. Because I want to care for my mother in her old age, this does not explain why I feel I ought to do so. To recognize that an 'ought' is involved here implies the recognition of an obligation independent of sentiment.

Why then was the theory ever held? The answer may be found in regarding it not as a theory of the first type but as a second type theory in disguise. In other words, properly understood, the theory states that, because the activities of procreation and nurture create sentiments of attachment, then early in the history of mankind such sentiments were expressed in the form of rules which, though extended to serve other purposes and distorted in various ways by the weight of other types of relationships which have been built upon them, survive to the present day. Individuals are in the majority of cases motivated to follow them because of the natural creation of 'original' sentiments in each generation.

In this form the extension theory can be seen to be a plausible but unverifiable 'conjectural history' type explanation. This does not mean that it is not of the greatest value to consider society from the standpoint of the way in which the psychological needs of its members are satisfied by their participation in the system of relationships that constitute it. But such a viewpoint does not enable us simply to derive culture from nature, nor, more specifically, a system of kinship relationships from psychological needs.

It may appear to some readers that what has just been said runs counter to the whole approach to kinship which is being followed here. This is not so. To say that kinship is only definable by reference to the sense that a society makes of the facts of biological relationship does not necessarily imply that that sense is necessarily reducible to it. We can learn two things from our criticism of the extension of sentiments theory. The first is that it is not possible to explain a kinship system in terms of the sentiments and activities which arise out of the co-operation of individuals in begetting and rearing children. The second is that it does not therefore follow that a kinship system is intelligible without reference to those sentiments and activities.

To account for the universality of kinship we must turn to the third type of explanation. Now, if we stick to the biological group, we might be able to argue as follows. For social life to be possible, language and the rest of society's accumulated possessions must be transmitted to the next generation and arrangements for its nurture during infancy and childhood must be made. Then in the absence of any alternative arrangements, which are not likely under primitive conditions, these activities will be performed by the biological group. Unfortunately what we have to explain is not the existence of relationships between members of the biological group, but the wider recognition of relationships. This can only be explained by relating the system of relationships to *other* systems of relationship in the society.

To put the point rather more crudely: if we find that a man distinguishes between somebody who is, say, his father's father's father's sons's son's son and another person who has no recognized agnatic[6] tie, instead of going away and puzzling about how it is that the feelings of duty and affection normally felt between father and son have become extended so that this man is a sort of brother, we ask rather rudely: 'So what?' Hearing that all sorts of legal, political and economic consequences follow from this relationship, the purpose of categorizing people in this way becomes clear, and the significance of the relationship in the society becomes clear also. After all, it is

[6] Relationship traced through males only.

only academics who make distinctions *for the sake of making distinctions*.

Now admittedly this does not answer the question 'Why should people use distinctions based on socially recognized biological relationships for this purpose?' Professor Fortes, in discussing a related problem, has pointed to the importance of this question and says that we cannot at the present time answer it. He himself suggests however that the answer lies in the homogeneous nature of those societies in which kinship is used as a basis for other types of social relationship. By homogeneity he means the extent to which one person can replace another in a given social position. Where individuals are socially undifferentiated 'there is nothing', he suggests, 'which could so precisely and incontrovertibly fix one's place in society as one's parentage'.[7]

We may note that this answer to the question is of a type which explains the cross-cultural regularity not in terms of an *initial historical situation* (all societies developed from kin groups), nor in terms of an *initial situation of the individual* (because every individual grows up in a kin group, kin relationships are primary and form the basis of other types of relationship), but in terms of *conditions which are necessary for an ongoing society to be possible.* In other words his explanation is a distinctively sociological explanation rather than an historical or psychological one. From this example it can be seen that structural explanations can provide understanding of social regularities which are found not merely within societies but between societies.

The example with which we began this chapter was chosen to illustrate the various problems, a discussion of which has formed its subject matter.

We began by examining the implications of that conversation and so started by pointing out the distinction between sentiments and obligations, between 'I want' and 'I ought' which was so important in evaluating explanations of the universality of kinship institutions. Now that we have looked at the meaning of kinship and its uses we can get a little more juice from it.

To start with, the fact that the speaker did not know the exact relationship that Florrie had to her suggests that, in the society concerned, kinship is not the chief means of 'placing' people in society. That is to imply that statuses are not allocated in this society on the basis of kinship. Moreover the fact that the speaker did not

[7] Fortes, M., 'The structure of unilineal descent groups', *American Anthropologist* 55, 1953, p. 30.

know whether Florrie was 'connected' through her mother or father suggests that either there is no system of intergenerational transmission of rights or, if there is (which is likely), then this system is either omnilineal or patrilineal, since in other systems it would be vital to know through which parent the relationship was. Hence we may guess both what type of system it might be and its importance to the society. From the way the speaker talks it seems likely that in the society concerned the chief importance of the recognition of kinship relations is to 'define and sanction a personal field of social relationships for the individual'. There is nothing peculiar about a system being put to this use. However, if we are right in assuming that this is the *chief* use to which it is put then this society differs markedly from most primitive societies. If it is the other uses to which a system is put which distorts the tendency to bilateral recognition then this reinforces our guess that the system of transmission is omnilineal or at most weakly patrilineal.

The method of using an example has been deliberately adopted because when we are talking about 'a kinship system', 'a type of marriage' or 'a type of family' it is very easy to forget that this is simply a way of referring to the patterns of thought and behaviour which are shared by a group of people and are reflected in conversations such as the one described. In order to think straight about such matters, we need continually to translate what we are saying into patterns of thought and action in order to see if we really understand what we are talking about and whether what we are saying is sense.

The example given is however very brief and thin. Though we can see quite clearly that certain things are involved in behaviour of the kind which the conversation describes, we cannot make more than guesses about the nature of the kinship system in that society. To discover this we should have to ask more questions of the same person, observe the behaviour of the same person and extend our range of observation much beyond a single individual, before we could produce an accurate description and arrive at a correct understanding of the sense which the members of the group, to which the speaker belongs, make of the biological facts of their existence and the way in which this sense is embodied in the rules governing their behaviour.

FURTHER READING

It has only been possible in the course of this chapter to deal with one or two issues which arise from the study of kinship by social anthropologists. No sociologist, and certainly no sociologist of the family, can consider himself equipped for the study of society without some knowledge of the work being done in his sister discipline. It is to be hoped therefore that advantage will be taken of the following introduction to anthropological studies in our field.

FOX, R., *Kinship and Marriage*, Penguin, 1967.

Readers who wish to read more about the problems involved in the definition of kinship will probably find following the vigorous and acrimonious controversy in *Philosophy of Science* both informative and enjoyable.

GELLNER, E., *Philosophy of Science* 24, 1957, pp. 235-243.
NEEDHAM, R., *Philosophy of Science* 27, 1960, pp. 96-101.
GELLNER, E., *Philosophy of Science* 27, 1960, pp. 187-204.
BARNES, J. A., *Philosophy of Science* 28, 1961, pp. 296-299.
GELLNER, E., *Philosophy of Science* 30, 1963, pp. 236-251.
BARNES, J. A., *Philosophy of Science* 31, 1964, pp. 294-297.
BEATTIE, J. H. M., *Man* 64, 1964, pp. 101-103.

The references to the discussion of the distinction between affiliation and descent are given below. The non-anthropological reader may find this rather hard going. The article that started it all, Fortes (1953), is well worth the effort.

FORTES, M., 'The structure of unilineal descent groups', *American Anthropologist* 55, 1953, pp. 17-41.
LEACH, E., 'Rethinking Anthropology', *L.S.E. Monographs on Social Anthropology*, No. 22, 1961, Chapter 5.
FORTES, M., 'Descent, Filiation and Affinity: A Rejoinder to Dr Leach; *Man*, 59, 1959, pp. 193-197 and 206-212.

The 'extension of sentiments' theory was the subject of controversy in which the two chief antagonists were Malinowski and Radcliffe-Brown. Malinowski's ideas on kinship are most succinctly formulated in *Man*, 1930. Radcliffe-Brown's approach to the study of kinship is most clearly exemplified in Chapter 3 of *Structure and Function*.

MALINOWSKI, B., Kinship, *Man* 1930, pp. 19-29.
RADCLIFFE-BROWN, A. R., *Structure and Function in Primitive Society*, London, Cohen and West, 1952, Chapter 3.
FORTES, M., 'Malinowski and the study of kinship' *in* FIRTH, R., *Man and Culture*, London, Routledge, 1957.
FORTES, M., 'Radcliffe-Brown's Contributions to the study of Social Organisation', *Brit. Jour. Sociol.* 6, 1955, pp. 16-29.

2

Marriage

'THERE was a right-old to do when our Jane got wed. The preparations went on for years, at any rate that's what it seemed like. You'd think with all that effort that on the day everything would have gone smoothly. Not a bit of it. In the first place who should call in that very morning but Mrs Crawshaw "to wish our Jane all the best". What she'd really come for was to find out why the Crawshaws hadn't been invited to the wedding. You know, when we were sending out the invitations, Mum and me clean forgot that, though John came from down South, he'd still got relatives up here. Anyway there she was, standing in the kitchen dressed up to the nines, with people cutting sandwiches all round her, going on about how even second cousins had been invited on our side but on her side all Mr Crawshaw's relatives had been ignored . . . and Jane was in hysterics and said she'd wanted a quiet wedding and it was nothing to do with all these people she didn't even know, and it was all Mum's fault, which upset Mum because Jane had been as keen on a proper wedding as any one; and she hadn't got anyone from the family to give her away—I mean Bert looked very nice in his tails and all, but its not like having your father or brother is it?

'Anyhow when we got to the church we went in and there was our side of the aisle filled to overflowing and scarcely three rows on John's side. I mean we'd kept the numbers on each side equal—for the invitations that is—but all sorts of people from around here dropped in to pay their respects like—it was just the same at Uncle Arthur's funeral—you never saw such a crowd—and you know how many people Mum knows—anyway we got the ushers, though why they call them that I don't know, to shift some of our lot over onto their side to balance it up a bit. Anyhow the service went off all right though Mum was worried because she cried half the time and smudged her mascara—I *told* her not to wear any—but when it came to speeches after the buffet back at our house and Bert, he was deputizing for our dad like, came to that bit—you know—about losing a daughter and gaining a son—she started off all over again and couldn't stop—it must have been the Sauterne—and then they nearly missed the train. Well what happened was . . .'

And so on.

In no society is marriage a relationship which is of purely personal concern to the persons thus joined together. In all societies it represents the creation of relationships between *groups* as well as individuals, a rearrangement of the relationships between persons (and hence of the rights and duties which are elements of these relationships) and it always involves a recognition of the changes that have taken place by the society as a whole as well as by the individuals and groups who are immediately concerned.

All these elements are indicated by the account of a wedding ceremony which prefaces this chapter. It is clear from the account that the ceremony is public: other people drop in at the church; a 'quiet' wedding isn't 'proper'. It is quite clear that two groups are involved: '*our* Jane wed'; there are references to 'our side' and 'their side' meaning 'our Jane's kin' and 'their John's kin'. Moreover it is clear that there is a notion of balance between sides, symbolized by the segregation of the two sides in the church and the shifting over of people from one side to another to make it 'look right'.

The rearrangement of relationships is quite clearly indicated. The girls family experience a sense of loss. The mother cries. One of the men of the girl's kin group '*give* the bride *away*'. The old tag about 'losing a daughter' is trotted out and evokes more tears. The loss which is being thus recognized is quite clearly seen as a loss of a member of the kin group, however unrealistic that loss may be in terms of daily interaction. It is not a complete loss however. Losing a daughter they gain, in a bilateral system, a son. They are gaining a father of grandchildren who will be *theirs*. But still the mother cries. The loyalty of the daughter is now to her new husband rather than to her mother. Whether *in fact* her mother's effective control (power) over her daughter is at an end, her *right* to it has been extinguished. She loses the right to her daughter's domestic services and to control her sexual behaviour. The rights to sexual access and to domestic services now pass to the husband, and the husband's kin acquire, like the wife's, rights in the grandchildren.

The bride however objects at the last minute to all these people who have quite clearly a legitimate interest in the proceedings. It is clear that, at that moment, she regards the whole thing as purely on the individual plane. For the 'happy couple', marriage is *not* concerned with inter-group relationships but with individual relationships. They doubtless see themselves to have a personal relationship which exists independently of the marriage. The marriage itself merely constitutes the social recognition of that relationship. It is not the creation of a social relationship within which a *new* personal relationship can grow.

The beliefs of both parents and children about this are probably not inconsistent. They both believe in love first and marriage afterwards, and not the other way round. There is only one snag in this doctrine. The whole notion of romantic love presupposes that the lovers have a freedom of choice. Complete freedom of choice implies that the social groups into which the children are born have a corresponding lack of power to determine whom their children marry. Now in no society known are such groups entirely uninterested in their children's choice of mate. They cannot be, because by virtue of the marriage they enter into relationship with the kin of their child-in-law. As we saw in the previous chapter the significance of this varies enormously, depending on the use to which kinship systems are put, but the principle is clear. Moreover, depending on the nature of the system, the children produced by the marriage will be affected by their ties of filiation to the other group. Inheritance of different types of property and group membership are often involved and in virtually all cases the children are evaluated by other people at least initially in terms of the evaluations made of *both* their parents.

Hence, we find in all societies either that marriage is hedged around by rules specifying which categories of people are eligible mates for the members of different groups or, at least, that the groups which constitute the society make strenuous efforts to control or influence their children's choice of marriage partner. It is a discussion of these themes that will be the concern of this chapter.

MARRIAGE AND THE TRANSMISSION OF RIGHTS

In the previous chapter we were concerned primarily with the way in which relationships *between* generations were recognized and used. No mention was made of another very important principle which concerns relationships *within* generations. In all societies there is a recognition of the importance of ties of kinship between children of the same parents, and in many societies sibs act together with regard to other groups.

These regularities can, once again, be looked at in terms of both sentiments and rights. Sibs are likely to be reared by the same mother and hence their loyalties are likely to be in the first place to their mother and to their age mates. (We may note here that sibs are linked twice—directly to each other and by loyalty to the same parent.) Hence biological conditions are likely to lead to the formation of a cluster of individuals sharing common loyalties. This cluster will obviously occupy the same territory and share the income from any property. With the decease of any one of the members, their share of any income will be appropriated by the surviving members of the cluster. Hence the members of the cluster will be held together both by common sentiments and by virtue of having common interests in the joint property of the cluster. Where such interests are socially recognized they may be said to constitute rights.

With the decease of the parent(s), it will obviously be to the advantage of the siblings to prevent the dispersion of their inherited property. But if the group is to continue they will have to produce a third generation. Ruling out for the moment an incestuous union between sibs, this means that they will have to bring in mates for the sisters or for the brothers. But other sibling groups will have the same problem. It is obvious therefore that the groups will not be able to retain all their members. At the same time bringing in an outsider will create problems as to the entitlement of the children of such a union to the property, since they will not be full members of the group in whom the rights to the property were previously vested; two sibling groups will have claims on the children, and the children will have claims on two sibling groups. Some sort of *arrangement* will have to be arrived at therefore between the sibling groups concerning the distribution of rights to property and in children. This arrangement is usually called 'marriage'.

The solution to the problem may be stated as follows:

(i) Let the sisters take lovers to procreate the children who remain full members of the original sibling group of the mothers.

(ii) Let the sisters take husbands on the understanding that the husband have no rights in the children.

(iii) Let the sisters take husbands and the men renounce rights in the children of the sisters and establish rights in the children of the wives.

(iv) as for (iii) but let the men retain some rights in the sisters' children and establish some rights in those of the wives.

These arrangements imply matrilineal (i and ii), patrilineal (iii) and, according to the details of the arrangement, either double unilineal or omnilineal (iv) systems of transmission. Artificially separated by the organization of these two chapters though they are, types of marriage and types of transmission are now seen to be merely different ways of talking about the same thing. For marriage involves the transference of rights between groups which determines the pattern of inheritance and group membership (descent) of the children of the union thereby created.

PATTERNS OF RESIDENCE: DOMESTIC SERVICES AND DOMESTIC AUTHORITY

Marriage is not merely concerned with a transference of rights in the children however. It also involves a transfer of rights in the persons of the spouses, as we saw from the example taken from our own society. Here we can make distinctions of a kind which are related to (but not the same as) the distinctions which were made with regard to the children.

The first type of rights in the persons of the spouses that we will consider are those which arise from the composition of the DOMESTIC GROUP. As far as the wife is concerned, the right to her domestic services is transferred by marriage to her husband. What this means in practice will depend on whether they set up house on their own or whether she finds herself living with her husband's parents and his brothers and their wives and hence under the authority of her husband's mother or in some other type of domestic group.

As far as the husband is concerned, the pattern of residence after marriage will determine whether he finds himself under the authority of his father, his wife's father, or on his own. Marriage, therefore, marks the re-ordering of domestic relationships as well as establishing those of descent and, if the domestic unit is an economic unit, of economic relationships as well.

There are only a limited number of possible patterns of residence. The wife may continue to reside with her brothers and the husband may merely visit her. Or the wife may continue to reside with her mother and her sisters and her husband may come to live with them. Or the wife may leave her natal group and live with her husband and his brothers. Or both husband and wife may leave their natal groups and set up a new domestic group of their own. These different solutions are termed nato-local, uxori-local, viri-local and neo-local respectively. They are, of course, related to the type of descent system. They are also related, however, to the type of property which is important, and its degree of partibility (whether it can be divided).

The way in which a given system of transmission will affect residence at marriage will depend on the uses to which that system is put. Often it is used to form exogamous groups whose members have to *act together* in economic or political matters. Such groups are usually described as *corporate* groups.

Since men have control in political and economic matters, priority is usually given to keeping the men together. A nato-local residence, pattern keeps all the members together. A viri-local pattern keeps the men together, an uxori-local pattern keeps the women together, and a neo-local pattern disperses the group. The only residence patterns that keep the men together are the nato-local and the viri-local. In patrilineal systems the viri-local pattern can be adopted. But in matrilineal systems, while this pattern keeps the men together, they lose control over the rearing of their heirs (the children of the sisters who have gone off to live with husbands in other groups). An uxori-local pattern can be an alternative here, provided that the geographical range of marriage is not too wide relative to the needs of the men of the group to meet together.

If the system of transmission is not used to form exclusive groups, but is primarily a means of transferring rights in property from one generation to another, then residence is no problem, provided the property is partible. If, however, it is not partible, then either only one of the siblings of the right sex can inherit, or, the siblings of the same sex will have to stay together and administer the property as a group. When this is the case, the same problems arise as when the system is used to form corporate exogamous descent groups since sibs cannot marry and they are forced to act together. Assuming that the men control the property and its effective control requires frequent contact, then a dispersion of the males by the adoption of uxori-local residence will, if the geographical range of marriage is large enough (and the available transport poor enough), prevent the exercise of such control.

If the propery concerned is a farm whose economic viability depends on its *size,* then, in order to inherit, the children of the owner of that farm will have to stay together to work it. In such a case, in a patrilineal system (provided the farm is large enough), the pattern of residence of the sons after marriage is likely to be viri-local. Or the property may not be a farm but a tenancy or the ownership of a dwelling house. In such a case it will not be the control but the utilization of the property which demands co-residence. In a bilateral system the married couple would presumably have a choice as to the type of residence they adopted depending on the suitability of the accommodation available, and their ability to set up a neo-local household.

It is important to recognize that *different* residential groups may be formed in societies with the *same* type of descent,[1] either because the system is used for different purposes or the conditions under which the system operates (the type of property, the distance away of other groups who provide wives, the effectiveness of transport) varies between the societies.

It is equally important to recognize that descent group membership is closely related to but quite distinct from membership of a residential or domestic group.

SEXUAL RIGHTS

The extent to which sibling groups act together is vividly exemplified in some societies which have forms of what is called PLURAL or POLYGAMOUS marriage. PLURAL MARRIAGE may be either the marriage of one man to several women, to which the name of POLYGYNY is given, or it may be the marriage of one woman to several men which is called POLYANDRY. Where the several women are sisters this is referred to as SORORAL POLYGYNY; where the several men are brothers, this type of marriage is called FRATERNAL POLYANDRY. The latter type of marriage is, however, very rare, and sororal polygyny is the more frequently found. Different types of plural marriage are obviously related to the type of residence pattern and descent system.

Plural marriage should not be confused with PRIVILEGED MATING. The majority of known societies do not regard, as we do (officially), sex as something which is only allowable within marriage. In the first place many societies allow pre-marital sexual intercourse with certain categories of people. In the second place, while the great majority of societies regard marriage as creating exclusive rights in the sexuality of the wife and, therefore, have strict rules which proscribe adultery, it must be remembered that marriage is primarily a transference of rights (even in the spouses) between *groups*. Hence, in a substantial minority of societies, sexual access to brothers' wives or wives' sisters, is not regarded as adultery. Here marriage transfers rights in the wife's sexuality not exclusively to the husband but to the males of the husband's sibling group, or rights in the females of a sibling group to a husband of one of them. It does not follow, however, that such transfers therefore constitute a case of plural marriage. On the contrary, the rights in the child born of a woman to whom her husband's brothers have had privileged access will, in a patrilineal society, be regarded as belonging to her husband on the principle

[1] This term is used here to include rules of exogamy.

that the 'social father' of a child is the rightful husband of its mother, whoever the genetic father may be. That is to say it is the marriage that establishes the *fatherhood* of the child, even though that same marriage may also have given rights of privileged *sexual* access to other members of the father's kin group.

We must take care, therefore, not to confuse the creation of rights in the children with the transfer of rights in the sexuality of the wife just because our society, stressing genetic paternity as the basis of social paternity, has to restrict access to the husband in order to ensure a 'proper' basis for social fatherhood.

LEGITIMACY AND PLACEMENT

So far we have considered three types of rights involved in marriage: rights in the children; rights in the spouses deriving from and reflected in patterns of residence; and sexual rights. We have not considered the first class of rights in any detail.

In the first chapter of this book we noted that it had been stated as a universal principle that a child must have a 'social father' or 'pater'. This 'principle of legitimacy' tied 'fatherhood' to 'membership of the procreative group' and to 'marriage'. We can now see why. Some agreement between the two kin groups of the man and the woman responsible for the generation of the child must be arrived at to reconcile otherwise conflicting claims in the child itself. However, the first solution to this problem that we put forward did not involve marriage, nor membership of the 'procreative group'. That solution was that the women take not husbands but lovers and retain all the rights in the children. Moreover, there is a society which approaches this situation, as we shall see.

Before we can deal with this problem, we need to be clear about the meaning of the term 'father' *as it is used in our own society*. First it implies that the man would be recognized by scientists as the genetic father of the child. Secondly, it implies that the man is recognized by the society as the procreator of the child. Now since different societies may have different beliefs about procreation and different ways of deciding difficult cases, we need, therefore, another term which means 'the man socially recognized as the genetic father (whether, according to our scientific ideas, he is or not)'. The term used for this purpose is GENITOR.

Thirdly, the father cannot be said to be a father unless the rights and duties are acknowledged and the appropriate behaviour expected by other people. This complex pattern of acknowledgement and expectation is partly what is meant by our describing a child born in marriage as legitimate. But equally, fatherhood can be regarded as being thus made legitimate. In for example a CONSENSUAL UNION between a man and a woman (that is to say where the two people consent privately to live together and produce children), the father is genetic father and genitor, and plays the role of father, but he is not thereby expected to play that role nor has any rights over his offspring, or they to him over and above those they have in a genitor. The man in such a case is an illegitimate father.

To speak of a man being an illegitimate father sounds very odd. Obviously, something more is involved in our notion of illegitimacy than 'lack of social expectations and of social recognition of rights and duties'. Now this 'something more' is apparently absent when we speak of 'illegitimate fathers' and, therefore, it must be something peculiar which follows from not having a legitimate father rather than from not having a legitimate child.

Now we can see why in a patrilineal society it should be necessary for a child to have a pater—otherwise he may find himself belonging to none of the recognized social groups which go to make up the society, and eligible for none.

In societies with other types of descent system this is not the case. However, we have seen that most societies have rules governing mating and marriage. Failure to produce at least a genitor for the child makes it look as if these rules may have in fact been broken. Hence there may be doubt as to whether the child in fact is a member of the society or whether he ritually unclean or something of this sort. Hence most societies withhold full social membership from children who cannot be 'placed' within the society or within a group within it.

The illegitimate father is not in this position. He may incur social opprobium but there is no doubt as to his rightful membership either of the society or to groups within it. We can now see a little more clearly what is involved in legitimacy. Legitimacy does not merely involve the recognition by others of rights and duties of parent and child. The 'third party' to any marriage, 'community' or 'state', is interested in the proceedings from 'its *own*' point of view, because in consequence of such proceedings, it will be possible to determine whether the children of the marriage belong to it or not.

The concept of legitimacy involves, therefore, two quite distinct ideas: the idea of social recognition of relationship between parent and child (of importance chiefly to the individuals concerned) and the idea of the child as a full member of society. In our society both are achieved by marriage, the husband being both pater and genitor. We shall refer to the second idea as the 'attribution of societal membership'.[2] The first will be referred to as 'the recognition of ties of filiation'.

In order that the child should be defined as properly belonging to the society, it will be necessary to arrange for some acknowledgement that he possesses the qualifications on which membership depends. If this depends on his having been engendered by a full member of the society, acknowledgement of genetic fatherhood by someone who thereby becomes genitor of the child will be enough. If, however, there is no notion of genetic fatherhood or it is not regarded as relevant to the qualifications for societal membership, the existence of a social father created by a marriage will be required.

In order that the child may have a proper set of kinship relationships, it will be necessary that someone should be recognized as the person through whom patrilateral ties may be traced. Once again the acknowledgement by a genitor may suffice. It may be said, therefore, that both types of legitimacy do not need to be tied to marriage and can be independent of it. Nor must marriage necessarily ensure legitimacy. If acknowledgement of genetic fatherhood is necessary to obtain societal membership, then this will not be achieved by marriage where access to the wife is not restricted to the husband, though the husband may be regarded as father for kin purposes. If there is more than one husband, marriage will not determine the person through whom patrilateral ties may be traced, though the child will be legitimate for societal purposes. However we define marriage[3] therefore, it may be said that legitimacy is independent of it.

To say this is not, however, to deny that marriage usually has the effect of ensuring both types of legitimacy to the offspring. That does not mean that it has to be done this way. We have to recognize that we are dealing here with three sets of rules: rules concerning societal membership, rules concerning kinship relationships, and rules concerning the rights established or transferred by marriage. It is only by examining the relations between these three sets of rules in particular cases that we can say anything about necessary relations between marriage and legitimacy.

To sum up: marriage frequently ensures the societal membership of children and the social recognition of their ties of filiation. It does not follow that marriage is the only way of doing either.

Now it may have occurred to some readers that it is very odd that the stigma of illegitimacy should have been so long retained in our own society where societal membership does not depend on parentage.

Now, when we are faced with a problem of this kind and can find

[2] I regret the 'barbarous neologism', but it is indispensable.

[3] Unless of course we define it as 'that which makes children legitimate'.

no logical connection between associated rules, there are two places we can look. We can look to the consequences of following the rules for the following of other rules, or we can look at the beliefs and ideas which are embodied in the rules.

We know that societal membership was not always attributed in the way it is now. Before the coming of the 'nation state', societal membership, or at any rate social acceptance, seems to have been assured by the ability to produce genitors, and few disabilities attached to children born outside marriage. It was the advent of both church and state as centralizing institutions that resulted in progressive legal disabilities being placed on bastards and, most important, made the parents not only criminals, but took the child away from them, raising it at public charge. Quite apart from beliefs which at first the church and later the Puritans inculcated concerning the iniquity of bastardy, the removal of the child from the parents made him unplaceable and destroyed the locally recognized and acceptable ties of filiation through a genitor. The legal requirement of the formal establishment of rights (which in a sense created bastardy) was reinforced by ideological sanctions.[4]

In order to account for the persistence of the stigma of illegitimacy, we might argue as follows. People are placed in one or other of the various categories or groups which go to make up the society on the basis of the group membership of their parents, and such placements play an important part in determining behaviour towards them. When children are young they belong to few groups and their memberships are determined by their parents. Children, therefore, 'inherit' group memberships in all societies whether or not the groups concerned are recruited on the basis of kinship. If you are born a Catholic, you can of course renounce your faith, but people will continue to say 'He is an *ex*-Catholic you know'. There is no possible way of ceasing to be an *ex*-Catholic. Hence, when we are introduced to some one we have not previously met, we ask, 'Who is he?' and the answer almost always involves reference to his natal group. In a small community this may involve tracing connections between the subject of your interest and other persons who are known to you. It may involve merely placing the subject in a category. But the more categories, the better you can fix his 'position'. 'That was Lord X, chairman of So and So' is a pretty useful reply, but if it were to continue 'third son of a German-Jewish East End tailor' that would be generally regarded as even more satisfactory.

It follows from this that lack of knowledge of the memberships of

[4] See Pinchbeck, I., 'Social Attitudes to the Problem of Illegitimacy', *Brit. Jour. Sociol.* 5, 1954, pp. 309–323.

one parent constitutes a severe drawback to the accurate placing of an individual. If we accept the currency of *ideas* which stress the importance of inheritance in determining character, then the lack of ability to place a person in terms of his parentage will arouse doubts as to one's ability to predict how he will behave. It is rather like buying second hand furniture—'you don't know where it's been'. What evidence one always has about the illegitimate is that their mothers have been at best unwise and at worst immoral; undesirable characteristics which may well have been 'passed on' to the child. Discrimination against these unpredictable and dubious people naturally follows.[5]

Recognition of parentage then has the consequence of enabling the child to be attributed not merely to the society but to a *position within* the society. Both of these attributions are quite properly called placement. Placement within a society is always necessary but there is no need for it to depend on the recognition of parentage. As long as parentage is recognized, however, and parents given charge over their children in their most formative years, it is highly unlikely that an individual's parentage will not constitute one of the dimensions on which he is 'placed'. The two senses of placement must be distinguished however. The need for the attribution of societal membership may be invoked to explain the origin of the universal human concern to trace paternity. Its usefulness as a means of placement within a society may be referred to to account for the persistence of that concern.

It can now be seen why there is always a third party in any marriage. The wider society is interested in what is going on because it will thereby be enabled to determine the societal membership and membership of groups and categories within the society of the children produced by the marriage. This last concern is, of course, shared by the natal groups of the spouses whose arrangement as to rights in the child has precisely the effect of determining his membership and hence placement. Even where individuals are not recruited to social groups *on the basis* of kinship qualifications (as in our own society) they are *in fact* recruited in this way, though not uniquely so. Hence the establishment of relationships between parents and children are of treble significance: to individuals, to kin groups and

[5] 'You can scarcely expect me to permit Cecily, a girl brought up with the greatest care and refinement, to marry into a railway station and form an alliance with a parcel!'—Lady Bracknell, on hearing that her ward's suitor, Jack Worthing, was found as an infant in a hand-bag left in a waiting room at Victoria Station and, although now rich through adoption, could not produce a genitor, far less a father. (Oscar Wilde, *The Importance of Being Ernest.*)

to the society. This point takes us back, therefore, to our discussion of the individual and society in the previous chapter. This is inevitable for in discussing marriage we are simply discussing kinship from another point of view.

THE DEFINITION OF MARRIAGE

The definition of marriage may seem a trivial problem, and so in a sense it is. More is involved than arguments about terms, however, and the problems which underlie that of definition are of crucial significance to our discussion of the family in the next chapter.

Marriage has been defined traditionally in terms of legitimacy and we have seen what problems there are with *that*. Moreover, even if we could arrive at a definition of legitimacy which was satisfactory, any definition, which made its defining characteristic the ability of the mates to procreate legitimate offspring, would run into trouble because it would include cases which we might very well wish to distinguish and the statement 'marriage is a universal social institution' would then become no more than 'legitimacy is a universal institution' put in a different way.

We have to be very clear about what we are doing here. We have to avoid the danger of thinking that, as Goldschmidt has put it, there is something called 'marriageness' which we could get at 'if only we could put it in a proper centrifuge and force out those extraneous substances that contaminate its cross-cultural purity'.[6] The inhabitants of Europe and America have an idea which they call marriage. People in other cultures have other ideas which are similar to, but not the same as, our ideas. Traditionally the argument has been about how dissimilar the ideas have to get to force us to stop describing their ideas as 'marriage'. Simple-minded laymen who point out that *any* dissimilarity is usually sufficient to stop *them* describing an idea as 'marriage' have usually been jumped on very hard and told not to be ethnocentric. Now the crime of ethnocentricity is indeed a grave one. It consists of explaining the concepts peculiar to one culture in terms of your own culture. This is, however, exactly what many of those who seek to produce a cross-cultural definition of marriage have in fact been doing since they use their own society's definition as a base. The correct question to ask is 'what concepts is it useful for students of society to devise in order to aid the understanding of different cultures'.

This precept still leaves us with serious problems. If you are not

[6] Goldschmidt, W., *Comparative Functionalism*, Univ. of California Press, 1966, pp. 25–26.

to be permitted to use your own society's concepts as a starting point, how can you even define an area of social behaviour which you wish to consider? The answer to this difficulty that has been adopted so far in this book is to look at the sort of problems with which men everywhere have to deal and the sort of sense they make of them. One of those problems is, as we have seen, to make arrangements for biological reproduction and for the transmission of material goods and cultural possessions from one generation to another. What has been previously called marriage clearly is concerned with the performance of these tasks.

Until recently few people adopted this approach. The protagonists in the battle were on the one hand those who tended towards the view that marriage was a 'bundle of rights', and that any cluster of rights from that bundle would be held to constitute marriage; on the other hand, there were those who sought some irreducible minimum or core of rights which characterized marriage everywhere. The skirmishing ground between these two sides was a number of hard cases. Let us look at these briefly.

The first class of cases was constituted by instances of transfers of rights which ensured the legitimacy of the child, but did violence to our own cultural notion of marriage. Examples of this class are woman to woman 'marriage' and 'ghost' marriage among the Zulu and Nuer. In both these cases the genetic father is not the pater or mother's husband, since the pater and husband is respectively, either a woman or dead. It is particularly odd to call these transfers marriage, because they do not include the transfer of sexual rights between *spouses* which is the most salient characteristic of our type of marriage.

The second class of difficult cases is made up of those in which the creation of rights in the child is distinct from the creation of an affinal relationship between the groups concerned. To put it another way, this type of case involves a separation of the legitimation of the child (that is to say the establishment of his societal membership and/or kin relationship) from the establishment of relationships of affinity between the natal groups of the spouses. In cases of this kind, we have a choice between calling either, both or neither of these orderings of social relationships 'marriage'.

Perhaps the most notorious case of this kind is Nayar 'marriage'.[7] The Nayars are an Indian caste found on the Malabar coast. The Nayar men's traditional occupation was that of soldiering, which entailed their frequent absence from their native village. They were

[7] Another case, recently the subject of discussion, has been the various forms of Sinhalese marriage. Cf Leach, E., 'Rethinking Anthropology', *L.S.E. Monographs on Social Anthropology* No. 22, 1961, Chapter 4.

also farmers, that is to say they resided on farms cultivated by tenants and serfs (members of other castes).

The Nayar inhabitants of the villages were themselves divided into sub-castes. The system of descent among the Nayars was matrilineal and formed the basis of the formation of exogamous descent groups (matrilineages). The commoner Nayars owed allegiance to either the lineage of the village head-man, or to that of the district chief or to the royal Nayar lineage or to the patrilineage of a Brahmin landlord. The Brahmins were a superior caste.

The domestic group was composed of a segment of the matrilineage composed of a group of sibs of both sexes, the sisters' immature sons and the sisters' daughters, and the sisters daughters' children. Note: the young men are away on military service and there are no 'husbands'.

When a female reached puberty a ceremony was performed in which each girl was paired with a man from a lineage linked to the girls lineage by similar previous ceremonies. The couple cohabited for three days. Thereafter the 'union' was dissolved. The only duty created between the couple was that of the woman to observe ritual pollution at her partner's death, *as if* he were her matrilineal kin. The man also acquired the right to be called by a term indicating kinship by his partner's children.

The ceremony was regarded, however, as admitting the girl to the position of adult woman in the society, and entitled her to take lovers from within her sub-caste but outside her lineage.

On the birth of a child, it was necessary that one of these lovers should acknowledge the genetic fatherhood of the child, that is accept the position of *genitor* of the child. If this could not be done, the child was not accepted as a member of his mother's lineage and caste. No relationship was, however, established between the child and his genitor by such acknowledgement.

The necessity of such acknowledgement lies in caste beliefs. If there was no acknowledgement, the genetic father might have been a man of lower caste than the mother. Hence, the child would not be a pure caste member and contact with him for some purposes would have involved ritual pollution. Hence, sexual relations between women, and men of a lower caste were absolutely forbidden. Relationships with men of higher castes were, however, favoured, different castes and lineages attempting to gain genitors in higher social groups and hence gain the basis for claiming superiority over others within their lineage or sub-caste. Sexual relationships between men, and women of a lower caste were not frowned upon provided the rules governing ritual purification were observed. The reason for this is clear. In a matrilineal system, the genitor's issue do not belong to his descent group so no harm is done.

Suppose, however, the father is a member of a *patrilineal* group. It would matter a great deal if the issue of the lower caste woman by a higher caste man became members of the genitor's kin group. This case does not arise among the Nayar. Whoever the genitor is, the child belongs to the mother's matrilineage.

It follows, however, that if we define marriage in terms of legitimacy, then both the puberty rite and the acknowledgement of genetic fatherhood are parts of marriage since they are necessary to ensure legitimacy, but where the genitor belongs to a patrilineal caste, then the last part of the 'marriage' is marriage for the woman but not for the man. Indeed the Brahmins regard their relationships with Nayar women as concubinage but *not* marriage, which of course must be with a woman of the same caste.

If we take the extreme 'bundle of rights' position we can say that both the puberty ceremony and the acknowledgement of genetic fatherhood are 'marriages', because both involve some of the bundle of rights involved in other types of marriage. Gough, from whose work on the Nayars the above (highly condensed) account is taken, wishes to adopt the alternative approach and define marriage as: 'a relationship between one or more other persons, which provides that a child born to the woman under circumstances not prohibited by the rules of relationship is accorded full birth status rights common to normal members of his society or stratum'.[8]

Goldschmidt has correctly pointed out that Gough has 'stripped the term marriage to a single criterion' and her definition simply states that 'marriage equals birth status rights to children'. This is our old friend legitimacy back again under another guise.

TOWARDS AN ADEQUATE DEFINITION

Instead of arguing fruitlessly about this problem, we need instead to ask: how do societies arrange for the orderly procreation and rearing of future generations and the transmission of material and cultural possessions?

This question may be further broken down into two sets of further questions:

First, how does the society (i) arrange for the determination of the attribution of societal membership to the child? (ii) arrange for the determination of the recognition of the ties of filiation of the child?

[8] Gough, K., 'The Nayar and the definition of marriage,' *Jour. Roy. Anthrop. Inst.* 89, 1959, p. 32.

(iii) arrange for the child's allocation to social groups within society? (iv) arrange for the transmission of property?[9] (v) arrange for the acculturation of the child both with regard to the culture of society as a whole and to the culture of the group within it to which the child belongs? (i) and (ii) are what is meant by legitimizing the child. (ii) involves (iii) if groups within the society are recruited on the basis of kinship, (ii) involves (i) if societal membership is determined by kin group membership; (v) is a corollary to (i) and (iii).

All of (i) to (v) may be what is vaguely indicated by the term 'placement', though it refers in particular to (i) and (iii). In some societies possession of property forms the basis of social group membership. In all societies distinctions are made between individuals and groups according to the extent of their control over economic resources. Hence (iv) is also always covered by the term placement, except where groups or individuals within the society cannot transmit property to members in the next generation.

Secondly, how does society (i) delineate rights of sexual access? (ii) arrange for the economic support of immature children and pregnant and nursing mothers? (iii) arrange for their domestic care and support?

While it is true to say of almost any of these tasks, that in most societies it is performed as the result of an arrangement entered into by two kin groups and publicly acknowledged, in few societies are *all* of these tasks performed as a result of such an arrangement, and seldom is any task performed *entirely* as a result of such arrangements.

The variability of the 'bundle of tasks' that these arrangements are concerned with is, of course, directly related to the variability of the uses to which recognition of ties of filiation can be put, and the enormous variation in ideas about kinship which men have.

If we are to use the term marriage it would seem to be *useful* to make it mean *the institutional means of providing for the performance of tasks concerned with procreation, rearing and transmission, where the means concerned involve a reordering of relationships of kin groups, and/or of the persons thought to be, already or potentially, the genetic parents of children.*

Such a definition has two elements. On the one hand it points out a class of tasks. On the other it specifies that the type of arrangement we are concerned with is one between kin groups or between persons linked through actual or potential genetic parenthood, as it is understood by the society concerned.

It is necessary to add a warning here about the use of the term

[9] 'Property' is used here to include 'offices'.

'institutional'. We have already noted that we cannot speak of a role being institutionalized except in relation to a group. Some of the problems involved in the definition of marriage arise because the arrangement entered into is not recognized by some official body, or by some group wider than that to which the spouses belong, whose members do recognize the arrangement. *Any* marriage definition can run into trouble on these grounds.

It can now be seen that questions concerning 'the universality of marriage' are questions with no precise meaning. They are questions whose answer depends as much upon sorting out what we mean by marriage, as it does upon going and looking.

FATHERHOOD, LEGITIMACY, PLACEMENT AND MARRIAGE

It may be helpful to conclude this discussion by briefly considering the relationships between the various terms with which we have been struggling in the chapter: fatherhood, legitimacy, placement and marriage. We have previously distinguished a 'pater' and a 'genitor'. There is no difficulty with the definition of genitor, but what exactly is a social father? We have answered so far: 'the man who has the rights and duties of a father as defined by the society concerned'. This will not do. Once again is presupposes a prior notion of 'fatherhood'. By fatherhood we could mean: the man through whom ties of filiation are traced; the man through whom rights to property are traced; the man whose acknowledged relationship to the child establishes its societal membership; the man whose acknowledged relationship to the child establishes its social group membership; or any combination of all these.

The notions of social fatherhood, marriage and legitimacy are systematically inter-related. The uses to which the recognition of ties of filiation are put will determine what marriage (the arrangement of rights between kin groups which provide for the recognition of ties of filiation) involves and this in turn will determine the social identifications which are necessary in order to permit the ties of filiation to be used in that way. That is to say it will determine what we mean by fatherhood. To speak of legitimacy is to speak of the recognition of ties of filiation by third parties. What actually follows from the recognition of a filiative tie as legitimate will depend on the uses to which such ties are put. Placement is a sort of catch-all word which covers every conceivable use to which the recognition of ties of filiation can be put.[10]

[10] Except, of course, the attribution of duties of maintenance and domestic care.

RESTRICTION ON THE CHOICE OF MATE: INCEST PROHIBITIONS AND RULES OF EXOGAMY

In the foregoing discussion we have had continually to recognize that most societies have rules which restrict the range of choice of partners for the purposes of both sexual and marital relationships. The most important category of such restrictions is that which includes prohibition on sexual relationships (and therefore, usually, marriage) within categories of close kin. Such prohibitions are found in all societies. They vary a great deal but they appear always to prohibit sexual relations between first-degree consanguineal kin. This regularity is not, however, an unquestionable biological condition of existence. If it is, then it is a very odd sort of biological condition.

It is not the case that primary kin *cannot* mate with each other. It is not even the case that primary kin never mate with each other. It is only the case that all societies have social rules which prohibit such mating. That is to say that in all societies men have some notion of genealogical relatedness and rules prohibiting the mating of persons within the categories distinguished as a result of such notions.

It would be a mistake to suppose that what has been described is a *regularity* in human behaviour. The apparent regularity depends on the way the principle is stated. It is stated in the way that it is, because societies have so many different rules prohibiting mating, that the only statement that can be made that covers this bewildering variety is that all societies prohibit mating in what *we* call the category of primary kin.[11]

Put more precisely, the question we have to consider is why there should be any overlap between the different categories within which mating is prohibited. This is really not a very difficult question to answer. *Given* that all societies do prohibit mating within certain genealogical categories, then it is highly likely that there will be some overlap. In fact the overlap is about as minimal as it can be. The question as to why there should not be an overlap would be much more difficult to answer.

The question that we have to answer is: why should all societies prohibit mating within certain categories (unspecified)? To put the question this way is to place such rules squarely where they belong: not as prior conditions which kinship systems have to take into account, but as elements in kinship systems themselves.

In dealing with this problem, we have not only to distinguish rules which forbid sexual intercourse within the prohibited category and

[11] For some indication of the variety see Murdock, G. P., *Social Structure*, London, Macmillan, 1949, Chapter 10.

those that forbid marriage. We have to take into account as well that such categories may not be mere categories but also groups. Hence, in our attempt to explain such rules, we must consider why such groups are formed and what follows from the successful co-operation of their members in their characteristic activities. We need to distinguish, in addition, *intra-* and *inter*-generational incest; that is, in the context of the *domestic* group, between parent-child and brother-sister (sibling) incest.

Let us look first at the domestic group. Now it can be argued that sexual intercourse between mother and son is not very likely to occur. Either the mother will be dead by the time the child is adult, or be sexually undesirable anyway. Moreover, it is important to recognize that power within the family will rest with the male who is not likely easily to relinquish his sexual monopoly of the mother. Neither of these explanations are satisfactory. In the first place, why forbid what is not likely to happen or nobody wants; in the second place the unequal distribution of power within the domestic group presupposes only unsuccessful attempts at incest, not a rule precluding such attempts.

We have not done with this argument however. The power of the father is made legitimate by teaching a belief in the rightness of his sexual monopoly of the mother. This if swallowed by the children would effectively prevent conflict within the family over access to the mother. It is after all the existence of the *rules* we are considering.

What about father-daughter incest? This prohibition is extremely difficult to explain simply in terms of the *domestic* group. The only plausible hypothesis is that put forward by Parsons concerning the psychological requirements of effective personality development. He argues, using an overtly Freudian framework, that the prohibition of sexual gratification with either parent is a necessary condition of the development of a capacity for normal heterosexual relationships, and hence for the continuance of society which depends on the capacity of its members adequately to reproduce.[12]

Let us now consider brother and sister incest. Within the domestic group Fox's[13] treatment of the subject is by far the most illuminating. It is, however, an explanation which is primarily psychological. It is this. Children brought up in close proximity are sexually unaroused by each other. Hence they mate out. Where, however, physical familiarity before puberty is prevented, and at puberty other

[12] This argument is set out in Parsons, T., 'The incest taboo', *Brit. Jour. Sociol.* 5, 1954, p. 101.

[13] Fox, R., 'Sibling Incest', *Brit. Jour. Sociol* 13, 1962, pp. 128–150.

sexual outlets are denied, there will be sexual arousal and a desire to act upon it. In this situation the desire will be so strong as to be frightening, resulting in strong prohibitions enforced by the anxiety attached to the idea of sibling incest itself. Where desire is weak prohibitions will be weak, where desire is strong prohibitions will be strong.

Now this type of argument is an ontogenetic one which seeks to derive the origin of a social rule in the conditions of action prior to its existence. However, it really includes another element also, that of other rules governing the physical intimacy of sibs. Therefore, the true ontogenetic argument here must concentrate on the 'familiarity breeds contempt' aspect.

Let us now leave these hypothetical explanations hanging in the air for a moment and consider the descent group aspect. It may be argued that inter- and intra-generational intercourse must be frowned upon within exogamous descent groups, lest it lead to permanent attachments which made exogamic rules difficult to enforce. If inter- and intra-generational intercourse is forbidden within the descent group, it will also be forbidden within the domestic group which it includes.

This type of explanation proceeds by attempting to show the necessity of rules forbidding intra-group intercourse, given the activities carried on by the group to which they refer. It is not an ontogenetic argument in any sense, however, because the fact that descent groups exist in society at a given time is purely contingent and not necessary. Given the existence of exogamous descent groups, it can be seen that rules forbidding intercourse serve to reinforce any prohibitions on marriage within the descent group. That different societies form different types of group out of different categories of kin explains the wide variety of prohibitions on intercourse, and the different activites which they perform in part explain the different degrees of importance attached to them.

There remain, however, two important problems: why exogamy? and why prohibitions on sexual intercourse within the domestic group when there is *no* exogamic rule applying to a wider group? There are three distinct approaches to this problem. First we could regard exogamy as an extension of the prohibition of sexual intercourse within the domestic group. Second we could regard the incest prohibition as a survival of a descent group society. Thirdly we would treat exogamy and domestic group prohibitions absolutely separately.

The first suffers from the same difficulties that have already been discussed with regard to the 'extension of sentiments' theories of kinship. The second suffers from the fact that there is no reason to believe that all societies were originally descent group societies. The charming thing about adopting the third approach is that we end up with similar explanations in both cases, though they are of a different logical type. Exogamy is not universal, hence we do not need to seek an explanation of the ontogenetic type. Hence our 'explanation' must merely show the place of this rule among the other rules of the society and the consequences of following it. This type of 'explanation' would point out that intergroup marriage establishes kinship, economic and political ties between groups that would otherwise have not been so connected, thus creating or strengthening ties within the groups which constitute the society.

The prohibition on sexual intercourse within the domestic group is similarly explained. At the core of every domestic group lies the biological group of parent(s) and children. Continuous inbreeding it is said would make impossible the establishment of ties of marriage between different biological groups (which is true) and only in such a way could relationships have been developed between biological groups (which is problematic). Hence, just as according to Parsons' psychological theory the incest prohibition within the biological group is necessary for the individual to have normal sexual relationships (outside it), so it is necessary for the groups themselves to establish relationships with other groups.

Now this isn't a proper ontogenetic argument at all, at least if we define such an argument as one which shows that a cultural or social characteristic is necessary in terms of some non-social law and the conditions of action of all men. It looks like an ontogenetic argument but it has evolutionary elements smuggled in. It implies that human society started with the biological group, and that kinship relationships were the first kind of social relationship, and hence primeval man could only form wider relationships on the kinship base, and (given all that) then a prohibition on intra-biological group intercourse was the only way in which it could be done. Such an historical account, though probable, is highly conjectural.

To deal with the domestic group, therefore, we must return to the arguments previously put forward. These were:

(i) Rearing children of different sexes together results in sexual indifference. They, therefore, mate out.

(ii) Son-mother intercourse is ruled out because of the power of the father which the rule of incest may be seen as legitimizing.

(iii) Father-daughter incest, it would appear, can only be explained in terms of a psychological theory such as is put forward by Parsons. However, it is perhaps not susceptible of, and does not require, such an explanation. It has been asserted to be the type of incest which is most common in practice, and it is likely that its frequency of occurrance is not entirely unrelated to the degree of importance attached to it by the societies concerned.

Now some societies regard father-daughter incest as pitiful or comic rather than wicked. Hence, it is by no means the case that all societies have a rule absolutely forbidding it. This suggests that the regularities we find between societies may be a factitious product of various structural features. That is to say that it can be explained in terms of *other* rules in the societies rather than in terms of their non-social conditions of action. We have already seen that there is likely to be a relationship between rules of exogamy and intercourse, not because the latter is extended to the former but because both are related to kinship beliefs and categories. Hence, dealing with the former may entail a disapproval of the latter. Moreover, where a high value is placed on virginity, father-daughter intercourse would obviously damage the chances of the girl in the marriage market, a fact which may be seen to entail a fatherly duty to refrain from intercourse in the girl's interests or as a duty to refrain from intercourse in the group's interests. Where the society places a high value on marital chastity it will be frowned on because it is inconsistent with the father's marital role, rather than because of the effects on or through the daughter. The chances of father-daughter intercourse being banned for one reason or another are quite high. So, we find that in most societies it is banned, but in others regarded as odd, since to have to resort to sleeping with one's own daughter suggests (according to different attitudes to sex and marriage) either that something is wrong with the marital relationship or that the man cannot get anyone else to sleep with him, or both.

Once again what we have done to deal with this problem is to relate the rules governing behaviour to other rules and both to beliefs and categories. The prohibitions on intercourse and on marriage are usually related not directly but through a set of beliefs from which both derive their force. At the same time we have recognized that even if a phenomena is universal it does not mean that there is necessarily one *casual* explanation for it.[15]

[15] This discussion makes no attempt to summarize the arguments which have been advanced. Two main classes of argument have been omitted: first, those arguments which are too silly to be worth discussing; and second, arguments which are concerned with the evolutionary consequences of non-adoption of the prohibition. The interested reader may find the latter arguments discussed in Fox, R., *Kinship and Marriage*, Penguin, 1967, Chapter 2. For a summary of the history of the anthropological debate see Seligman, B., 'Incest and Exogamy: a reconsideration', *American Anthropologist* 52, pp. 305–316.

OTHER TYPES OF CONTROL ON MATE SELECTION

It is, of course, not only that marriage within certain categories of individuals is prohibited in all societies. In many societies marriage with certain categories is also preferred. In many instances, where marriage is an alliance between groups, then this alliance may be reaffirmed by marriages between the same groups in each generation. As a consequence an individual's mate will also be his consanguineal kin, hence the rule of marriage may be expressed in terms of consanguine kinship. These rules may be of considerable complexity and sometimes define exactly whom an individual must marry (prescribed marriage).

In addition to systems of preferred or prescribed marriage, Goode[16] has noted four ways in which the choice of marriage partner of a child may be determined by its parents or kin-group. The *first* of these is child marriage. Here the contracting parties enter into an arrangement before the child has had time to establish any attachments to members of the opposite sex. *Secondly* a similar effect may be achieved by isolation of the child (in this case usually a girl) so that she has no contacts with others of the opposite sex who are potential marriage partners and is dependent upon her family to arrange a marriage for her. The degree of seclusion may vary from the extreme seclusion forced upon women in some primitive societies, to the less obvious but still effective control over social contacts exercised by parents among the upper classes in Victorian Britain. Goode points out that the degree of control over choice of marriage partner is related to the amount of property possessed by the parents. As we saw at the beginning of this chapter, marriage could be regarded as rooted in property, since it is concerned with the regulation of the transmission of rights between generations and groups. It is of interest to point out here that only in capitalist, late capitalist and communist societies, do the majority of the population not possess any property (except short-lived consumer durables) with whose transmission they have to concern themselves. In most technologically primitive societies, the parents or the group to which they belong do possess property which is of considerable importance to them.

Isolation shades imperceptibly into the *third* type of control which involves supervision without segregation. Here an attachment to people of the opposite sex before marriage is permitted, but every possible precaution is taken to ensure that it only occurs with the right partner. Goode in fact calls this type 'chastity', drawing atten-

[16] Goode, W. J., 'The Theoretical Importance of Love', *Amer. Sociol. Rev.* 24, 1959, p. 38.

tion to the way in which supervision is aided in its effectiveness by cultural notions of shame, sexual purity and so on. These ideas may, however, be used to legitimize complete segregation as much as to make supervision effective.

The *last* type of supervision is the type with which we are all familiar: that of parental influence. This relies on the inculcation of moral norms concerning premarital sexuality, an attempt at indirect supervision, and possibly segregation (what else are girls' boarding schools?) and the use of a network of informers to keep tabs on the child's activities. The parent is aided in this task by the extent to which the child's social contacts, as we have already seen in our discussion of placement, are in fact determined by the social position of his parents.

In this type of system the choice of marriage is formally free and in fact is free as long as the partner comes from the right social category or group.[17] The notion of the romantic love, it may be pointed out, aids parental control in so far as it presupposes that somewhere there is the 'right man'. Since the theory does not specify how the man's rightness is to be determined the way is wide open to the advice of more 'experienced' people. Hence the mother's line, 'I don't want to interfere, love, I just want to be sure he's the right man', is not greeted as one might expect in a free system by a rebuff but by the reply, 'I know Mum—if only I could be sure.' Harmony is preserved but at the expense of a certain ambiguity in the use of the term 'right'.

The incidence of these different types of control over choice of marriage partner can be understood in terms of the ideas that the society has about sexuality on the one hand and the uses to which the system of marriage and affinity is put.

[17] For an excellent description of the simultaneous operation of the principles of 'love' and occupational homogamy see Hollingshead, A. B., 'Class and Kinship in a Middle Western Community', *Amer. Sociol. Rev.* 14, 1949, p. 469. The whole topic of mate selection is discussed further below (Chapter 6).

3

The Family

THE discussion of what we mean by the family itself has been left extremely late in this book and for good reason. There is probably no other term with which we shall have to deal that is less clear than this one (except possibly 'placement'). If the reader looks back over the preceding pages he will discover that we have been able to discuss a large number of topics usually covered or referred to in texts on the family without even mentioning the word. The reader may also have gained the impression that social anthropologists in general are not a great deal concerned with the family. Sociologists are very much concerned with it. The reason for this difference in focus of interest lies largely in the nature of the societies that members of the two disciplines study.

'Family' is a word which, unlike 'kinship', is much used by the inhabitants of the technologically advanced societies with which sociologists are concerned. It might be thought therefore that confusions might arise from differences between popular and academic uses of the term. But popular usage is itself extremely complex. We have already seen that people can refer to their relatives as 'the family'. 'All the family turned up for the funeral.' In the next breath they will say, 'Of course I knew *my* family would come, but I never expected all *my husband's* family to show up.' Apparently we have one family which is simultaneously two families—his and hers. 'But of course my brother didn't bring his family along—they're much too young.' Here the reference is to offspring. 'The neighbours were very good too. The Jones came, and their two children. It was very nice the whole family turning up like that.' Here the usage is more restricted than 'relatives', or 'his relatives', but includes both parents *and* offspring. 'Of course, the children will be leaving home soon. It's always sad to see the family break up like that.' Here the reference is not only to parents and children, but to their co-residence, that is to the household. 'Anyhow they won't be living too far away—I always think its nice if you can keep the family together.' So apparently the family hasn't 'broken up' after all. Even though the members are dispersed they still do not cease to be members of the family—whatever that means.

Confused as it may appear to be, the usage of the term 'the family' and the patterns of social behaviour to which it refers are a distinctive part of our (Western) culture. To recognize this is to recognize that we cannot apply it without further definition to other cultures and this is partly the reason why it is a confusing term to use in cross-cultural studies. (The reader may remember that we had similar trouble with 'father' and 'marriage'.) Yet it would be both pedantic and absurd to refuse to use the term in the study of those societies who have a concept of 'family' which closely approaches our own. Nevertheless any definition must be in terms of other, more general concepts. It is for this reason that a consideration of the family has been postponed for so long.

CATEGORIES, ROLES AND RELATIONSHIPS

It will be remembered that in discussing the preliminaries to our study of the family we noted that all social behaviour implies categorization of some kind. All categorization implies making distinctions: classifying people, for example, as the same or different from one another in some way. Our interest in categorization lies in the fact that it is necessary to classify people if we are to have expectations about how they are going to behave.

Similarities in people's behaviour can arise in many different ways and hence many different types of category can be distinguished. The rich, the infirm, bus conductors, southerners, are all examples of different types of category. People are classified according to the relative amount of money they have, according to a physical characteristic, according to the social role they play, according to their relative spatial position and so on.

To classify people in this way makes it possible to divide people up into exclusive categories in each case. The rich cannot also be poor, nor the infirm fit, nor bus conductors bus drivers, nor southerners northerners. The bus conductor example is however a little different from the others. Of the others we can say that we are classifying people on different 'dimensions': wealth, physical fitness and so on. In distinguishing between bus drivers and conductors, though we are distinguishing categories on the basis of the social role their members play, we cannot say we are classifying people on a 'social role' dimension because there are many social roles and to play one role does not imply that you do not also play another. We are either distinguishing bus conductors from non-bus conductors or we are distinguishing bus conductors from bus *drivers*. You cannot be a bus conductor and a bus driver and a bus inspector at the same time. This is so because the roles are interdefined. To say that a man is a bus conductor implies that he is playing one of a set of roles. Roles, therefore, are not separate and unrelated things, for they are sets of expectations about how people should behave to other people. To know what it is to be a bus conductor is to know how one should behave to a bus driver, etc., but is not to know how one should behave to a school-teacher or to a welder. Nevertheless it is still true that classifying someone as a bus driver does enable us to establish an exclusive category of people.

We have already noted that, when two categories of people share the same expectations about how they should behave to one another, we may say that a social relationship exists between members of one category and members of the other category. We could put it more precisely by saying that a type of social relationship exists between the categories and relationships of that type exist between members of the categories. Where the categories are based on the performance of the same role it is the existence of the role which makes possible the relationship. Because we recognize a man as a bus conductor, we know what to expect from him and how to behave towards him.

The concepts to which the terms category, relationship, and role refer are therefore logically interrelated. If we turn now to kinship categories we immediately see that they differ in some respects from the other types of category we have considered.

Membership of a kinship category depends on the possession of a common characteristic which distinguishes members from members of other categories of the same kind. That something is, however, that their members stand in a certain recognized real or fictive biological relation to a particular individual, or Ego. Kinship categories do not therefore constitute a set of exclusive categories in the way that bus conductor, bus driver, bus inspector, etc., do.

The people who compose the category of bus conductors play the same social role. It follows from the way in which the roles are allocated that, having distinguished a *role*, we could then distinguish exclusive categories of *people* using the role they played as the basis of our distinction. If we tried to do this with kinship roles, then, having put on the one side all the people who played the role of brother, we could not put on the other side all the people who played the role of father without shifting some of the fathers over because they were also brothers.

When we refer to a kinship category therefore we are not distinguishing exclusive categories of people in the society as a whole. We are distinguishing categories of people who are exclusive only when seen from the point of view of the individual.

This is so because the roles concerned are allocated on the basis of the unique biological relation that one person has to another. Social relationships between members of different categories of kin are possible because the members share common expectations about how members are to behave to each other. But, because of the way in which the roles are allocated, because they follow a pattern of unique biological relations, this allows me to infer only how I should behave to *my* father and not how I as a child should behave to all the members of an exclusive category of people called 'fathers'.

Because biological relations ramify bilaterally, each individual has a unique set of persons to whom he is biologically related. From this it follows that however widely or narrowly these biological ties are recognized for the purpose of forming categories of recognized kin, no two persons will have the same set of persons to whom they recognize a kin relationship.[1] Hence the recognition of biological ties alone cannot form the basis of recruitment of individuals to an exclusive category of people whose members share the characteristic of recognizing a kin relationship to each other. A kinship position has properties similar to that of a spatial position—no two points can ever have the same relation to *all* the other points on the same surface.

It is because of these properties that those societies who use kinship as a basis for the allocation of individuals to exclusive categories, have to cheat, and ignore ties either through men or women. They then usually try and get the best of both worlds by distinguishing individuals in terms of bilateral filiation.

From all this it follows that whatever we mean by the term family it is not and cannot be an exclusive kin-category of people.[2]

[1] This statement does not of course hold where there is a rule of endogamous marriage, i.e. Ego has to marry within his recognized kin or when the range of marriage is restricted by non-social factors, e.g. isolation as in an island community. Siblings will of course share the same recognized kin in *ascending*, though not in descending generations.

[2] On the problems of descent in bilateral systems see Freeman, J. D., 'On the Concept of the Kindred', *Jour. Roy. Anthrop. Inst.* 91, 1961, p. 192; also Davenport, W., 'Non Unilinear Descent and Descent Groups', in Farber, B. (Ed.), *Family and Kinship Organisation*, London, Wiley, 1966.

CATEGORIES AND GROUPS

When we say that a plurality of people share expectations about the way in which different categories of people within that plurality behave, we imply that the members of the plurality concerned have some of the characteristics of a social group. We do not necessarily imply, however, that the categories within the group are themselves also groups. This is an important point because to say that a group exists is to imply some sort of categorization. The notion of group is meaningless apart from the notions of member and non-member. Such categorization may occur before the formation of the group, or be based on the recognition of relationships between members of the group which distinguish them from non-members but it must be there.

Now we have already had cause to distinguish various types of group in our consideration of kinship. We have referred to the domestic group, the residential group, descent groups, and the procreative or biological group. The first three types of group, if their membership is recruited on the basis of recognition of biological relations, must be recruited by ignoring (for the purposes of group formation) some ties of equal genealogical closeness. This may be done *in the same way throughout the society, that is to say be governed by a societal rule, or it may be done as a result of agreements arrived at by the related persons concerned, which are peculiar to them,* but done it must be. The biological group is a special case, however.

It should be noted that the types of group distinguished are characterized by reference to the activities which they undertake rather than to their membership. They are terms which figure largely in any answer to the question, 'What do people use the system of kinship recognition for, and how do they use it?' Once again however the biological group is something of a special case.

It is true of the biological group but of no others than the activities which distinguish it prescribe its membership. Those activities demand a man, a woman and a sexual relationship between them. The biological necessity of care for offspring demand their presence also. Now it does not follow from these biological considerations that these individuals must form a group. But such considerations do prescribe in part the way in which the different members of such a group must behave; that is to say what may be expected of them; that is to say the roles they must play. The terms 'father', 'mother', 'child' are not merely names of genealogical positions, the content of the roles attached to which may vary from society to society. They are also names of activities, and hence specify in part the content of roles. These roles do effectively determine the membership of the group if it is recognized that they do so by specifying universal activities as well as certain types of biological relatedness.

It is to this set of roles that the term 'nuclear family' in part refers. We should note however that it only succeeds in referring to an exclusive category of people by virtue of reference to the *activities* of the members.

When a set of people interact with one another over a period of time they come to share expectations about the way in which *each other* will behave. When a set of people share expectations of this sort we may describe them as a group. Obviously procreation and rearing involve continuous interaction. Hence by virtue of the activities which define the membership of this set, the members are likely to constitute a group whose ways of behaving both share elements in common with other sets of the same kind and differentiate one set from another.

To refer to a nuclear family therefore is to refer to a group which carries out certain activities which define its membership, and determine to some extent the content and distribution of the roles played. To speak of *the* family is to refer to the class of such groups; *a* family is any particular group which is a member of that class.

To ask 'is the nuclear family universal?' is to ask whether the biological activities, which occur in all societies, universally result in the creation of groups having the membership defined by those activities.

The nuclear family refers to the biological group. It is not a group based on a category of kin but on a class of interrelated activities. The weak link in this group is however the man. There is no biological need to wait around for nine months for the birth of the children. The nuclear family has in fact at least two subgroups within it composed respectively of man and woman, and mother and children. The existence of these two sub-groups need not necessarily overlap in time. If they do so overlap this is because of the nature of the relationship between the man and the woman. The existence of the nuclear family as a group depends therefore on an arrangement being reached whereby the man helps the woman while she rears the children. Marriage as we have defined it is usually[3] such an arrangement. The relationships which characterize the nuclear family are therefore parent-child and mates.

[3] See Chapter 2, p. 53.

KINSHIP AND THE FAMILY PROCESS

By defining the nuclear family in terms of its activities we have determined that it will be extinguished before the death of its members. Eventually, the woman or women will become infertile. Eventually the children will be reared. Hence the activities of the nuclear family will cease and its members will no longer constitute such a family. This does not mean they will all no longer be members of *a* nuclear family however. The children will make arrangements with persons of the opposite sex and in turn produce children, thus becoming members of their own nuclear families. This process is illustrated in Diagram 2 (pp. 71–2). Each circle represents the members who at one time made up a nuclear family. It will be seen that each individual is a member of two such groups and that each group is connected to two groups in the ascending generation and with as many groups as there are children in the descending generation.

In the diagram three or four generations are shown. The speed with which generations follow one another varies very considerably. If mating takes place as early as sixteen and the average age of death is as late as the seventies, it is possible that there will be four generations alive at the same time. If on the other hand mating takes place later and the expectation of life is short, the parents are unlikely to survive sufficiently long to do more than see the infancy of their grandchildren. In either case parents will usually live to see the founding of at least their children's nuclear families. Hence the extinction of the nuclear family with maturation of its children does not mean that its original members will no longer exist.

We noted earlier that we could call a nuclear family 'a group' because the performance of its characteristic activities involved the growth of shared expectations among its members. The shared values and expectations which have grown up as the result of nuclear family membership will not disappear because the activities cease to be performed. There will still be a sense in which the members of the defunct nuclear family can be called a group.

To refer to a group is to refer to the things that a set of people share. We distinguished the things that the members of a nuclear family share which made them a nuclear family, i.e. the biologically necessary activities and the other expectations, beliefs and values which they come to share as the result of a period of interaction. This last category of things shared is not of course destroyed by the cessation of the first set of activities. It is useful to have terms which distinguish these two sets of common properties and the terms customarily used are NUCLEAR FAMILY and ELEMENTARY FAMILY. The nuclear family shares biologically based activities and consequently ceases to exist, after one generation. The elementary family shares those things which have become common to its members during the period of interaction involved in the performance of these biological activities. The members of both nuclear and elementary families are the same: it is the sources of their solidarity that differ. In Diagram 2, the mother, father and children groups shown may be called elementary families.

The members of a given biological group start off as members of a nuclear family, become members of a family which is both nuclear and elementary and end up as members of an elementary family. It is only fair to warn the reader that this distinction is often not clearly made and the terms used are often used to mean exactly the same thing, viz. a set of persons playing the roles father, mother, children to one another.[4] Some sociologists may regard this distinction as pedantic, but it is of fundamental importance because it makes clear the different types of solidarity which exist between the different members of a family group at different stages of its development.[5]

To the reader who has dutifully waded through the chapter on kinship this may have a familiar ring. We seem to be coming back to the 'extension theory' of kinship. And so in a way we are. For Malinowski argued that he had witnessed with 'his own eyes' this process of extension. What he could only have witnessed in fact was this development of sentiments among the group which was performing biological activities which outlasted the performance of those activities and persisted among the members even when the younger generation had founded nuclear families of their own.

We noted in Chapter 1, however, that we could not explain kinship in this way. Similarly we cannot explain the behaviour of members of families entirely in this way either. For their behaviour to one another is not determined solely by the activities they carry out. Nor is it determined solely by the values and expectations which they come to share which distinguish one family from another. It is also determined in part by the expectations as to the behaviour of people performing the biological activities of mates and parents which are shared by the society as a whole.

The behaviour of the Jones family (to put it another way) can be

[4] Also called the *immediate* and the *conjugal* family.

[5] Readers familiar with Durkheim's '*Division of Labour*' may recognize similarities between this distinction and that between organic and mechanical solidarity. For an example of the utility of this distinction see below Chapter 4, p. 99.

understood partly in terms of the biological conditions of their action, partly in terms of their social conditions of action (that is the expectations of others which they have learnt and acquired through the membership of their society), and in terms of the unique set of experiences which the members have come to share as a result of their acting together under those conditions.

To put it yet another way we could say that a nuclear family is a set of people who play biological roles, and institutionalized social roles to one another and, in so doing, develop beliefs and values which inform sets of expectations (roles) which are peculiar to them (or if you prefer it are institutionalized only within that family).

We cannot therefore explain the existence of these general expectations about the behaviour of family members in terms of the generation of sentiments among them through the performance of common biological activities. We can only explain their existence completely if we explicitly recognize that it is partly through the prior existence of kin roles that they come to have the relationships to each other that they do. (See Chapter 1, pp. 31–4).

We are then dealing with a continuous process of family formation which we may call THE FAMILY PROCESS: the creation and extinction of nuclear families; the development of elementary families; the creation of new members by birth; the loss of existing members by death; the establishment of affinal relationships by marriage; the supplementation of these ties by ties of filiation as the children are born, and affines become kin's kin. It is by this process that the exact shape of the set of relations which constitute the web of kinship in any given society at a given time is determined. But at the same time it is only by virtue of the definition of kinship roles and the rules governing marriage and so on that this process is regulated and controlled.

We may now use the terms which we have defined to help us understand the use of the term family in popular speech. It now appears that such usage is less confused than highly complex, and it is so because of the complexity of the situation which it describes.

Each individual belongs first to one and then to two elementary families. He is born into one family, his FAMILY OF ORIGIN and creates his own FAMILY OF PROCREATION (Diagram 1a). (The family of origin is sometimes referred to as his FAMILY OF ORIENTATION. The family of procreation is sometimes referred to as his FAMILY OF MARRIAGE.) Together, Ego's families of origin and procreation constitute his KINSHIP CORE; viz., all his first degree kin (Diagram 1a). Ego's family of procreation is linked, however, not only to *his* family of origin but also to *his wife's* family of origin. Hence the overlapping kinship cores of Ego and spouse constitute a T-shaped cluster or core of three overlapping elementary families linked by his mating arrangement (Diagram 1b).

Diagram 1. FAMILIES OF ORIGIN AND PROCREATION THE KINSHIP CORE.

Fo. Family of Origin; Fp. Family of Procreation; ●s. Spouse; C. Ego's Fo; R. Ego's Spouse's Fo; D. Ego's and Spouse's common Fp.

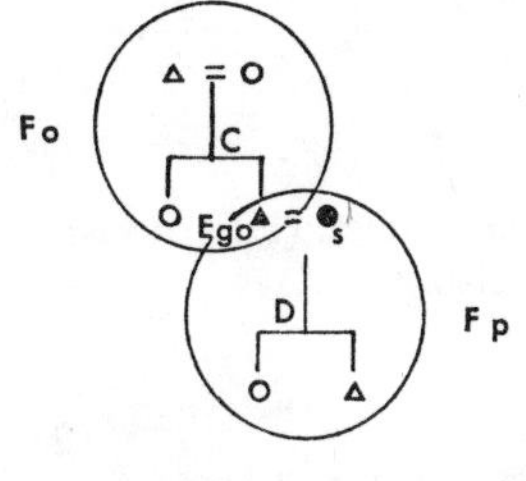

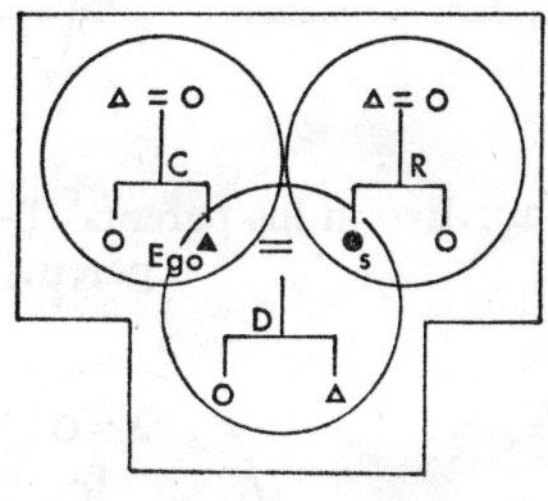

1a 1b

1a. Ego in his families of origin and procreation (Ego's kinship core).
1b. The overlapping kinship cores of Ego and Spouse (their T-core).

At birth, Ego is a member of the T-core of his parents, all the members of which are his consanguineal kin (Diagram 2a). With his marriage and the birth of his children, Ego is a member of an additional T-core constituted by *his* families of origin and procreation and *his spouse's* family of origin (Diagram 2b). With the birth of his grandchildren, Ego now becomes a member of several new

Diagram 2. THE FAMILY PROCESS.

(For explanation of letters, see Diagram 1).

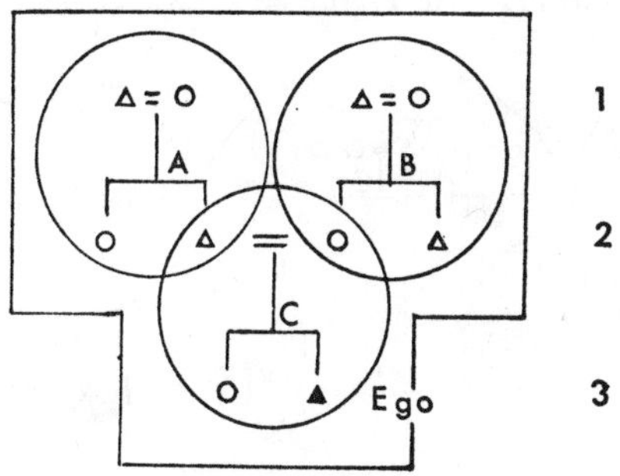

2a. Ego in his parents' T-core.

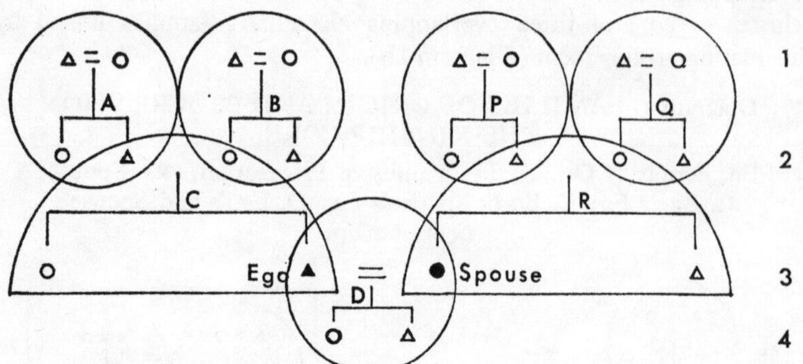

2b. Ego in his parents' T-core and his own T-core. (His spouse's parents' T-core shown also.)

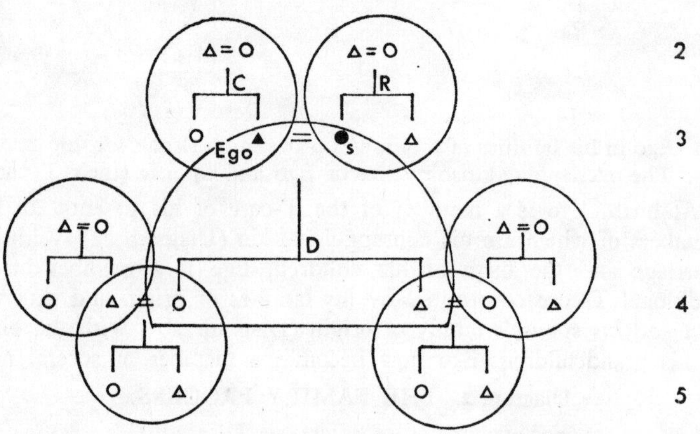

2c. Ego in his own T-core and those of his children.

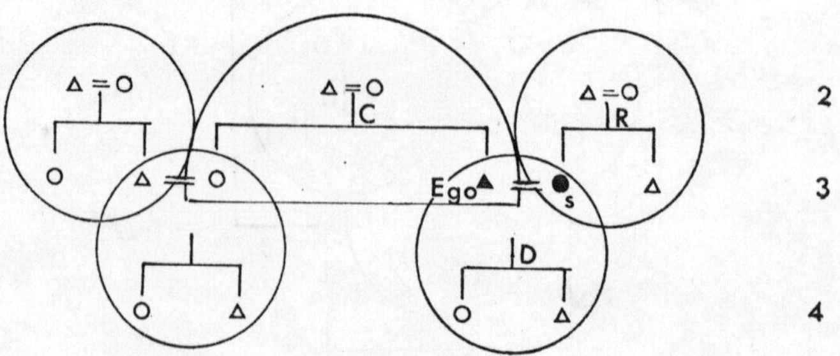

2d. Ego and his own and his siblings' T-cores.

T-cores—as many as he has mated children (Diagram 2c). With the birth of his nephews and nieces he becomes a member of as many new T-cores as he has married sibs (Diagram 2d).

At any given point in time we may think of a given Ego as occupying a position in a complex cluster of interlocking T-cores each constituting the kinship core of a married couple. We may see Ego as moving throughout his life through the typical positions which constitute a T-core; starting off as grandchild, becoming a parent and ending up as a grandparent. Or we may think of Ego starting off as a grandchild in his parents' T-core (ABC), becoming a parent in his own and mate's T-core (CRD) and an uncle in his sibs T-cores (Diagram 2d), and ending up as a grandparent in his children's T-cores (Diagram 2c).

The behaviour of an individual is not then to be understood simply with reference to his membership of any one elementary family, nor simply with reference to his membership of categories of kin, but with reference to his position in an ongoing process through which both categories and groups are formed. As a consequence we need to regard the terms 'father', 'mother', 'sibling' as each referring not to single roles but to *role sequences,* which affect behaviour not merely within the elementary family but also affect the pattern and content of interaction with other kin outside the elementary family or kinship core which is being considered.

We must stress again however that neither an elementary family nor a kinship core of an individual or couple constitutes an exclusive category of kin, except from the point of view of the individual or couple concerned. Ego's family of origin is first-degree kin to him but second-degree kin to his children. The second-degree matrilateral and patrilateral blood kin of Ego's children are not blood kin but affines to each other, and so on. Moreover Ego is simultaneously a member of two elementary families and may be a member of many more than two T-cores.[6]

THE FAMILY PROCESS AND GROUP FORMATION

So far we have been concerned simply to try to understand what is involved in the concept 'family'. And we have broken the notion down into other related concepts. We have not considered what types of family it is useful to distinguish. We have merely developed concepts which will be useful in distinguishing such types.

Any typology of the family will be concerned to distinguish the

[6] See Stacey, M. (Ed.), *Comparability in Social Research,* London, Heinemann, B. S. A., S.S.R.C., 1969.

various uses to which what we have called the family process can be put, either by whole societies or by pluralities of individuals within them. Before we can consider this further we have to return to the composition of the biological group itself. The procreation and rearing of children is *not* a use to which the family process is put: rather to speak of the family is, we have seen, to speak of the consequences which these activities have for the formation of social groups. In contrast the formation of domestic, residential and descent groups depends either on the existence of the biological group or on the recognition of kinship relationships, or both.

As far as the biological group is concerned we have noted that it can be seen as composed of two subgroups: mates, and mother and children. Continued interaction between father and mother and children is not a biological necessity. The smallest biological group is in fact 'mother and children' rather than 'parents and children'. The conditions of survival of the mother and children are frequently such as to require a man to fend for them. There are two candidates for this task: the mother's brother or other male kin and the mother's mate. In the Nayar case we find the mother's male kin performing this activity.[7] We may find it shared between them as is the case where residence after marriage is natolocal as it is among the majority of the Ashanti.[8] In the majority of societies these activities are performed by the husbands, except where their presence in the domestic group conflicts with the necessity to keep the men of the descent group together. (See Chapter 2, p. 42).

Fending for dependent females and children requires some measure of co-residence. Obviously rearing is even more dependent on co-residence. A consideration of the membership of the *biological* group cannot therefore be divorced from the conditions which lead to the formation of the *domestic* group. This does not mean to say that the two types of group cannot be distinguished from one another. Because performance of the biological activities which characterize the biological group require the performance of activities of the domestic group it does not mean that members of a domestic group are necessarily restricted to the members of the biological group. Indeed the nuclear family is frequently 'submerged' in a larger domestic group.

Where various types of plural marriage are practised, then the basis of the domestic group will not be a simple nuclear family but a

[7] See Chapter 2, p. 51.

[8] See Fortes, M., 'Kinship and Marriage among the Ashanti', in Radcliffe-Brown, A. R. and Forde D. (Eds.), *African Systems of Kinship and Marriage*, London, Oxford Univ. Press, 1950.

compound nuclear family composed of a man and his wives or a woman and her husbands. The polygynous family we may regard as a set of co-resident groups of mothers and children and a set of groups of mates, the groups of mates being linked by a common member, and each group of mates overlapping a group of mothers and children.

To describe a group as a DOMESTIC GROUP is to classify it according to the activities which it characteristically performs. This set of activities is not the same as those of the biological group although they overlap. Characteristic of the domestic group is the provision of shelter, food and clothing for its members. Where these activities are provided separately for subgroups within the group, as in the case of a polygynous group where each wife cooks for herself and her children and is not under the authority of another wife and each mother-child group has its own dwelling, the group is more properly a residential group rather than a domestic one.[9]

Similarly in our own society, where a married child, spouse and children live in the same *house* as the parents of the child, they are not said to be members of the same HOUSEHOLD unless they eat together and share a common housekeeping. To share a common housekeeping implies that the food is prepared by the same person or persons and purchased from a common fund. Even where they do form a common household they cannot be said to be a domestic group in the full sense of the word unless the house is owned jointly or, if owned by one of the members, the other members share it as of

[9] There is some disagreement (as usual) about the definition of the term domestic group. Fortes has defined it as 'essentially a house-holding and house-keeping unit organized to maintain and *bring up* its members.' (My stress.) Other authors have used it to mean 'relatives who share a common residence'. Fortes definition, apart from the italicized phrase, is the same as that put forward here. Stacey has suggested the adoption of the latter of the two definitions as more useful. We have regarded the rearing of the children to be characteristic of the biological group rather than of the domestic group. It seems more useful for theoretical purposes to classify groups in terms of their activities and make membership an independent variable, and to distinguish sharply the activities of biological and domestic groups. Of Stacey's definition it may be said that it is highly unlikely that unrelated persons will share the accommodation of one of them 'as of right' as well as a common housekeeping. Hence all domestic groups by our definition will also be domestic groups for Stacey. Unfortunately her definition would include households of relatives that were not domestic groups because the members did not share common rights in the occupancy of the property. This difference does not matter a great deal since such rights are rare in the type of society for which Stacey's definition is designed, but the distinction between the two definitions is important for cross-cultural studies.

For discussion of these definitions see Stacey, M. (Ed.), *Comparability in Social Research*, London, Heinemann, B.S.A., S.S.R.C., 1969.

right and without conditions as to tenure and payment. Because in many societies with which sociologists are concerned all the various characteristics of the domestic group are frequently not found together, they usually distinguish the 'composition of the household' from the 'ownership' and type of 'tenure' and do not use the term domestic group. It is important to remember however that these two items do not exhaust the characteristics of the domestic group and that we need to know the terms on which the other members of the household participate in the occupancy of the dwelling.

Such pedantry has its purpose. When, as is frequently the case, members of the elementary family continue to form domestic groups after the extinction of the nuclear family, this may be explained in terms of the ability of the group to provide certain services for its members which they could not obtain elsewhere. At the same time the examination of the rights and duties which subsist between members of the group is essential to a complete understanding of the behaviour of its members.

Domestic groups and households may be classified according to their composition. They may be composed of a nuclear family alone. If this is the normal type of household, then it follows that there must also be found 'denuded elementary family' households composed of people whose children have formed their own nuclear family households, or siblings one or both of whose parents have died, or individuals who have lost parents by death and sibs (if any) by death or marriage.

Though we may find elementary family households, the elementary family (as we have defined it) cannot be a principle of household formation since the marriage of the children must add new members to the household. Adherence to the principle, that the members of the elementary family must *exclusively* constitute the household, is therefore impossible. Where children's spouses and grandchildren are also brought into the household we may describe the household as a *composite* household.

If the members of the elementary family are kept together we shall find that the household reflects the shape of the family process. Because it is not possible for all family households to retain all their members some of the children must leave home at marriage, (whether this is governed by residence rules or left to choice). Even so there must be a rapid growth in the size of the household except where the family size is two or less and there is an even balance between the sexes of the children. Depending on these factors, and the incidence of death, such composite households will grow too large for the dwelling and have to split up. In consequence of the large number of factors which are operative, the actual incidence, size and number of composite households in any society will vary enormously even where there are strict rules of residence. Where this is not the case, as in our own society, the variation may be even greater.

The crucial factor which appears to constitute a necessary condition of the dissolution of the composite household, is the ability of the children to create households of their own. In order for this to be possible it is necessary for them to be able to command economic resources such that they can acquire a separate dwelling. But they also have to constitute a viable social group which can perform without such aid from the parents or sibs as is dependent on co-residence, the characteristic activities of the biological and domestic groups, the performance of which are the necessary conditions of their children's and/or their own existence.

Their ability to do this will depend on the strength and stability of the marital relationship and the degree to which the spouses are able to perform the tasks allotted to them by the family system in which they participate. Where, for example, marriages are arranged by the kin of the spouses, the spouses having no previous relationship with one another, the establishment of such a relationship will be a condition of their nuclear family forming an independent household. Discussing the reasons why bilateral Sarakatsani shepherds of Greece continue to live after marriage in the households of their parents and do not until much later set up, with their wives, households of their own, Campbell remarks that, among other reasons, 'it requires the passage of time and the birth of children before it can be said in any real sense that an elementary family has been founded.'[10] Of course the Sarakatsani whose marriages are arranged are an extreme case. Nevertheless this example draws attention to the way in which in our own society co-residence after marriage may be related in part to the length of courtship and the extent to which marriage creates a relationship as opposed to merely ratifying an existing one.

The ability of the spouses to perform their domestic roles required by the formation of an independent household may be related to the definition and performance of the parental role itself. Where the role of the mother is extremely permissive and stresses the provision of services for the children to the exclusion of their training through requiring their participation in household tasks, children of both sexes will be dependent on the mother, and the husband, deprived of

[10] Campbell, J. K., 'The Kindred in a Greek Mountain Community', in Pitt-Rivers, J. (Ed.), *Mediterranean Countrymen*, Mouton, 1963, p. 93.

his mother at marriage, dependent on his wife. Hence the new wife will be faced with a situation in which she is formally responsible for the provision of domestic services to the husband, from whom she can expect no help. The apparent permissiveness of the mother has the effect of giving her power over the child by reducing her daughter's independence, and moreover, establishes an obligation on the child's part to repay the services which she has received. Such patterns of dependency have been described in Britain and may occur among some types of Italian family, and prboably also in some parts of Spain.[11]

It is important to recognize that the provision and exchange of domestic services is not dependent upon residence in the same dwelling. A newly married couple may be enabled to take up separate residence at marriage even though they are not fully able to perform marital roles adequately, provided that they live near enough to the parents of one or other of the spouses to continue to receive services from them. Such arrangements may make the application of careful definitions of the household difficult to apply. Meals may be prepared and consumed alternately in different households, children may sleep in the grandparents' dwelling and so on.[12] Even where the arrangements made do not go as far as this, residence in the locality of one set of parents may lead to the development of RESIDENTIAL GROUPS sharing domestic services, their membership being determined by arrangements between the parties concerned. Since what is taking place is the continuance of a relationship of dependency between mother and daughter, the pattern of residence is likely to be uxori-local.[13]

Composite households and residential groups sharing domestic services may also come to benefit the parental generation by providing care and support for aged parents, though it would not seem that groups consisting of parents and more than one married child come into existence for that purpose. Hence relations between the households and families in such groups are characterized by an

[11] For a summary of data from British studies susceptible of this interpretation see Klein, J., *Samples from English Cultures*, London, Routledge, 1965, Vol. I. See also Kenny, M., *A Spanish Tapestry*, London, Cohen and West, 1956, Part II, Chapter 4; and Tentorio, T., 'La famiglia nella cultura italiana contemporanea', *Quaderni di Azione Sociale*, XV (i), pp. 53–54.

[12] For example see Rosser, C., and Harris, C., *Family and Social Change*, London, Routledge, 1965, pp. 151–154.

[13] The studies which have described this type of pattern in greatest detail are Young, M., and Willmott, P., *Family and Kinship in East London*, Routledge and Kegan Paul, 1957; Townsend, P., *Family Life of Old People*, Routledge and Kegan Paul, 1957; Marris, P., *Widows and their Families*, Routledge and Kegan Paul, 1958.

exchange of services, though there may be considerable variation in the timing of the flow of services in different directions. In some cases the early flow of services from parents to children is reversed as the parents age; in others the flows overlap and in others services flow in both directions right from the marriage of the children. The timing, content and direction of these flows are important in determining the nature of the relationships between family members[14] (see below Chapter 7).

We have already had occasion to refer to the existence of property holding groups. A domestic group is of course such a group since it holds the occupation of its accommodation. All domestic groups are also ECONOMIC groups in the sense that they purchase and *consume* goods as a unit. Where a group's members act together to exploit productive resources owned by all or one of them, then the group may be regarded as an economic group in the *productive* sense. In some societies most economic production is undertaken by groups of kinsmen recruited through the family process. Property and employment are obtainable primarily through one's membership of such a group. A kin group may own property without working it. In such a case it is a PROPRIETARY group. Alternatively it may constitute a work group without owning the property required. In such a case it may be termed a WORK group.

If inheritable property is partible and is not worked by its owners there will be no necessity for those who inherit it to constitute a group. However in such a society they will be unable to support themselves until they inherit. In this situation the man must either postpone marriage[15] until he inherits or must come to some arrangement whereby he receives a portion of his inheritance before his father's death or receives employment from him which enables him to support a family. If the size of the family property is small this will not be possible. In such a case a man must obtain employment outside the family—which may be difficult—or work for his father,

[14] See Sussman, M., 'Relationships of Adult Children with their Parents', in Shanas, E. and Streib, G. F. (Eds.), *Social Structure and the Family*, London, Prentice-Hall, 1965; Stehouwer, J., 'Relations Between the Generations and the Three Generation Household in Denmark', in Shanas and Streib, *op cit.*; Rosenmayr, L. *et al.*, 'Inter-generational Relations and Living Arrangements in the Course of the Life Cycle', *6th International Congress of Gerontology*, 1963.

[15] If they have to postpone marriage until the death or retirement of parents, extended economic groupings will not of course be formed. For a description of such a situation see Williams, W. M., *The Sociology of an English Village*, London, Routledge, 1956; also Rees, A. D., *Life in a Welsh Countryside*, University of Wales Press, 1950. Another way out of this difficulty is the practice found in

which will entail remaining under his authority. Here the elementary family will be an economic group, in the sense of the co-operative exploitation of resources, i.e. a work group but not a proprietary *group*. If the property is not partible but can support the son's nuclear family a similar situation will obtain.

If there is more than one inheriting child, it will be frequently impossible for them all to be supported by the property, thus forcing one or more of the sons to 'travel', that is to say, to seek some other means of earning a living. Where both men and women can inherit he may of course solve the problem by marrying an inheriting daughter.

The consequences of property inheritance have been related to the partibility of the property. This is however a vague notion. Land for example may be divided and if as is frequently the case it is regarded as impartible this is so because of the system of agriculture used, or because of beliefs concerning the undesirability or wrongness of dividing it. According to varying conditions and beliefs therefore, the rules of inheritance may restrict inheritance to one of the children, thus preserving the property intact.

Where families are economic groups, marriage will take on an enormous economic significance, since it will become an alliance between economic interests. Where the daughter's inheritance takes the form of a dowry (a marriage payment by the bride's family to the groom), this may sometimes be in the form of land. Judicious alliances between families may therefore increase the size and profitability of the holdings and affinal ties may provide a source of important economic help in times of crisis and difficulty.[16]

The family process may therefore become a means whereby various elementary families become linked by common economic interests thus leading to the creation of economic groupings wider than the elementary family itself. At the same time, where the members of the family not only own but together *work* the capital, the authority of senior members of the elementary family or cluster of families is

some parts of Norway where the inheriting son enters a relationship of concubinage with a woman on the understanding that he will marry her on inheritance. See Park, G. K., 'Sons and Lovers: Characterological Requisites of the Roles in a Peasant Society', *Ethnology* 1, 1962 p. 412.

[16] For an analysis of family farming in England see Williams, W. M., *Ashworthy*, London, Routledge, 1963. On the importance of marriage as alliance see, for example, Stone, L., 'Marriage among the English Nobility in the Sixteenth and Seventeenth Centuries', *Comp. Stud. in Soc. and Hist.* 3, 1961. For an example of the economic significance of marriage see Arensburg, C. M. and Kimball, S. T., *Family and Community in Ireland*, London, Peter Smith, 1961.

also that of an employer. Control over the capital upon which the children depend gives senior members the power that the capitalist always has over the proletariat. Frequently in rural communities, successful exploitation of economic resources requires co-residence and hence we may find overlapping elementary families together constituting residential and domestic as well as economic groups.[17]

In the same way therefore that biological activities form the basis for the development of interpersonal relationships which outlast the performance of such activities, so those relationships may in turn provide the basis for the formation of groups concerned with the performance of other types of activities. Since such groups are formed through the 'family process' and constitute an extension of the elementary family, the formation of such wider groups have been described as extended families. It is to a discussion of the extended family that we next turn.

In the preceding discussion we have distinguished types of family groups according to their activities and shown the way in which such groups are formed through the family process. It is necessary to stress the need for one further distinction however. Such groups may be formed *ad hoc* according to need, i.e. according to the material conditions under which people act. They will also be affected however by the social conditions of action—that is to say the rules governing kin recognition, inheritance and so on. Such sets of rules will of course have to fit the non-social conditions of action. Given a certain type of agricultural technology and a certain type of soil and a certain birth rate, equal division of landed property may result in such fragmentation of holdings as to result in death through starvation for the population concerned. Such rules are therefore related to but not completely determined by the material conditions of action, and hence constitute a separate type of condition.

When we find that the members of a society form groups wider than the elementary family by means of the family process, we have to ask whether the type of group formed is *required* by the rules governing the family process or merely *permitted* by such rules. In many primitive societies unilineal systems of transmission make possible the existence of rules which require the formation of exclusive kin groups. In societies which have bilateral systems of recognition it is logically impossible to have rules which require the formation of such groups unless some non-kinship criterion is added.

[17] See for example, Kooy, G., 'The Traditional Household in a Modernized Rural Society', *Recherches sur la famille, III*, Gottingen, 1958. Also van Deenen, B, *Die Ländliche Familie unter dem Einfluss von Industrienähe und Industrieferne*, Berlin, 1961.

In such societies therefore groups wider than the nuclear family are permitted but are not necessarily required. Hence when we find, for example, a tendency to uxori-locality we need to ask whether it is the type of activity that demands such a pattern or whether it is required by the system of rules governing the family process. It is one of the 'advantages' of a bilateral system that it is extremely flexible, since it provides the means of group formation without specifying *either* the membership of the groups *or* the activities which they must perform. In a bilateral system where there is no rule based on a non-kin criterion prescribing the formation of exclusive kin groups, the activities of kin groups wider than the nuclear family must be explained in terms of their activities and the conditions of their action created either by *other* social institutions or by material conditions.

THE EXTENDED FAMILY

There is probably no other term, except 'family' itself, about which there is more confusion than the EXTENDED FAMILY. Throughout our discussion so far we have seen the family not as a category of kin but as a *group*. In a bilateral system it is not possible to define the membership of groups on the basis of the rules governing kinship alone. We must therefore define such groups both in terms of the family process *and* in terms of different types of activity.

The term 'extended family' has been used by sociologists in the study of bilateral kinship in Western society, to point out a particular type of family which had been found. The term has been used to describe European families in which inheritance was patrilineal, which were characterized by the formation of composite households, and which performed the activities of productive economic groups.[18] Such households were formed either of parents and one son or of all or some of the sons and their wives, living and working together as a joint domestic and economic unit. The first type of extended family was described by Le Play as the STEM-FAMILY (*famille souche*).[19]

'Extended family' has also been used by anthropologists in connec-

[18] Litwak for example has defined the 'classical extended' family in terms of 'geographic propinquity, occupational dependence and nepotism, a sense that extended family relations are most important, and an hierarchical authority structure . . . ' Litwak, E., 'Occupational Mobility and Extended Family Cohesion', *Amer. Sociol. Rev.* 25, 1960, p. 9.

[19] These two types of extended family households have been described as 'extended multi-generational' and 'direct lineal multi-generational households' by some European rural sociologists, who have argued that the former is more characteristic of agricultural households, cf van Deenen, *op. cit.*

tion with the JOINT FAMILY which is found in Hindu India. The term 'joint family' refers to the co-residence in the *same dwelling* of lineally related persons of the same sex under the authority of a single head. This last additional criterion is of course implied in the sociological use of the term 'extended family' since the sharing of property owned by a senior member will entail that the senior male will hold authority over the other members of the group. In anthropological parlance the term extended family is relatively seldom used, but has been defined as 'the dispersed form corresponding to the joint family', whatever that means exactly.[20]

We have already noted that co-residence in the same dwelling may not be an absolutely necessary precondition of the co-operative exploitation of a common economic resource, even where that resource is land. Hence the lineally-linked nuclear and elementary families may form only a patrilocal group resident within a *locality,* or if they do not contribute labour but merely exercise control over the property, they may not even have to form a residential group of this kind. The term 'extended family' was developed to deal with such a situation.

The difficulty created by the above definition of the joint family is that it does not specify the types of solidarity which characterize it and hence does not define the type of social relationships, including authority relationships, which it exhibits. In consequence it becomes extremely difficult to know, once the criterion of co-residence in the same dwelling disappears, whether the linked elementary families concerned are dispersed *joint* families, that is to say whether they are extended families or not.[21]

Similar problems have confused the use of the term 'extended family' in the study of Western society. Sociologists speak of extended family relationships, extended kin relationships, extended family networks and extended kin networks, as well as of extended families. In Britain some students have restricted use of the term to the domestic group, or to a residential group performing domestic activities, or defined the extended family in terms of interaction.[22]

This confusion has arisen partly because in the last twenty years or so sociologists have re-discovered the existence of links between nuclear families which were previously thought to have atrophied in

[20] *Notes and Queries in Anthropology* (6th Edition), London, Routledge, 1951, p. 72.

[21] See Goode, W. J., *World Revolution and Family Patterns*, London, Collier-Mac, 1963, pp. 238–243.

[22] For a discussion of different definitions and reference to their sources see Rosser, C. and Harris, C., *op. cit.*, pp. 29ff.

urban industrial societies. Hence a great deal of time has been spent refuting the proposition that in such societies the nuclear family is isolated.[23] There has been a great deal of discussion about what links are recognized and what they are used for, but little discussion of the different ways in which the family process can lead to their maintenance.

In their study of Swansea, Rosser and Harris define the extended family as 'any grouping wider than the elementary family'.[24] The use of the term 'grouping' here is significant in that it does not make clear whether the extended family is a social group or a set of people who recognize relationships to another. Such vagueness of definition may be justifiable for delimiting a field of research interest, as was the purpose in this case. It is not however adequate for theoretical purposes.

The family process can be used by society as a whole to define the membership of groups by the use of various descent type rules, or individuals themselves may form groups as a result of arrangements made between them for specific purposes. In the latter case the arrangement and the purposes will define the membership where the principles of descent and inheritance are not adequate. It would seem useful to describe such groups as 'extended families'. Extended families may be of different types according to the different activities they perform. They may vary in size and membership according to the length of generations and the principles of descent and inheritance even where the activities performed are the same.

Where we do not find social groups being formed through the family process however this does not mean that, because there is no extended family, the nuclear family is therefore isolated. In the first place the universal family process will continue. Hence we shall be able to discover overlapping elementary and nuclear families. Hence the spouses of the nuclear family will always be members of their elementary families of origin, all of whose other members are outside the nuclear family. The nuclear family will not be 'isolated' therefore because it will overlap other family groups even though, together with them, it does not constitute an extended family.[25] Moreover the children and spouse in the nuclear family will recognize relationships to Ego's parents and sibs, even though they do not share the common values, beliefs, expectations and activities which

[23] Further discussed below, see pp. 98ff.

[24] *Op. cit.*, p. 32.

[25] Goode makes this point very clearly, though his use of the term family is not clear. See Goode, W. J., *World Revolution and Family Patterns*, London, Collier-Mac, 1963, pp. 170–171.

distinguish Ego's elementary family. Hence nuclear families will always be linked to other elementary families both by ties of common group membership and by the recognition of blood or affinal relationship. If we were to describe such links as 'extended family ties' because they are the ties which are used to form the various types of grouping wider than the elementary family which we call the extended family, we should have no way of referring to *relationships within extended families,* for which this term is better reserved. Perhaps 'extended kin relationships' could be used to denote *ties between members of overlapping elementary families* when such families do not constitute extended families.

The notion of an 'extended kin network' is however important and useful and is one that is closely related to the formation of extended family groups. This term is vaguely used, often in a metaphorical sense, though there have been recent attempts to define it and related concepts with more precision.[26] A network may be regarded as a set of interconnected points. The points are people and the connections social relationships. These relationships however are not necessarily of the same kind. A might be the friend of B who was the brother of C who was the work-mate of D who was the husband of E who was the sister of A and the brother of B. Some but not all of the relationships in the network described are relationships which involve participation in a group. A and D are work-mates and share work group relationships with others who are in turn connected with the members of the network through C and D. Logically a network is unbounded; that is to say it goes on for ever. All the members do not recognize relationships with all the other members but are all linked with varying degrees of closeness depending on the number of relationships involved. Taking any individual as our subject, we can see the network from his point of view as being composed of individuals at one, two, three, removes from him. He will necessarily come into contact only with those people with whom he has direct relationships. Ego and his directly linked members are referred to as 'a set'. They are not necessarily a group. They are not even necessarily linked to each other; the only thing they necessarily have in common is a relationship to Ego.

In fact of course a network may not go on for ever, it may be 'bounded'. Similarly it may not be true for a given Ego that the members of his set have no relation to each other except through

[26] On the notion of network see Mayer, A. C., 'The Significance of Quasi-groups in the Study of Complex Societies', in Banton, M. (Ed.), 'The Social Anthropology of Complex Societies', *A.S.A. Monograph* No. 4, London, Tavistock, 1966, p. 97.

him. They might all have relationships to every other member of the set. In such a case Ego's set would not only be a set but also a 'close-knit' network. If in a network this is true of the sets of all the members of the network then the *network* may be said to be close-knit.

It is obvious that the bilateral recognition of kinship produces a kinship network, since each individual has overlapping sets of recognized kin, and that this network will be unbounded.[27] It also follows that because of the degree of overlap the network will be relatively close knit. Not all but most of Ego's recognized kin will recognize relationships to most but not all of Ego's kin.

Whether or not it is true that many of the relationships which go to make up a network are group relationships, the fact that a plurality of individuals recognize relationships with one another means that they are well able to act together in certain situations even where they do not constitute a group. Because a set of individuals act together it does not imply that they are a group, unless that co-action is dependent upon their sharing established valued expectations governing that co-action. Frequent co-action on the part of the same individuals in similar situations will of course lead to the formation of such shared expectations. Hence, by virtue of their membership of groups (elementary families) which overlap one another, individuals come to be members of close-knit networks. Such networks may provide the opportunity of co-action and repetitative co-action may lead to the establishment of groups wider than the elementary family, that is to the establishment of extended families.

If this process has been seldom explicitly described this is partly because clear distinctions have not been made between extended families of different types and extended kin networks. It is well recognized that the gatherings of kin, for example at marriages, do not constitute the gathering of a kin *group* since all the attending kin have in common is relationships (of different types) to a particular Ego. However a succession of marriages will see a considerable overlap in the kin attending them, resulting in the same people meeting again and again in the same situation. Similarly the mobilization of kin resources in time of crisis by a succession of related Egos may have the effect of activating relationships between the kin so mobilized. How far and in what way the movement of information, sentiments and resources along a kin network have consequences for the formation of more permanent groups remains to be investigated.

The extended family is then a *group* formed through what has been described here as the family process, whose membership is defined by an arrangement of the members in relation to the activities of

[27] Unless continuous inter-marriage takes place.

the group in the situation in which it has to act, and is not required by the rules governing the family process. It is not a category of kin. Types of extended family can be distinguished by the use that they make of the overlapping family cores which the family process creates and the nature of the activity undertaken by its members. The extended family is not necessarily a *corporate* group, that is to say a group whose members act as a unit in some way, though it may be. Such groups are usually domestic groups, household groups, property controlling groups, and economically productive groups or any combination of them. Where their activities require co-residence they may also constitute residential groups. The list of activities is not however exhaustive. If we do not know of other types it is probably because we have not looked for them.

THE UNIVERSALITY OF THE FAMILY

We have already noted that to ask 'Is the nuclear family universal?' is to ask whether the biological activities, which occur in all societies, universally result in the creation of groups having the membership defined by those activities. We have also noted that the nuclear family is made up of two groups consisting of the mates and the mother and children which do not have to overlap in default of an arrangement made between the mates. In order to consider the problem of the nuclear family's universality, we have to elaborate a little further what is meant by the term 'rearing' which refers to the activity which constitutes what has been described as the biological role of the mother.

It is clearly not a biological necessity for the rearing to be performed by the same persons as the genetic mother. The child can be fed by a wet-nurse or by a bottle, and cared for as far as its physical needs are concerned by a person or persons not related to it. It is a condition of the survival of the child that these biological needs shall be met. It is not biologically necessary that the mother should meet them. Rearing however involves more than the satisfaction of the biological conditions of survival. It involves also the satisfaction of conditions required for the development of the personality of the child in such a way that he may be able to co-operate with other individuals for the purposes of survival and procreation. Whereas the biological conditions of survival can be clearly specified, the conditions of adequate psychological development for survival are a matter of some dispute. It would appear however that a stable relationship between the child and another person, who can respond not merely in physical or cognitive but also emotional terms to the child, is a necessary pre-condition of adequate personality development.[28] Once again it does not have to be the mother.

It is difficult to argue therefore that the non-social conditions of action are such as to determine the necessity of the existence of a group which satisfies the conditions for the survival of the children. All that necessarily follows from these conditions is the copulation of a man and a woman and the existence of a stable group consisting of an adult person and immature persons whom the adult rears. We may perhaps add another adult person who maintains the first adult and the children.[29]

It seems to us that the genetic mother and father are the obvious people to perform the activities specified, but that is not to say that they have to be. There is no reason to suppose that the nuclear family is universal on the grounds so far put forward.

If we turn to the evidence, we find that while these activities are usually performed by the genetic parents they are not always so performed. The 'hard cases' we discussed when considering marriage are also hard cases from the point of view of the nuclear family. In discussing marriage we saw that there were a variety of possible types of arrangement which could be used to provide for the achievement of various tasks necessary for the replacement of the members of the society and the transmission of their possessions. The status of the genetic father can be reduced to that of a lover and his role in the biological group taken over by the mother's male kin on the one hand, or the mother's male kin can be pushed right out of both the biological group and the household and the activities of maintenance be performed by the genetic father. Looked at in this way the Nayar no longer appear an 'exception' but are, as Levy and Fallers have rightly put it 'merely an extreme case of a quite widespread pattern',[30] i.e. of the extrusion of the genetic father in favour of the mother's male kin.

While it is true that in no known society is the genetic mother not

[28] For the evidence on effects of deprivation of material care on humans cf. Yarrow, L. J., 'Separation from Parents in Early Childhood', in Hoffman, M. L. and L. W. (Eds.), *Review of Child Development*, Russell Sage Foundation, 1964; and on monkeys see Harlow, H. F., 'Social Deprivation in Monkeys', *Scientific American* 206 1962.

[29] Freudians would wish to argue that adults of both sexes are necessary for adequate personality development, cf. Parsons, T., Bales, R. F. and Shils, E. A., *Family, Socialisation and Interaction Process*, London, Routledge, 1956.

[30] Levy, M. J. and Fallers, L. A., 'The Family: Comparative Considerations' *American Anthropologist* 61, 1959, p. 649.

expected to nurse and care for her child, in virtually all societies satisfactory arrangements are made for these activities to be undertaken by other persons when the mother is not available. Problems of a psychological kind only seem to occur when the arrangements provide material care without providing for a stable affective relationship between the child and an individual.[31]

There seems no reason to suppose therefore that, if a society decided to breed children on baby farms and had them reared in small groups composed of children and a man and a woman, none of whom were related to each other, this method would not be perfectly successful as far as the physical and psychological development of the children were concerned. If however such attempts repeatedly were to break down and the family tended to reappear, it would suggest either the existence of some psychological characteristic present in men and possibly other primates which leads to the formation of family groups; or it would suggest that the formation of family groups has consequences for society, such that it cannot continue to exist without 'the family'.

We need to look around therefore for such attempts, since unlike students of the physical world we are unable and would not wish to conduct experiments, since this would, in our case, involve the manipulation of human beings. Even if we were to try and do so however, we would be up against severe difficulties. In the first place all existing societies use kin groups to achieve the performance of child rearing and maintenance. Hence all our subjects would have expectations about the *right* way to rear children and these expectations might very well be the source of any return to the family pattern which we found. Secondly whether or not it is true that the existence of any society is dependent upon the existence of the nuclear family, it is certainly true that all societies operate on the assumption that child rearing activities will be performed by the family or at least the mother and her kin. Moreover, most societies rely heavily on the family for the purpose of cultural transmission. Upsetting the family would, like upsetting any one of a series of linked institutions, certainly create problems for the society concerned, and hence predispose its members to return to the old family pattern. Therefore we would need to use for our experiment a completely new society. There is of course no such thing. If we started off with a population of infants who were physically reared and shown affection but never spoken to, and then, when adult, placed in an environment in which they could survive through gathering activities, we should simply

[31] Yarrow, L. J., *op. cit.;* also Bowlby, J., *Maternal Care and Mental Health*, W.H.O., 1951.

have created an animal band,[32] and all the evidence from studies of primates suggests that they would probably form biological groups for the purposes of rearing and maintenance.[33] It is the simplest way of achieving such tasks. If they failed to perform such activities they would of course die out.

The two classic experiments sometimes described as 'attempts to abolish the family' have been the attempt made by the Soviet government to radically alter family institutions in the twenties of this century, and the attempts at the communal raising of children in Israeli kibbutzim (collective farms).

In Russia the revolutionary social changes undertaken by the Bolsheviks were from the very beginning accompanied by attempts to destroy the pre-revolutionary form of family: steps were taken to degrade marriage by abolishing the ceremonies which had previously accompanied it, divorce was made obtainable virtually on request of either partner, abortion freely permitted, children urged to place party loyalties before that to parents and kin. By the 1930s Soviet Russia had a high abortion rate and an extremely high divorce rate, a falling birth rate and a high rate of juvenile delinquency. In the mid thirties, marriage ceremonies were restored, freedom of divorce was curtailed, and abortion legally abolished.[34]

It is extremely difficult to see what, if anything, these facts prove. It could be argued that the rise in divorce and the increase in abortion showed the instability of the nuclear family when not socially sanctioned. On the other hand it could be said that because such changes were reversed it shows that Soviet leaders recognized the indispensability of the family. That, however, implies that the family is indispensable, and we do not know what the Soviet leaders thought. It has certainly not been shown that high divorce, abortion and delinquency rates were caused by the changes in family law, though rises in the first two rates were of course thereby made possible. It is much more likely that the rises in all three rates are closely related to the appalling housing conditions under which the Russian people lived at that time.

[32] In fact this would be impossible since such bands only survive through the possession of a rudimentary culture which is learnt in each generation.

[33] For a summary of studies on primate kinship see Reynolds, V., 'Kinship and the Family in Monkeys, Apes and Man', *Man*, N.S. Vol. 3, No. 2, June 1968.

[34] Cf. Timasheff, N., 'The Attempt to Abolish the Family in Russia', in Bell, N. W. and Vogel, E. P. (Eds.), *The Family*, Free Press, 1960. His account is highly tendentious. See also Fletcher, R., *The Family and Marriage*, London, Penguin, 1962, pp. 35–38, for an account based on a different source; also Geiger, K., *The Family in Russia*.

Another interpretation is possible however. In the early days of Jewish settlement in Israel, the kibbutzim stressed collective ties over and against family ties. Unlike the Russian population, the inhabitants were all young and lacked any extended kin ties. With both the creation of stable community groups and the development of three generational kin ties within the kibbutzim, there has been a shift of emphasis away from the collective towards the family. Marriage is more important, women's and men's roles are more sharply distinguished, parents spend more time together in their improved living quarters, and a greater part of the care of the children devolves on the parents rather than on collective agencies.[35]

It must be recognized that the family is, like all kin groups a divisive structure within the society (see below Chapter 5, page 144). Both our examples are instances of the stressing of societal solidarity as against family solidarity made necessary by special societal circumstances. These are not attempts to abolish the family, and the emergence of more conventional family forms proves little.

There is one other line of argument open to us however. In order to explain the nature of the family we have had to argue that where, in consequence of the performance of activities of rearing, mates and children come to form a social group, this group persists even after its characteristic activities have ceased. It does not persist solely because the persons concerned are recognized as biologically related. If therefore we wanted to 'farm' children, we should have to rear them in groups composed of them and a man and a woman. When the activities or rearing were over, we should expect to find that the grouping persisted. We should have therefore a social group made up of male and female 'rearers' and their reared young. In other words we should have a group with the same sex generational structure as a family. It would be absurd, since the co-residence of the 'rearers' is required, not to use persons having a sexual relationship with one another as 'rearers'. You would end up therefore with a family with only the biological links of parenthood missing.

It would seem therefore very difficult to avoid having the family as a social institution even if one wanted to. There is however one note of caution that must be sounded. There seems no reason why, once the child had been partially reared, he should not transfer or extend his relationship from his early rearer to someone else. The task of cultural transmission might, and in some cases is, transferred to another member of a wider kin or other kind of group. In such

[35] On the kibbutzim, see Talmon-Garber, Y., 'Social Change and Family Structure', in Farber, B., *Kinship and Family Organisation*, London, Wiley, 1966.

cases the nuclear family will be submerged in a larger group and may not, and indeed in some cases does not, ever act as a unit *vis à vis* any other social group. It is wrong therefore to think of the universality of the mother child group as necessarily implying that in all societies mother and children (with or without additional male adult members) always acts as a unit.[36]

We may conclude by referring to one of the most stimulating of recent discussions of this topic. Reiss[37] has argued that the key activity of the family is what he calls 'nurturant socialization of the new born'. By this he means the provision of affective care necessary for the normal personality development of the child. Even if the agent of such socialization is not genetically related to the child, the group which performs this activity will acquire the characteristics of a kinship group. Hence the family is a kinship group which performs this activity. Men are usually present but not absolutely necessary, and from the child's point of view the presence of the genetic father is not necessary at all.

[36] Levy and Fallers (*op. cit.*) make this point against Murdock who stresses the universality of the nuclear family. They do not distinguish different types of learning involved in the whole process of rearing and cultural transmission (socialization). They do, however, distinguish 'phases' of 'socialization'. For a further discussion see below (p. 95). Seeal so the discussion of the Dutch 'familie' and 'gezin' in Kooy, *op. cit.*

[37] Reiss, I. L., 'The Universality of the Family: a conceptual analysis', *Journal of Marriage and the Family* 27, 1965, p. 443.

PART II THE FAMILY AND SOCIETY

4

The Family and Industrial Society

In our discussion of the universality of the nuclear family in the previous chapter, we noted that one way in which the widespread existence of this group might be explained was by examining the degree to which society was dependent upon its existence. This line of argument was not however pushed very far because it was possible to show that it is extremely difficult to avoid having something remarkably similar to the family if humankind is to reproduce itself at all. We now turn to a consideration of the relation of the family and society in more detail. In so doing we shall have to consider both the consequences that the family has for other social institutions and the consequences which those institutions have for the family.

THE FUNCTIONAL THEORY OF THE FAMILY

The 'functional theory' of the family seeks to explain the existence of the family by showing that it has certain SOCIAL FUNCTIONS. To say that an institution has a social function is to say that the performance of the activities (governed by that set of expectations concerning the way people should behave to one another, to which we refer when we speak of the institution concerned) has certain *effects* on the other social institutions which go to make up the society. However it says more than this. When we speak of the social functions of an institution, we are not concerned with *any* effects the activities which it governs may have. We are concerned with those effects without which a society could not exist.

That isn't quite the end of the story however. The expectations which govern the performance of the activities which are necessary to the existence of *any* society must not only ensure the adequate performance of such activities. They must also 'fit' the other sets of expectations which govern the performance of other necessary activities in the *particular* society concerned.

If we can show that the activities performed by a particular institution must be performed in any society, and that, given the nature of the other institutions in that particular society, then the institution we are interested in must be of the type that it is, we may then be said to have explained the institution concerned. Frequently, if not always, we are unable to show that an institution must be of the form that it is in order to 'fit' other institutions. We may then speak of there being a range of 'functional alternatives', i.e. different ways of performing the necessary activity all of which fit other social institutions. We are sometimes able to reduce this range by considering the relations between the ideas upon which the different expectations or rules governing the activities in different institutional spheres depend.

Because such explanations or partial explanations involve both the relation of parts (the institutions) to one another, and establishing that the activity of one part is necessary for all the other parts to exist, such explanations are called STRUCTURAL-FUNCTIONAL explanations.

Any society is a group. When we speak of a group we are always referring both to a set of persons and to the things which they share. The members of a society share common beliefs and values and common expectations about how the activities which they share should be carried on. We have to distinguish carefully between the conditions which have to be fulfilled if the people and their descendants are to continue to *co-operate* together and the conditions which have to be fulfilled if the *individual members are to survive*. The fulfilment of one set of conditions is however a condition for the fulfilment of the other set; men cannot survive as biological organisms or reproduce themselves as men except through membership of a society, nor can a society survive unless its members survive or successfully reproduce. We need to distinguish between these two sets of conditions because we do not need to explain in distinctively *social* terms the existence of activities which are necessary to *individual* survival.

We can now turn to the family. We can list the activities which must occur to ensure the survival of the society's members and the activities which must occur to ensure the survival of the society, and examine which of these the family universally performs and whether any other institution could perform such activities. Alternatively we might look at the activities which the family in fact performs, and examine how far they are indispensable to the society.

Whichever way we do it, we have to have some list of activities which are necessary for the survival of a society and its members. Such lists are compiled by attempting to elaborate what is logically involved in the notion of a society. Most theorists prefer to take the more modest course of describing the effects that family activities universally have. This is in fact very modest since they are often able to get out of explicitly stating how they decide which of the activities that the family performs have effects which are 'functional'.

In his book 'Social Structure',[1] Murdock argues that the family performs four characteristic functions: the sexual, the economic, the reproductive, and the educational. Murdock argues that the sexual drive is a powerful impulse and cannot be left without restraints and that the nuclear family provides for its satisfaction and at the same time controls it. However the establishment of sexual rights in the spouses by marriage is only one of a very large number of controls on sexual intercourse which are found, as Murdock's data show.

He goes on to argue that the nuclear family is everywhere characterized by economic co-operation between man and woman based on a sexual division of labour. By this he means that apart from child-rearing the woman also produces goods and services for the family. This is simply not true of marriages among classes which can afford servants where even the wife's managerial role can be whittled down to that of a mere customer. Nor is economic co-operation between the sexes confined to cohabiting pairs.

It is indisputable that it is a condition of the survival of the population of a society that it must reproduce. It is also true that the family universally controls reproduction.

In the term 'education' Murdock explicitly includes 'socialization'. These two activities may be seen as satisfying two conditions: one that children develop psychologically in such a way as to make it possible for them to constitute members of *a* society, and the other that they should be made members of that *particular* society by virtue of their having acquired the values, beliefs, expectations and accumulated knowledge which constitute its culture.

If it is granted that the sexual, reproductive and educational activities are necessary conditions of the continued existence of either the society's members or of the society itself, it still does not follow that this amounts to an explanation of the family, because there is no reason why all these functions must be performed by the same

[1] Murdock, G. P., *Social Structure*, London, MacMillan, 1949.

institution, and unless they are it will not have the characteristics of the family.

This point is explicitly recognized by Kingsley Davis.[2] Davis lists four functions of the family: reproduction, maintenance, socialization and placement. The first three functions fulfil the conditions of the perpetuation of the *membership* of the society and on which the existence of the society *indirectly* depends. The last two functions serve to fulfil the conditions of transmission between the generations of both culture and social positions, upon which the continuance of the society *directly* depends. Only the family could provide for the performance of this set of tasks, but 'all of these functions could be performed independently of each other'.

It becomes clear that the 'functional theory' neither claims to explain nor succeeds in explaining the existence of the family. What it does make clear is the way in which changes in the family will affect all other institutions in the society.

In view of the discussion in the preceding chapter it could be argued that a more useful explanatory approach is to start with the biological and psychological conditions of the perpetuation of the members of the society and then show that something very much like the family must emerge if members of the society are to reproduce, and that once established the family will inevitably start to perform the functions of cultural transmission and placement.[3] Its biological activities determine its structure and its structure determines its direct functions.

It is significant that Davis starts with function and then goes on to discuss the way in which the structure is related to the function. In fact one must start with the activities of the individuals and not the functions of an institution (making love and bearing and rearing children—not 'replacement'), show how these determine the structure of the group and only then start worrying about the effects on society.

Though we cannot reduce society to its members (it's something more than a lot of people), the idea of society is only intelligible in terms of the individuals that go to make it up and their activities. A function is not an *activity* but a special kind of *effect*. Unless we get this very clear we shall end up by talking about the family performing functions for society in the same way as we speak of Mrs Brown cutting the sandwiches for the Women's Institute, which is always a sure sign that we have lost touch with social reality.

[2] Davis, K., *Human Society*, London, MacMillan, 1948, pp. 394–395.

[3] For a succinct and cogent statement of this point see Parsons, T., *The Social System*, London, Tavistock, 1952, pp. 160–161.

THE NOTION OF 'FIT' BETWEEN FAMILY AND SOCIETY

Our discussion of the functions of the family gives us some pointers to the way in which the family affects other social institutions and processes. We have already noted that the particular form a social institution takes can be understood in terms of the necessity of its 'fitting' other social institutions.

In order to be clear about this we need to examine the different ways in which institutions may in general be said not to 'fit' one another. In the first place the expectations or rules governing an activity may be logically inconsistent.

The second type of lack of fit is the case where the rules are not logically inconsistent but where in fact it would be physically impossible to obey both rules.

The third type of lack of fit is the case where it is neither logically or physically impossible for everyone to obey both rules, but where the chances of the majority of people governed by both rules being able to obey them both is low.

The fourth type of inconsistency is the case where the performance of activities are related because the performance of one activity constitutes necessary conditions of the performance of the other. All institutions which have social functions must, logically, be interrelated in this way.

The cases so far discussed have been examples of different types of incompatibility between rules governing activities, and in the last three cases the incompatibility has been determined by the material conditions under which the activities have been undertaken. Rules are not only related to one another 'through the physical', as Gellner has put it, but also because the rules themselves are related to more general beliefs and values to which they give specific form. For example an attempt to compel married women to work and to direct labour would be regarded in British society as an attack on the liberties of the individual and upon the sanctity of marriage. In other words it would be rejected because it did not fit, not so much the precise pattern of expectations which governed activities of different kinds, but because it was inconsistent with general beliefs which those other expectations reflect.

When we turn from general considerations to examine the actual fit between different social institutions in particular societies, it becomes apparent that if we are to argue that the family has a particular form because no other form would fit the economic institutions with which it is associated, then we must specify in much greater detail the exact ways in which rules and beliefs may be said to 'fit'. While there have been many attempts to deal with this problem, few have been sufficiently precise to enable us to determine what empirical evidence would support or falsify the hypotheses which derive from them.

PARSONS' THEORY: THE CONFLICT OF VALUES

Parsons has argued that the isolated nuclear family is the type of family which is most adapted to (i.e. 'fits' 'best') the other institutions found in industrial societies. What Parsons means by 'isolated' is of crucial importance here, since it is widely held that the work of students like Sussman[4] and Litwak[5] in America and of Young and Willmott[6] in Britain have shown that the nuclear family is not isolated.

Parsons writes: 'This relative absence of any structural bias in favour of solidarity with the ascendant and descendant families in any one line of descent has enormously increased the structural isolation of the individual conjugal family. This isolation... is the most distinctive feature of the American kinship system...'[7]

What Parsons means is quite clear. Because the American kinship system is in his words an 'open, multilineal, conjugal system'—that is to say because there are no rules prescribing or favouring marriage with particular relatives or categories of relatives ('open'), and no single line of transmission is preferred ('multilineal')—there are no principles which *by themselves* can lead to the formation of kin groups wider than the nuclear family. Hence the nuclear family is *structurally* isolated. That is to say the rules governing the behaviour of individuals provide for the formation of nuclear family groups only. This is the social situation in which people are placed in our

[4] Sussman, M. B., 'The Isolated Nuclear Family: Fact or Fiction?', *Social Problems* 6, 1959, pp. 333–340.

Sussman, M. B. and Burchinal, I. G., 'Parental Aid to Married Children: Implications for Family Functioning'.

Idem, 'Kin Family Network: Unheralded Structure in Current Conceptualisations of Family Functioning'. (Both reprinted in Farber, B., *Kinship and Family Organisation*, London, Wiley, 1966).

[5] Litwak, E., 'Geographical Mobility and Extended Family Cohesion', and 'Occupational Mobility and Extended Family Cohesion', *Amer. Sociol. Rev.* 26, 1961, pp. 9 and 258.

[6] Young, M. and Willmott, P., *Family and Kinship in East London*, London, Routledge & Kegan Paul, 1957.

[7] For descent read 'transmission'; for conjugal read 'nuclear', in the terms so far used in this book. 'The Kinship System of the Contemporary United States', in Parsons, T., *Essays in Sociological Theory*, London, Collier-Mac: Free Press, 1964, pp. 184–185.

society. What they do in this situation is another matter. They may use the family process to form all sorts of extended family groups, but they get no help from the rules which govern it. *Structurally* the nuclear family, based on the marriage bond between husband and wife ('conjugal'), is the basic unit and *structurally* it is isolated.

Similarly if we look at what Parsons says in discussing kinship in industrial societies in general we find him writing that the 'extent of kinship solidarities' and the 'most stringent kinship obligations' are limited 'to the conjugal family of procreation isolating this in a *relative* sense from wider kinship units'.[8] Here he is referring both to the formation of groups and to the recognition of obligations (that is, to relationships). What he is implying with regard to the latter is less clear however. If he means by 'conjugal family of procreation' a 'nuclear family', then his statement implies that Ego's most stringent obligations to his children become less stringent after the children's maturation. If he means by 'conjugal family' an 'elementary family', then he specifically provides for the existence of stringent obligations between two elementary families, one of which is nuclear, and hence denies the isolation of the nuclear family (where isolation is taken to mean that obligations between its members are more stringent than obligations to kin outside it).

It is fairly clear from the whole passage that by 'conjugal family' he means 'nuclear family'. In other words what he is saying is that Ego's duties to his spouse and *immature* children are more stringent than his duties to his parents. Let us suppose that this is true when Ego's children are immature. What happens when they marry? It is clear that *the children's* obligations to Ego will be less stringent. But why should *Ego's* obligations to them be less stringent than before?

The confusion arises through not making a clear distinction between nuclear and elementary families. Our family system implies the *primacy* of obligations within the nuclear family. Since this family is extinguished before the death of its members by the maturation of the children, it follows that relationships between parent and child are not fully reciprocal throughout the whole family process, the duties of members of Ego's generation to the descendant generation having primacy over their duties to the ascendant generation. That does not mean to say that they have no duties to the ascendant generation, nor that they are not important, nor that they are not equally stringent. It merely points to the fact that neglect of duties to the ascendant generation can be justified if those duties are

[8] Parsons, T., *The Social System*, Free Press, 1964, p. 186. For the distinction between nuclear and elementary family see Ch. 3, p. 69 above. My stress. 'Relative' means 'relative to agricultural and primitive societies'.

shown to conflict with Ego's duties to the descendant generation.

There is therefore another confusion—that between the *ranking* of obligations and their degree of 'stringency', if 'stringency' means 'their importance and the degree to which they are sanctioned'. Parsons is not so much wrong as conceptually confused. Tidied up a bit, what he says is that in industrial societies the kinship system makes no provision for the formation of kin groups wider than the nuclear family and that obligations between members of the nuclear family take *precedence* over those to kin outside it.

Let us now turn to the characteristics of the economic system which according to Parsons necessitates this type of family. The simplest one to deal with may be described as 'occupationally induced geographic mobility'. This is assumed by Parsons to be a characteristic of industrial societies. He confines his discussion to pointing out that any kin group wider than the nuclear family would inhibit geographic mobility of individuals and that the nuclear family is the unit of mobility. Here Parsons is of course using 'family', 'group', 'unit', as referring to a household or residential group. This as we have seen simply does not exhaust the possible types of kin group and the argument simply does not therefore stand up. If it can be shown that an industrialized economy can only function if there is a considerable movement of people between jobs and that such movement must involve frequent geographical mobility, and that the age at marriage is such, and the age of retirement such, that fathers and married sons are working at the same time, then it follows that even extended stem-family *households* will be impossible in a large number of cases. It would be very difficult to show that all these conditions *must* be fulfilled under any industrial system. It may be accepted however that a high degree of geographical mobility must disperse the sibling group.

There is evidence however that 'restricted' family types are more frequently found in hunting and gathering societies than in societies which are non-mobile. Mobility seems to be an intervening variable here however and the crucial independent variable to be property ownership which is closely related to the type of organization of economic production.[9]

Industrial society is characterized by the existence of specific institutions set up to perform economic activities. From this it follows that in such societies the family cannot in the majority of cases be a *productive economic unit*. This point, which Parsons makes repeatedly, is a reference to the characteristic difference between

[9] See Nimkoff, M. F. and Middleton, R., 'Types of Family and Types of Economy', *Amer. Jour. Sociol.* 66, 1960, p. 215.

industrial and pre-industrial societies. It is of the first importance to note that the use of kin groups to co-ordinate economic activity distinguishes the latter type of society. With regard to the problem of fit it is uninteresting, since it merely points out that two different social instutitions cannot both have the *monopoly* of the same activity.[10]

Parsons' main arguments however do not depend upon inconsistencies between rules governing the activities of economic and kinship institutions. Rather they centre on the conflicts of value which arise because of the difference in type of the much more general ideas upon which each institution depends, and which govern the way in which roles in the society are allocated.

Parsons sees the growth of successful industrial activity as associated with the adoption of values which he calls 'universalism' and 'achievement'. We have noticed that social relationships involve categorizing people and that kinship categories were categories of a special sort—'relational' categories. That is to say one does not behave in the same way to all the people who are fathers, but distinguishes between fathers according to the relationship they have with particular other people. It is the relationship to the particular person that determines the behaviour rather than the membership of the category alone. Our old friends the bus conductors are treated *universally* in the same way irrespective of differences in their relations to *particular* other people.

We would think it shocking if bus conductors distinguished between different sorts of passenger in the fares they charged—if for example a conductor let all his first degree kin travel free but charged double to the man he'd had a row with in the pub on Saturday night. We would think it equally shocking however if he showed no more filial affection towards his mother than he did to anybody else's mother.

The belief that it is wrong to differentiate between people in the same category on the grounds of their relation to you is what Parsons means by 'universalism'. The belief that we ought to differentiate between people in this way is its opposite, 'particularism'. It is obvious that the family constitutes a set of particularistic relationships, while the economic institutions reflect universalistic values.

By 'achievement' Parsons means the belief in the rightness of varying one's behaviour towards other people on other grounds than their

[10] The importance of this point is considerable in understanding the relation of different types of activity to one another in 'modern', as opposed to 'descent group' societies. It is not fully grasped by Litwak (see below). The distinction is elaborated by Parsons in *The Social System*, London, Tavistock, 1952, p. 176.

possession of inherent qualities, which he calls in contrast 'ascription'. The landlady who says, 'I'm sorry, I don't care if you are the Secretary General of the United Nations and Louis Armstrong's brother; I won't have no coloureds here,' is behaving universalistically —she refuses to be influenced by the relationship of the man at the door to a particular person. Nevertheless she is also behaving 'ascriptively' because the way she chooses to categorize him depends on his inherent qualities and not upon what he has achieved.

Kin relationships depend on categorization on the basis of inherent qualities (being born of . . .), and not upon achieved qualities. They are governed not by achievement values but by ascriptive values. We have already shown that they are also governed by particularistic values. Modern industrial enterprizes are governed by universalistic and achievement values. As a result individuals who are both members of families and workers in industrial enterprises will be required to hold two contradictory sets of values at the same time.

If they act in accordance with those values, further sets of problems arise. From time to time they will be confronted with difficulties in the economic sphere when a relative asks for help in getting a job, or comes in to the shop where they work and asks for special treatment. Within the family they may find that they have to suspend judgements on their kinsfolk which depend on the values which govern their behaviour at work. For example sons may be more successful than fathers, or one brother more than the other brother. The values that stress the approval of one brother have to be put in cold storage and kinship values relied upon when the brothers meet.

Parsons wishes to argue that this makes life extremely difficult, but that if you restrict the family group to the nuclear family you do not get these difficulties *within the family group* because the children are immature and the wife busy raising them. As a result there is only one occupation-holder in the family and all the members share the same amount of prestige and economic power—that which derives from his position.

If the most stringent family ties are those between members of the nuclear family, no two persons playing roles opposite one another in the same economic institution will be connected by such ties.

Major conflict is therefore avoided by two types of segregation. The nuclear family is cut off from wider kin in the sense that the most stringent ties are confined within it, and because its members do not perform economic roles opposite one another it is also segregated from the economic system except for the husband. In this way intrusion of family values into the sphere of work is avoided and work values do not disrupt the solidarity of the family.

Parsons' argument has two parts. *First* it argues that the two sets of values which he specifies are inconsistent, and that the two sets of values are held respectively by the two institutions concerned. Parsons is on fairly firm ground here. He is not saying that in industry no one is ever refused a job because of his colour or given one because of his particular relation to the foreman. He is drawing our attention rather to the fact that such behaviour is not *justified* in terms of dislike of 'the blacks' or the rightness of looking after one's own. It is *justified* rather, by saying 'he wasn't up to the job' or 'he's the best man I could get'. This is precisely why it is so difficult to establish how much discrimination and nepotism there is.[11]

The *second* part of his argument also has two parts. First it could be argued that 'strain' between the family and economic institutions could be avoided if the different sets of values are segregated, that is to say if the occasions on which they apply are quite clearly demarcated. Parsons stifles this objection at birth by saying that the values of the economic institutions are the *dominant* values in industrial society. This point of view, while attractive, is not supportable *a priori*. It is rather a hypothesis which demands investigation of the extent to which different groups and categories carry over the values which characterize the economic sphere into other spheres of activity. It seems likely that such an investigation could throw considerable light on the empirical variation in the types of family found in different sectors of industrial society.

Secondly Parsons not only assumes that the values he specified characterize the economic sphere, he also assumes that people actually *act* upon them; in other words he assumes that extended kin are differentiated from one another in occupational terms, and that people in industry act universalistically and promote and recruit on an achievement basis sufficiently often to make that differentiation a reality.

The American studies which show that help and aid are transmitted to married children are, as Pitts has pointed out,[12] in no way inconsistent with Parsons' hypotheses, provided such aid does not intrude into the occupational sphere. Such aid is not inconsistent with the elementary family structure since it flows from the senior to the junior generation, and is merely a continuation of a pattern

[11] It should be noted, however, that to justify behaviour in this way can imply that 'achievement' is a means or that it is an end. Parsons wishes to argue that in industrial societies men value achievement as an *end*. It could be argued that they necessarily value it only as a means. If it is a means, they must at least sometimes act in accordance with it.

[12] Pitts, J. R., 'The Structural-Functional Approach' in Christensen, H. T., *Handbook of Marriage and the Family*, Chicago, Rand McNally, 1964, pp. 88–90.

established in the nuclear family. Pitts points out however that the aid is very often designed to *further the more speedy establishment of the independent nuclear family*. It is still structurally isolated in the sense that care is taken not to diminish its autonomy and subsume it into a wider kinship group. Financial aid in particular is not dependent on proximity, and in the middle classes, where this kind of aid is common, it has the effect of 'evening out' over time the incomes of families whose earnings increase progressively over the life cycle by transferring wealth from the 'rich' oldsters to the 'poor' youngsters.[13]

On the other hand the widely reported reluctance of many working class families to move when employment is no longer available in the area is evidence of the way in which ascriptive ties to neighbours and kin create problems in the economic sphere and is at the same time consistent with the evidence of the importance of the exchange of domestic services among working class families.

Parsons' theory may then be criticized less because it assumes a single pattern of behaviour which has been shown to be false, than because it states merely that there must, in industrial societies, be an *absence* of rules determining extended family groupings and ties and hence gives us no means of explaining the wide variations in actual family groupings which are found.

Before we leave Parsons' theory, for the present, it is necessary to note one other major element in it. A central place in Parsons' general sociological theory is occupied by the idea of socialization, and this process, in which the family plays such an important part, is discussed at length in a collection of essays edited by Parsons.[14] In his introductory discussion, Parsons stresses the importance of the family *not* being completely isolated from the occupational structure. It is obviously necessary that a family member should occupy a position and play roles in the economic sphere, if there is to be an economic sphere outside the family. Such an overlap is also necessary, Parsons argues, because it makes it possible for a child within the family to learn and make part of himself (internalize) the values which govern activity in the economic sphere. In a society where most activities are ordered with reference to values different from those of the family, the family has the job of transmitting the opposite values to those on which it itself is based, and it can only do this if at least some of its members take part in those activities.

[13] For a description of this process among the British middle class see Bell, C., 'Mobility and the Middle Class Extended Family', *Sociology*, Vol. 2, No. 2, 1968, p. 173.

[14] *Family, Socialisation and Interaction Process*, London, Routledge, 1956.

This is not to say that the family is *exclusively* charged with the internalization of such values, but it constitutes a major sphere of social life in which this takes place. For Parsons, therefore, the family must not be completely segregated from other social institutions because, if it were, new members of the society would not be socialized and hence could not take part in the activities which characterize other social institutions.

LITWAK'S THEORY: PRIMARY GROUPS, BUREAUCRACY AND 'SHARED FUNCTIONS'

Before considering another 'theory of fit', we must pause to note briefly another sense in which the family in industrial society may be said to be isolated. In primitive societies it is frequently the case that the majority of roles and group memberships are allocated on the basis of kinship, and every type of co-operative activity undertaken by kin groups. Hence at one time (particularly in the nineteen thirties) sociologists were very fond of describing the family in industrial societies as having lost its functions.[15] Here 'function' is used loosely to mean 'activities' though some of the lost activities are social functions in the strict sense. There are many splendid different lists to choose from but there is general agreement that kin groups have lost religious, political, economic and educational activities to specialized institutional *groups* called churches, political parties, businesses and schools.

We have already noted however that these institutions are dependent on the family and that Davis's four core functions can all be performed by other institutions either in whole or part. Litwak's[16] argument runs as follows: there is no reason to suppose that there is a residual set of functions which only the family can perform, neither is it correct to assume that the family has lost in entirety its other functions. In support of the first proposition he can cite the development of new social institutions such as day nurseries, and child welfare clinics who perform part of the activities of maintenance and socialization and the development of psychiatric agencies to take over the activity of 'tension management' which Parsons sees as a

[15] Cf. Ogburn, W. F., 'The Changing Functions of the Family' in Winch, R. F. *et al.*, *Selected Studies in Marriage and the Family*, London, Holt Rinehart, 1962, p. 157; McIver, R. M. and Page, C. N., *Society*, London, Macmillan, 1957, Ch. 11; Burgess, E. W. and Locke, H. J., *The Family from Institution to Companionship*, American Book Co., 1953.

[16] 'Extended Kin Relations in an Industrial Democratic Society' in Shanas, E. and Streib, G. F. (Eds.), *Social Structure and the Family*, London, Prentice-Hall, 1965, p. 290.

characteristic activity of the family. He can also point to the fact that placement is, in an 'achievement' society, no longer entirely determined by birth.

In support of the second proposition he can point to evidence which shows that without family support throughout the educational process, the child is likely to 'drop out'; that family type is an important factor affecting religious activity; that motivation to work is partly determined by family background and so on. He wishes to argue therefore that the family in industrial societies is characterized less by a *loss* of functions than by a *sharing* of functions. The key process in whose terms this sharing by the family of the functions of other groups may be explained is, one might add, socialization.

Who is doing the sharing? Litwak's answer is important because it makes clear what both he and Parsons regard as the distinguishing feature of industrial societies, an important point on which we have so far remained (deliberately) unclear. The sharing, says Litwak, is being done by the *primary group* on the one hand and by various types of *bureaucratic* institutions on the other. The term primary groups means 'groups characterized by intimate face to face association and co-operation' which 'are fundamental in forming the social nature and ideas of the individual'.[17] The term bureaucracy is used in the sense that Max Weber defined it. That definition cannot be dealt with here. It involves however an organization composed of a number of social positions ('offices') hierarchically arranged in terms of authority, occupied by people appointed on the basis of their technical qualifications, who are promoted according to achievement, in which the official's sphere of competence is strictly defined.[18] relationships are impersonal—without affection or enthusiasm, and in which the official's sphere of competence is strictly defined.[18] It is an institution governed therefore by values of universalism, achievement, specificity and affective neutrality in Parsons' terms; the polar opposites of the values governing family relationships.

Stripped of its theoretical language, what Litwak says is that the family is a basic social institution upon whose activities all other social institutions depend, that all activities which go on in a society cannot be provided for by bureaucratic institutional groups and must therefore be performed by non-bureaucratic groups and that the

[17] Cooley, C. H., *Social Organisation*, London, Schocken Books: Bailey Bros., 1962, p. 23; 'forming the social nature' is, of course, 'socialization'.

[18] Cf. Weber, M., *The Theory of Social and Economic Organisation*, London, Collier-Mac: Free Press, 1964, pp. 324–341.

Note: This is not a summary of Weber's treatment. Certain elements of his characterization relevant to this discussion have been selected for citation here.

distinction between what the former can do and what the latter can do does not depend on the type of activity (political, religious, economic, etc.) but upon the extent to which the activity is sufficiently patterned, repetititive and predictable in its occurrence, and the extent to which the need for it is easily recognizable.

'Shared functions' then are really 'shared activities'. If the family was isolated or segregated from other institutions in society as Parsons has said it must be, Litwak goes on to argue, then neither type of institutional group would be able to perform its activities effectively and *such segregation depends on each type of institution having entirely separate activities.*

This would seem to be a gross misreading of Parsons. Parsons we have seen is concerned with the maintenance of the solidarity of the family group by the elimination of economic differentiation, and the segregation of particularistic and ascriptive behaviour within the family.

On the first count, the performance by the family of activities which contribute to the successful performance of activities by other institutions is quite different from the performance of roles in those institutions, that is the membership of such groups.[19] On the second count, Litwak's whole argument depends on the greater efficiency of the family in situations when a particularistic orientation is required. It is precisely because the family has a *monopoly* of particularistic roles that other institutions have to rely on it when their ways of behaving governed by universalistic values are inadequate.

The segregation of the family to which Parsons refers does not involve a complete loss of activities to other institutions, as Litwak rightly points out. What it refers to is the confinement of particularistic and ascriptive ways of behaving to persons playing kin roles to one another, the belief that it is wrong to give primacy to ties of kinship when playing any other institutionalized role, and the ensuring that no two people in the same nuclear family play roles in bureaucratic institutions opposite one another, thus preventing them

[19] Because a child's mother sees that he takes the medicine ordered by the hospital she may be said to be engaging in 'medical' activities which she shares with doctors and nurses. This is quite different from being a doctor or nurse because then she would be required to show no more affection to her own child than to any other child (strictly speaking), when she was on duty. Hence her activity in giving him the medicine in no way diminishes the segregation of family and bureaucratic *roles*.

If my son grows cabbages in my back garden and sells them for profit then he is engaging in an economic activity, but he is not playing a role in an *economic organization.*

ever having to choose between loyalty to closest kin and the *im*personal standards demanded by their occupation.

What the family has lost is not religious and economic *activities*. It has lost the control and co-ordination of such activities. That is to say that these activities are no longer performed by family members as a *group*.

Litwak has performed a valuable service in pointing out that the development of specialized bureaucratic institutionalized groups (which perform the activities which the family group once performed) does not imply that such bureaucratic groups have a monopoly of their characteristic activities, and that therefore the range of activities which family groups in such societies perform may still be very wide. But Litwak's confusion of 'function' and 'activity', and 'activity' with 'group membership'[20] leads him to reject some of Parsons arguments on which his own theory in fact depends. At the same time he fails to distinguish the sharing of an activity and the effect that the performance of that activity has on the activities of other institutions in society, a mistake which derives from the loose use of the term 'function' with which he begins his argument.

The unwillingness of bureaucratic institutions to accept in practice that they do share 'functions' with the family and that untrained and non specialized individuals acting particularistically and ascriptively can be of assistance to them in the successful performance of their activities may be seen to be one of the sources of the belief that the family has lost its functions. The prevalence of such unwillingness would seem strongly to support Parsons' thesis that the two sets of values are extremely difficult to combine, and the 'loss of functions' theory may be seen to have the effect of making their non-combination legitimate.

GOODE'S THEORY: POWER, AUTHORITY AND LEGITIMATION

Goode's[21] approach to the problem of fit between the family and other social institutions characteristic of industrial society involves an examination of the effects of industrialization upon different economic categories ranked in order of their command over economic resources.

[20] See footnote to p. 107.

[21] Goode, W. J., *World Revolution and Family Patterns*, London, Collier-Mac: Free Press, 1963, esp. Ch. 1 and 'Conclusions'. See also his 'Industrialisation and Family Change' in Hoselitz, B. F. and Moore, W. E., *Industrialisation and Society*, UNESCO/Mouton, 1963, p. 267; and 'The Process of Role Bargaining in the Impact of Urbanisation and Industrialisation on Family Systems' *Current Sociology* XII, i.

Goode argues that the new economic institutions in an industrializing society will be in the hands of those who control property and wealth in the society before industrialization. As a consequence the upper economic categories will be able to control their children because the children's membership of upper categories will depend on their inheriting property or jobs in the new economic institutions. At the bottom of the economic scale however the fact that the parents have nothing to offer their children will mean that the basis of the parents' power over the child, which previously depended on control of jobs and what property there was, will be gone. Because parents and kin generally have little to offer the child, the advantages of maintaining kin connections will be small and in consequence it will be lower strata families that first begin to move towards the 'conjugal' family form.[22]

Goode's emphasis, because he is concerned with change and its sources, is on the degree of 'fit' between the needs of the individual members of society, and the extent to which they satisfy them under any given system. The question he wishes to ask is 'How far and in what way does any given family system satisfy the needs of individuals?' and he seeks to explain change in terms of the value to individuals of different family systems—or of the same system among different categories—in maximizing the satisfaction of their needs.

Now Goode is very well aware that though we may specify certain basic 'human needs', the way in which the satisfaction of these needs is to be achieved and the levels of achievement which are considered satisfactory will vary with the society or group within it, according to the beliefs, values and ideas that the members of the society or group share. However because no system is entirely satisfactory, and all systems require sacrifices of individual interest to that of the group, certain ideas such as equality and individualism have an almost universally popular appeal. Such ideas once evolved or introduced tend to favour *both* a family form where the subordination of the

[22] It is interesting to note that Litwak in an early formulation (Litwak, E., 'Occupational Mobility and Family Cohesion', *Amer. Sociol. Rev.* 25, 1960 p. 12, footnote 11) argued that the workers would be the *last* to be affected by industrialization, since they would be 'the last to feel bureaucratic pressures'. Both are probably right. Goode's point is that industrialization destroys the power and legitimation of the classical extended family and Litwak is certainly wrong in supposing the Bethnal Green 'extended family' to be a 'classical' survival. However the lower level of skill of manual workers is likely to mean that less job and geographical mobility is required than in the middle class and hence the 'modified' extended family will suffer less disruption of activities dependent on proximity than will be the case in the middle class. See below 'Discussion', also Chap. 5.

individual to the family group is reduced to a minimum and the development of other social institutions which promote free enquiry and freedom of economic activity on which the rapid changes involved in any industrial system depend.

Although Goode is too shrewd to take an extreme theoretical position on this issue, he seems to go some way towards a position which would hold that the 'conjugal'[23] family and the industrial system of production fit each other not directly but through the ideas and values built in to both systems and *in addition* that the development of such ideas are a necessary or even sufficient condition of the development of both types of system.

It must be stressed however that he explicitly lists the arguments that we have considered so far: geographical mobility makes it difficult to keep in touch with kin; occupational mobility leads to a differentiation of kin groups wider than the nuclear family; and the loss of control of important activities by kin groups diminishes the importance of such groups to their members. He also adds a new and important consideration. Industrialization creates a large number of different jobs and occupationally differentiates kin. Hence the chance of any individual being *able* to assist a kinsman is diminished, because in most cases they will be in different occupations.

Goode's theoretical approach may be explicitly linked with our discussion of different types of fit (p. 97) by focusing on the notion of *power*. If we define power as 'the ability to affect the behaviour of another even against their will' and we define authority as 'power which is made legitimate in terms of beliefs and values held by the people concerned', then we may see the role of ideas which Goode stresses as affecting the basis of legitimation of family authority and the effects of changes in other institutions as attacking the bases of that authority (that is to say the power of parents over children and men over women) which characterizes most non-conjugal family systems.

To give a concrete example: when the children believe that each individual has a right to act in furtherance of his own happiness they will no longer accept that their parents have a right to determine whom they shall marry. This may cause difficulties at home but the

[23] The critical features of the conjugal family as defined by Goode are the same as those which constitute Parsons' definition of the American family, viz. multilineality, openness, and conjugality—the latter referring to the primacy given to marital obligations over obligations to sibs and parents. Conjugality presupposes that the nuclear family is not subordinated to any wider kinship group, nuclear family subordination not being required by the rules governing the family process nor by the activities of family groups.

victory for the children will become complete when they can earn a perfectly satisfactory living, even if their parents cut them off with a shilling, because they can both work in a factory. Whether beliefs as to the rightness of parental authority will hold an extended family group together, even though the children have the power to be independent, depends on how dissatisfied the children are, which in turn depends partly on their economic position and partly on the values they have. The values get in in two ways therefore: they not only legitimize authority; they partly determine the level of dissatisfaction of those under authority. Since values which are likely to maximize their dissatisfactions are likely to be a prerequisite of industrialization itself, dissatisfaction, the acquisition of economic power and the withdrawing of legitimation from parental authority all go together.

The redistribution of economic power within the family is the result of changes in the material conditions of action of the children and hence Goode shows how both the types of fit between conditions of action and between ideas—*both* operate together *and* interaffect one another.

It is important to recognize that the process which Goode describes, attacks both the existence of groupings wider than the nuclear family in systems where the rules governing the family process *require* their formation and the existence of certain types of extended family in bilateral systems where such groupings are *permitted*. The existence of the first is undermined because the sources of legitimation of the rules are undermined as well as the conditions of the groups carrying out their activities changed. The existence of extended families under the authority of a single head are undermined in bilateral systems not by withdrawing legitimation from the system of rules governing the family process *as a whole* but by changing the ideas on which the authority of people occupying certain positions within it depend, as well as changing the material conditions of action.

DISCUSSION

If we may venture to criticize Goode's approach, which is elaborated here to a greater extent than he himself has attempted, it would be that like most students of the family he pays too little attention to the process of industrialization itself. The factors which are implicitly assumed in the above discussions of the relationship between industrialization and the family but are never explicitly mentioned, are the degree of job differentation and the increase in the level of skill. The more that jobs are differentiated (that is to say the more different types of job there are) and the higher the level of skill required, the less substitutable one worker will be for another. When substitutability is low, it will be difficult to 'fit' men to jobs. The more difficult it is, the more necessary it will be to appoint them purely on merit and the more moving of people around will be involved. It is upon this factor that Parsons' characterization of industrial society depends.

Now it is perfectly possible to conceive of a society in which a large number of the work force were engaged in non-agricultural occupations where the ratio of skilled to unskilled workers was very low, and where the managerial skills required were of a rudimentary nature. In such a society, except in the case of the skilled tradesmen, members of the managerial classes and members of the working classes would be interchangeable within their class, and, assuming a minimum level of education, even between classes.

In such a society it would be by no means necessary for the majority of the population to be mobile between jobs, nor would individuals in different jobs be very significantly differentiated in terms of economic power except across class (property owning) lines. It would therefore be perfectly possible to transmit property and jobs on the basis of kinship (ascription)[24] and for kin groups to form common households or residential groups of other kinds. The vast mass of the population, unable to amass enough wealth to enter the property owning classes, would be virtually immobile and hence tend to disvalue achievement and to value ascriptive solidarity with kin, neighbourhood and ethnic groups.[25] The necessities of manufacturing would not require the performance of universalistically oriented roles. It may be argued that the existence of primarily economic relationships between individuals and groups which would characterize such a society implies a universalistic categorization. On the contrary, while it cannot be denied that people would be categorized in terms of ability to pay or deliver the goods, this does not mean to say that distinctions would not be made within categories (particularism) on the basis of kinship, friendship, membership of peer groups and so on. (In fact except perhaps in the very large companies, one would

[24] For a description of the functioning of an extended kin group in an industrial society at the managerial level which explicitly recognizes the importance of substitutability, see Leyton, E., 'Composite Descent Groups in Canada', *Man*, 1965, p. 98.

[25] For examples of rejection of the dominant value by the unsuccessful see almost any community study, e.g. Elias, N. and Scotson, J. L. *The Established and the Outsiders*, London, Cass, 1965; and Gans, H. J., *The Urban Villagers*, London, Collier-Mac: Free Press, 1962.

be hard put to it to think of a non-particularistic field of business activity.)[26]

It may be suggested that Britain about 1850[27] bore a marked resemblance to this type of society, and that our present day society at the very least bears strong signs of continuity with such a society. If this assertion is correct it would seem to indicate that it is vital to make explicit what elements in industrialism affect the family. The empirical evidence about the continued existence of extended kin relationships and groups in industrial societies may point less to the inadequacies of our theories of the family than to suppressed and erroneous theories of industrialization. It is true that industrial societies are characterized by the growth of bureaucracies but it is not true that all or even most of the enterprises in such societies are bureaucracies and, as Weber himself was at pains to stress, even those that exist are far from pure and likely to slip over into other types of organization.

Let us very briefly try another approach. The basic requirements of industrialization, it would be generally agreed, are a surplus of capital, the requisite financial institutions, willingness to employ capital in productive uses on the basis of maximizing its return, enough people and/or good enough communications to constitute a mass market and provide a labour force, an educated *élite* capable of technological innovation, a set of ideas which will legitimize the activities of control and co-ordination of productive processes, and a surplus of agricultural produce.

Successful industrialization would not appear to require in all its stages that people act universalistically and that roles are allocated in all cases on the basis of achievement rather than ascription. If universalistic and achievement values seem to be associated with industrialization, then this is because of their effect in the *initial* stages of serving to legitimize the authority of the industrializing *élite*. It does not necessarily follow that people begin acting in the way approved by such an ideology.

The first problem is to win the acceptance of the new ideology, but if this policy is successful sooner or later the people at the bottom begin to notice that this is not the way society is run at all.[28]

[26] For an example of the particularistic and kin based working of the British establishment see Lupton, T., 'Kin Connections and the Bank Rate Tribunal', *Transactions of the Manchester School*, 1959–61.

[27] Japan too is remarkably particularistic see Abegglen, J. G., *The Japanese Factory*, London, Collier-Mac: Free Press, 1958.

[28] Cf. Merton, R. K., *Social Theory and Social Structure*, Collier-Mac: Free Press, 1949, pp. 131–160 (esp. 141–149).

At that point, which America has now reached, you have trouble.

Now one of the reasons that they are now having trouble is that in order to keep the profits rolling in (in a competitive economy) you have to improve your technology. This leads to an increasingly differentiated job structure and an increasingly high level of necessary skill. In order to achieve this you have to start acting universalistically and recruiting on the basis of achievement rather than ascription. This threatens those areas of the society where power is based on ascribed rather than achieved characteristics, and makes it difficult to maintain certain exceptions to the universalistic principle at the bottom.

It may therefore be that we have yet to see the full effect of industrialization on the family. The *first stage* of the industrialization process requires primarily *a concentration of capital,* and the development of *an ideology to justify those who now control it*. This is the process with which Goode, in his penetrating and detailed study, is chiefly concerned. It destroys the economic base of the authority structure of the family while the new ideologies, which justify the concentration of capital and its control, remove its legitimation. It may therefore be seen to be destructive of the traditional kinship systems of descent group societies.[29]

In some cases the ideological changes and in others the economic changes precede industrialization itself. Indeed they may be a precondition of autonomous industrial growth. Hence one may find the 'conjugal' family before industrialization. Where industrialization is induced from outside, then the importation of foreign capital may result in the short term coexistence of large kin groups with industrial production, since the basis of their economic power (their property) will not have been removed to provide capital for industrialization. Those actually working in industry may very well establish extended family groupings in the towns created to provide labour for the new industries (where job differentiation and level of skill are not too high) after the first disruption of kin ties created by the initial rural-urban migration has been overcome.

The *next stage*[30] of industrialization demanding *a more exact fit*

[29] See Moore, W. E., 'Industrialisation and Social Change', in Hoselitz, B. F. and Moore, W. E., *op. cit.*, pp. 337–341.

[30] To speak of stages implies a developmental theory of industrialization which is seen as being determined (once the process is begun) by the development of technology. It does *not* imply a developmental theory of society.

Where industrialization is undertaken by a foreign power, universalistic behaviour may be demanded of the *workers* in the early stages of industrialization. Such requirements do not often apply to promotion however since this is usually affected by ethnic considerations. See Moore, W. E., *op. cit.*, p. 306.

between work skills and job demands will result in the need to act in accordance with the values of universalism and achievement. Even in this case there will still be large areas of industrial society (mainly service industries) where both level of skill and job differentiation are low, and the adoption of such values may not be required.

Whichever phase of industrialization the society is in therefore, we may expect to find great variation between different occupational areas in terms of the degree of skill required and in the extent of job differentiation. Correspondingly we should expect to find wide differences in family form between different occupational categories.

In the first phase we should also expect to find wide differences between types of industry in the extent to which achievement, etc., values are adopted and even wider differences in the extent to which they are acted upon. At the same time we should expect to find considerable variation in the extent to which different groups within societies are proletarianized by the concentration of capital and variations between societies in the degree of concentration of capital related to the degree and mode of industrialization. As a consequence the sociologist may be faced with a baffling number of family types all associated with 'industrial production' if that term is widely defined.

The Parsonian characterization of industrial society may be regarded therefore as an analysis of an extreme type of society to which actual societies will approximate more and more as industrialization progresses, but perhaps never reach. Similarly the type of family which he sees as fitting industrial society would only *necessarily* be found throughout a completely industrialized society. Even this type of family, it will be recalled, does not involve isolation from all kin in the simple-minded sense that Parsons' vulgarizers have assumed.

The identification of the key characteristics of industrial society, which demand the values Parsons defines and have the disruptive effects which he predicts, would enable us to place both societies and groups within societies on a continuum with regard to those characteristics, and hence explain variations in family structure which are found between and within societies.

The key characteristics put forward here are hypothetical, and a great deal of research into both historical and contemporary materials would be required to provide adequate opportunities for the falsification of hypotheses concerning their importance. The level of skill required and the degree of job differentiation are ways of referring indirectly to the conditions of action of men in societies with advanced technologies. Where the technology is advanced, production through the utilization of that technology can only be achieved by creating a large number of different jobs each requiring a high level of specialized skill. Hence the technology requires a differentiated job structure which constitutes the social conditions of action of the men in the society. In order to fill the jobs they *have* to adopt universalistic and achievement oriented values, and move men about to get not the *best* but the *minimum* adequate fit between jobs and men. This will involve a high degree of occupational differentiation among kin and a high degree of both intergenerational and geographical mobility. These characteristics require both the adoption of the values specified by Parsons and create the same conditions of action for people in their kin roles that he specifies. They thus involve both the types of lack of fit between family system and industrial institutions that we began by considering: inconsistency between ideas reflected in the two types of institution and inconsistency between the conditions required for each to carry out its characteristic activities.

THE CONJUGAL FAMILY: CAUSE OR EFFECT?

Those readers who recall the admonition at the beginning of this chapter to consider the effect of the family on other institutions as well as their effect on the family should by now be somewhat uneasy. Although we have been discussing 'fit' we have been discussing the fit of the family to society and not the other way round. It is a curious fact that family sociologists seem to have a tendency to see the family as a dependent variable. In contrast, economic historians who are not interested in the family *per se* tend, on the other hand, to see it as an independent variable. The reason for this difference is clear: in order to evaluate the effect of one institution on another you have to specify the conditions under which the activity governed by the second institution can take place.

Now we have already elaborated the conditions which are necessary for autonomous industrialization to occur (see above p. 113). A little thought shows that the family, because of the functions it has, must be of considerable importance in creating those conditions.

In the *first* place there must be a surplus of capital, which can be employed in industrial uses. Whatever the family form, it is likely that such capital will be owned and controlled by individuals or families, rather than companies and organizations, since prior to industrialization the need for control of the productive processes by such means will not exist. Hence the extent to which such capital is dispersed among a large number of individuals as opposed to being relatively concentrated will depend to a great extent on the system of inheritance that prevails.

Where the patrimony is divided among all the children or among all the sons, the system will favour a more equal distribution of wealth than where only one child can inherit. Since the economy must by definition be primarily agricultural, most property will be in land. In a money economy the effect of a single heir system will be to concentrate the profits in the hands of the single heir or, if dispersed through dowry or in gifts to non-inheriting sons, to make it available in liquid form for investment either in an enterprise owned by the inheritor or, through a money market[31] of some kind, in enterprises owned by others.

The type of inheritance system does not of course determine the matter. But the less capital there is available in the society as a whole and the less developed are financial institutions, the greater its influence will be in making available relatively large sums for investment.

In the *second* place the family as a socializing agency will have a vital role to play in influencing the beliefs and attitudes of individuals which will determine the propensity to save and to invest and the willingness to innovate and take risks.

Thirdly the family as a reproductive agency will affect the size of the population and hence the size of the labour surplus which can be utilized for non-agricultural production.

Fourthly the family has an important role to play in determining the reaction to the new systems of production involved in industrialization and in their legitimation.

The problem of the effect of *systems of inheritance* on population growth is an interesting one. The more children one has under a system of equal division, the more one's property will be divided at one's death. Hence it has been argued that there is a strong incentive under this system to keep the size of the family down. On the other hand it could be argued that under such a system the children could at least all marry, while under the single inheritance system many of the non-inheriting children would have to remain celibate.

If you think about it it will appear that both views are correct. Under the equal system there will be more marriages but fewer children per marriage; under the single system there will be fewer marriages but more children per marriage. Of course where division proceeds too far so that the portions cannot support a family it may prevent marriage. It is impossible to balance these factors out and

[31] The existence of such sums seeking investment is, of course, a condition of there being a money market.

draw any firm conclusion. It is quite clear however that a single system will force the non-inheriting children to 'travel'. *If* there is population growth relative to the land available this will produce a landless labour force, whereas under the same conditions the equal system of inheritance will produce a subdivision of holdings.

Given population growth therefore, a single system is likely both to provide a labour force and prevent the dispersion of property, while an equal system is likely to tie labour to the land and prevent the accumulation of large sums for investment in default of any financial institutions capable of capitalizing peasant hoardings.

Professor Habbakuk has pointed to an association between single inheritance systems and early industrialization (England and Germany) and between equal inheritance systems and late industrialization (France and Russia); and between single inheritance systems and migration (Eastern Czechoslovakia) and between equal systems and domestic manufacture (Western Czechoslovakia and mediaeval East Anglia).[32]

It may seem surprising that the family should, on account of its socializing function, be considered important. Surely the family is simply an agent which transmits whatever ideas go to make up the culture of society? On the contrary it seems possible that the family form, particularly the system of inheritance, can vitally affect those ideas.

Family structure can of course affect the efficiency of socialization. It seems likely that the extent to which a child shows evidence of a concern with achievement is related to the size of the family, but only within the same social class. The social class of a child determines what is transmitted and in America there is some evidence that achievement values are more associated with the middle than the working classes. The smaller the middle class family however, the more achievement-oriented the child is. This fact is quite easily explicable—the smaller the family the more time each child spends with his parents and the more intense the ties with them and hence the better the transmission of whatever they are transmitting—in this case achievement values.[33]

How can the family determine what is transmitted? In order to understand this we have to look again at systems of inheritance. Where a child knows from birth that all he has to do is to sit back and wait to inherit, his whole activities and those of his parents are

[32] Habbakuk, H. J., 'Family Structure and Economic Change in Nineteenth Century Europe', *Jour. Econ. Hist.* 15, 1955, p. 1.

[33] Rosen, B. C., 'Family Structure and Achievement Motivation,' *Amer. Sociol. Rev.* 26, 1961, p. 574.

going to be directed towards fitting him for his role as inheritor—whatever that may involve. Where however a child knows from the earliest age that he is not going to inherit but has to go out into the cold wide world and fend for himself, both he and his parents will be concerned to prepare him for independence which willl depend on his own achievements. The value of achievement will therefore be systematically stressed. Inheritance systems which determine the inheriting child by sex and birth order make possible the ANTICIPATORY SOCIALIZATION[34] of the other children to fit them to the achievement-oriented roles which they will have to adopt. Inheritance systems which do not do this, either because the inheriting child is chosen on the death or retirement of the father or because all inherit and it only becomes apparent later that their portion will be too small and they will have to find other means of support, will preclude satisfactory anticipatory socialization.[35] Hence it would appear that the single inheritance system not only provides a mobile labour force, keeps capital in large lumps, but also imbues this labour force with the values of achievement necessary for entrepreneurial activity.

While it would be mistaken to regard this as established beyond doubt, it does provide an hypothesis supported by some evidence which shows that there is an intimate relation with the structure of the family of the content of socialization. It also suggests ways in which change can be autonomously generated in so far as it points out that an ascriptive particularistic society can produce achievement-oriented universalistic individuals.

Lastly we turn to the effect of the family upon the activities of specialized institutions of economic production. It has been argued that one of the advantages of the conjugal family is that it contains only one worker and therefore is mobile, both occupationally and geographically. We have argued that such mobility is not necessarily required by industrialization. If we look at Britain, the only pure case of autonomous industrialization there is, we find that although the first fifty years of industrialization showed an enormous population redistribution, it also showed an enormous population growth. The rate of growth of the population of the towns was far greater than that of the rural areas[36] and hence much of the 'redistribu-

[34] i.e. the learning of behaviour and values appropriate to a position or situation *before* occupying the position rather than *through* occupancy of the position.

[35] Kasdan, L., 'Family, Migration and Entrepreneurs', *Comp. Stud. in Soc. and Hist.* 7, 1964-1965, p. 345.

[36] See Habbakuk, *op. cit.*

tion' was the result of differential growth rates rather than mass migration. Much of the migration that did occur would seem to be the result of relatively small movements in a uniform direction rather than movements over vast distances. This is not merely a unique historical circumstance. Unless the country concerned is able very swiftly to export manufactured goods in exchange for imported food, most of the rural population will have to stay put on the land in order to feed themselves and the non-food producers in the towns. Since the need to inherit is likely to retard the age at marriage in conjugal family systems this entails that the age at marriage will drop among the landless town labourers and hence a large part of the population increase will come from the rural surplus already engaged in industrial production in the towns. Hence this stage of industrialization does not require massive rural-urban migration. Since the level of skill required in the first stage is likely to be low, there will be no great need for occupational mobility either.

In fact we find that in Britain, so far from destroying the family, industrial enterprises used it. The family had already been used by merchants as a productive unit to whom they put out raw materials for manufacture. The use of machines driven by mechanical power involved simply the gathering of family units under one roof. In early mining, family and kin groups were extensively used as sub-contracting teams. Among entrepreneurs the family was extensively used since, in the absence of an adequate capital market and of any law of limited liability and given the scarcity of capital, the family was the obvious institution to use for forming partnerships and raising capital. So far from the family being inconsistent with economic institutions, the latter depended heavily on the former.

It is of course true that the development of the early enterprises into industrial bureaucracies resulted in the destruction of the family as a work group; men, women and children being employed instead as individuals, and that this pattern rapidly became widespread. It should be remembered however that the large factory was not the characteristic mode of production in the nineteenth century, which was rather the small workshop, and that kinship probably remained of considerable importance to both workers and employers in their economic activities until well into the twentieth century.

In view of these facts it would seem hard to argue that a conjugal family form is *for these reasons* (i.e. its permitting occupational and geographical mobility) a necessary *prerequisite* of industrialization. With regard to the legitimation of authority, the creation of the new industrial enterprises involved the creation of social positions and classes whose authority could not be derived from any traditional source, but this would have been the case whatever family system existed prior to industrialization.

While the family form which pre-exists industrialization may very well be one of its determinants,[37] it would not seem that this is because some forms prevent mobility. It is probably due more to the family's basic functions—reproduction and socialization—and the way it discharges its pre-industrial economic function, the type of inheritance system being of particular importance, than because of direct inconsistencies between the values built into the roles of industrial economic institutions and the family or because of the former's demand for geographical and occupational mobility.

We may conclude this discussion by referring to a point that was made in the previous chapter which is of crucial importance here. When the lack of fit of the extended family with the industrial system is discussed it is frequently not made clear whether what is being referred to is the extended family which is *permitted* by the rules governing the family process or the extended family which occurs because such rules *require* its existence. If the family process is governed by a rigid set of rules which determine the membership and activities of groups wider than the nuclear family, such groups will be unable to meet the *varying* demands made upon them at different *stages* in the industrialization process. If however, as is usually the case in a bilateral system, family groups are formed not as a result of the rules governing the family process alone but as a result also of the activities of the family members, then as the economic institutions in society change this produces a change in the activities of family members and also of the composition of groups wider than the elementary family.

The importance of the existence of bilateral systems as a precondition of industrialization lies therefore in the fact that they permit individuals to form different types of group performing different types of activity at different stages of the industrialization process, rather than because the structural isolation of the nuclear family in such systems implies that extended family group do not exist.

[37] For a discussion of the type of family in America which suggests that the characteristics of the contemporary American family predate industrialization, see Furstenburg, F. F., 'Industrialisation and the American Family: a look Backward', *Amer. Sociol. Rev.* 31, 1966, p. 326. For evidence that the conjugal family can diffuse itself independently of industrialization see Greenfield, S. M., 'Industrialisation and the Family in Sociological Theory', in Farber, B. *Kinship and Family Organization*, London, Wiley, 1966, p. 408.

5

Family, Mobility, Community

It will be our business in the course of this chapter to consider further some of the problems touched on in our discussion of the family in industrial society. In particular we shall consider different kinds of mobility and the way they affect the solidarity of the family and of other ascriptive groups within the society and the way in which such groups interaffect one another.

DIFFERENTIAL MOBILITY IN THE NUCLEAR FAMILY

We have already noted that Parsons has argued that in industrial society the *unit* of social mobility is the nuclear family. That is to say it is the nuclear family which moves up or down between strata and not isolated individuals. We can now see a little more clearly why this must be. The members of the nuclear family in any society are spouses and immature children. The children have neither power, authority nor prestige *in the society as a whole* apart from their parents. Their position in the society is ascribed on the basis of their parentage. Secondly, the family is a unit of residence and consumption. Young children can have no style of life independently of their parents. Where prestige is attributed on the basis of style of life, therefore the child's prestige will be the same as the parents'. Changes in the parents' style of life and in their degree of power and prestige will mean changes of the same order for the children. As the parents move, whether it be geographically or socially, so must the children.

In societies where the kin group is wider than the nuclear family and is a unit both of ownership and production, the individual's ranked position in the society will be determined by his group membership and he will be able to affect it only by affecting the position of the group to which he belongs. In societies where property and economic activities are not shared by members of corporate kin groups but belong to individuals, it will be logically possible for the membership of kin groups to be internally differentiated in terms of property, ownership and occupation.

Where the nuclear family is structurally isolated in Parsons' sense, the differentiation of individuals recognizing ties of kinship to one another will have consequences for the formation, through the family process, of groups wider than the nuclear family. Within the nuclear family it will be logically possible for husband and wife to occupy different positions within the stratification system. Whether it is in fact possible will depend on a variety of factors, of which two of the most important are the rights accorded to women in the society concerned and the rights given to *married* women.

Before we go any further it must be made clear that we are not referring to the power or authority or prestige of the wife within the family. We are referring to the rights which determine whether a wife can hold positions outside the family which confer authority, or can exercise power in the society as a whole—not just within the family. Of course the class of rights we are considering affect very considerably the position of the wife within the family, but the position of the woman in society and in the family need to be sharply distinguished.

It might be thought that in an omnilineal system, women must be able to hold property. It must be remembered however that lineality is a principle of transmission not a principle which determines control. In a system where the men are dominant, the property may be transmitted through the women without their ever getting their hands on it, though they may indirectly enjoy benefits that it brings. In nineteenth-century Britain, for example, property which belonged to a woman was normally controlled by her father until her marriage, upon which it became the property of her husband. In this case a woman was not legally debarred from controlling property. It was rather that, since women were considered by virtue of the disabilities imposed by their sex to be incapable of managing wealth, inheritance by women was normally made conditional on male control until marriage. *Legally,* disabilities were imposed upon *married* women who were debarred from holding property. They could still inherit property however, and as a result the only women who had any legal control over property were widows. Hence the importance of rich widows to poor young adventurers.

Now, in most industrial societies, any formal disabilities placed upon women as regards possession or control of property or the occupancy of jobs have been removed. At the same time it is still true that the proportion of women who hold jobs is small compared with men and the proportion of working women that hold jobs ranked high in terms of power and authority is also small.[1] As Bernard Shaw once put it: 'the women said we will not be dictated to—and went out and became stenographers.'[2]

Two things therefore need to be explained: why industrialization is accompanied by the 'emancipation' of women and why, once emancipated, women do not more often succeed in utilizing the opportunities thus made available to them. With regard to the first it could be argued that industrialization creates non-domestic jobs which women can do, and that in the early stages of industrialization women are more amenable to the authority of new employers than men.[3]

Goode has argued[4] on the other hand, following the sound principle that human behaviour is never determined by the conditions of action alone, that there have been many occasions in human history where women have been employable and labour short and women have still not been employed and that therefore beliefs and attitudes must constitute an additional factor. He draws attention to the changes in ideas which are a necessary condition of industrialization and argues that the growth of individualistic ideas is responsible for the removal of disabilities placed on women.

While we may see such notions at work in the reformist movements in the nineteenth century, it is absurd to explain the employment of female labour in mines and factories in terms of ideas about the individual rights *of the women*; such employment needs to be explained in terms of notions concerning the rights of employers and the destruction of old ideas governing the relationship of master and servant. We may accept the importance of the spread of individualistic ideas in destroying the old relationships within the family which militated against the employment of married women, but their acquisition of rights in the sphere of employment derives from the spread of collectivist rather than individualistic notions.

Granted the emancipation of women, why are the opportunities provided not more used? The answer to this question takes us back to the family. In the first place there are obvious advantages in a sexual division of labour within the family: that is to say in one

[1] See Goode, W. J., *World Revolution and Family Patterns*, London, Collier-Mac: Free Press, 1964, pp. 55–66, for a summary and discussion of evidence on these points.

[2] He was of course referring to middle class women.

[3] See Bendix, R., *Work and Authority in Industry*, London, Wiley, 1956; London, Harper and Row, 1963.

[4] Goode, W. J., *op. cit., loc. cit.*

partner specializing in child-rearing and household management and the other in providing the material means of support. Except where the earnings of the husband are high or the wife's potential earnings through employment outside the family are high, it will not be possible to employ someone to take over the child-rearing and household management tasks. Since the wife must be periodically absent from employment through child-bearing she is the obvious candidate for the family-oriented role.

This argument, while incontrovertible, needs to be treated with caution. It does not apply with equal force at all stages of the family cycle. The wife can work in the early stages of marriage if child-bearing is postponed. The availability of the means of contraception and the fact that it is effectively opposed by only a few religious sects mean that in Western societies it increasingly is postponed. One of the results of this postponement is that it makes possible earlier marriage and reduces the necessity of parental support and hence consent. Nor does it apply during any time that may be left after the last child has been born and reared. If the age at marriage is low and the family size small (i.e. four or under) and the expectation of life is long (i.e. sixty or over at the age of marriage) then there will be a substantial period towards the end of the marriage when the wife's presence at home is not demanded by the cares of the nuclear family household and an even longer period where the wife's presence is not demanded by care for pre-school children.[5]

In industrial societies the age at marriage is low, the family size is relatively small, the expectation of life long and there are schools. The wife therefore, even if she plays the family-oriented role will be able to work for a large part of her married life. However her career will be interrupted by child-bearing and this interruption will affect the chances of reaching a high position in her profession when she resumes work.

The activities which characterize the nuclear family may be seen therefore to favour a sexual division of labour and to favour the adoption by the woman of the family-oriented role, and the performance of this role would seem to militate against continued employment and to diminish a woman's career prospects. Moreover, where the woman's and the man's skill are both high, then *his* mobility to obtain employment may result in residence which prevents the pursuit of *her* career. As a result of all these factors women have

[5] For details of variation in the occupation of married women over the cycle see Kelsall, R. K. and Mitchell, S., 'Married Women and Employment in England and Wales', *Pop. Stud.* 13, 1959–1960, p. 19.

lower activity rates[6] than men and fewer reach the higher level job.

This isn't the end of the story however. Even if the woman works, the role which is most visible will be her domestic role. As a result the expectations which the children will acquire through being socialized in such a family will be that the family role of the wife is the dominant one. As a result they will regard working as an 'optional extra' for women rather than as an integral part of a woman's adult status.[7]

In the economic sphere the identification of the woman with the domestic role and men with the occupational role will favour the recruitment of women to jobs which are related to the domestic in some way—jobs which are connected with taking care of people, rather than involving the efficient manipulation of people and things. At the same time the periodic absence from work involved in accidental pregnancies or domestic crises may give substance to beliefs as to the unreliability and expensiveness of female labour, while women's association with particular types of jobs tends to give rise to beliefs about their having specialized aptitudes and abilities.[8]

If we now add to these considerations the fact that all known industrial societies have developed from societies where economic activity was controlled by men, women being confined very largely to the domestic sphere and where the superiority of men was taken for granted, we have a perfectly adequate explanation of the low female activity rates and women's lack of success in reaching the top jobs. How much of it can be attributed to the persistence of earlier notions (feminists would say male prejudice—but it is really female prejudice as well) and how much to the incompatibility of the conditions for the successful performance of family activities and for the successful performance of career activities it is impossible to say. It seems reasonable to suppose however that it cannot be explained entirely in terms of beliefs and values and that, even if there were no 'prejudice' on the part of either sex against the employment of women, they still would have a smaller proportion in the top jobs and have lower activity rates.

Two further points must be noted however. First, provision of communal care for children (i.e. day nurseries) or the substitution of

[6] An activity rate refers to the proportion of people old enough and not too old to work who are actively employed.

[7] For a discussion of sex roles see—Parsons, T., 'Age and Sex in the Social Structure of the United States', in Parsons, T., *Essays in Sociological Theory*, London, Collier-Mac: Free Press, 1964, pp. 89–103.

[8] See Chombart de Lauwe, M. J., 'The Status of Women in French Urban Society', *Intern. Soc. Sci. Jour.* 14, 1962, pp. 35–36.

communal for family care (as in the kibbutzim) are the pre-condition of women working on the same terms as men. Provided the numbers employed caring for the children are smaller than the numbers thereby released for other work, such care will result in a real increase in the labour force if the women are prepared to go out to work. Feminists tend to suppose that women must want to escape from the home into the outside world and that if they do not use the opportunities this must be through prejudice or ignorance. Goode once again has pointed out that the satisfaction obtained from work by the poorly educated and low skilled is small. In such cases the rewards from work are extrinsic rather than intrinsic, i.e. they work for the money.[9] If they did not need the money they would not work. If they do not need the money they very often do not work, as the absenteeism rates show. In this situation why should a married woman consider the opportunity to work an inestimable boon? At the beginning of industrialization women and children were forced into the factories because a low wages policy meant that if they all did not work they all would starve.[10] It is not unreasonable to assume that the crucial factor determining whether married women work is the degree to which their household's income provides what they consider a reasonable standard of living. We must be careful not to suppose, because middle-class women obtain satisfaction from their jobs apart from the financial rewards, that this is true of everyone else.[11]

The second point that must be considered is whether or not the activities of child care can be undertaken by people outside the nuclear family or by an extended family. This depends of course on a large number of factors. In the first place proximity of residence is required. This opportunity is only available to those whose level of skill and that of their husbands is not so great as to require mobility which would prevent the provision of such services. Secondly it will depend on the shape of the family cycle. Where the parent is so old as to be retired when a woman's children are young, then her mother or mother-in-law may be able to provide help with the

[9] See Parker, S. R. *et al.*, *Sociology of Industry*, London, Allen & Unwin, 1967, p. 153.

[10] Women were not forced into economic activity. Women had been engaged in farming and manufacturing activities undertaken by the family for centuries. They appear to have been employed in mining also. See Hewitt, M., *Wives and Mothers in Victorian Industry*, London, Barrie & Rockliff, 1958.

[11] For discussion of evidence on motivation of married women to work see Parker, S. R. *et al.*, *op. cit.*, p. 51. See also Gavron, H., *The Captive Wife*, London, Routledge, 1966, p. 107; also Chombart de Lauwe, *op. cit.*, pp. 38, 40.

children and the house. In a society where married women work, if her parent is under retiring age, this may not be possible because she may also be at work. If the age at marriage is low in both the woman's and her parent's generation, then if the mother postpones her return to work in order to care for her daughter's children while the daughter works there will of course be no net gain in female employment as a result.

Such services may however be of advantage to the family concerned. We have already noted that the middle class family can 'even out' its income over time by transferring income from rich oldsters to poor youngsters.[12] The working class family does not enjoy a rise in real income over the life cycle and cannot provide help to young married children of a financial kind. It can however provide domestic services. When the children have married the income may be the same but the expenditure has diminished. Help can be provided to the young family either by the mother returning to work and giving part of her married earnings to the married child or domestic services can be provided which enable the young couple to go out to work. Since financial aid would be a denial of the autonomy of the nuclear family, domestic service is likely to be a popular choice. If the parent is, however, still raising children of her own, it will be the only possible choice. Hence we would expect to find working class mothers going out to work while their children are young more frequently than middle class mothers, where near kin are not too dispersed to help.[13]

In industrial society therefore though married women may work and frequently do work at different stages of the family cycle, few married women follow careers. It is highly unlikely that the woman is going to be *occupationally mobile* through employment outside the family. Where she does not work her rank position will be the same as that of her husband. Where she does work, she is accorded the same position as her husband if that position is *lower* than his. This is possible because, since her main adult role is a family one, her occupational role is considered unimportant. If however it is *higher* than her husband's it can no longer be pretended that she isn't really trying, and she has to be evaluated on the same criteria as he is. This creates a situation in which it is difficult to place the children

[12] See above, Ch. 4, p. 104.

[13] See Thompson, B. and Finlayson, A., 'Married Women who work in Early Motherhood', *Brit. Jour. Sociol.* 14, 1963, who found a higher proportion of women with young children working in the lower occupational groups; Gavron, H., *op. cit.*, found fewer but her account suggests little aid was available from kin in the areas she studied.

and most important of all threatens the equality of the husband. (In fact it upsets beliefs about male authority and superiority as well, but there are problems enough without bringing in this factor.)

It has to be recognized that the sexual division of labour[14] has a very important side effect on the marital relationship. Where there is a complete division the relationship can never be competitive. Each spouse has a clearly defined sphere of competence. Secondly it is a relationship of exchange and complementarity. Obviously in the sexual sphere there is an exchange. But in the domestic sphere there is equally an exchange relationship, in which each partner gratifies the other's needs. Where the wife successfully pursues a career, this interdependence is greatly diminished.

A marriage may be seen as being held together by both what the spouses have in common and by an exchange based on difference. Differential occupational mobility of the spouses therefore introduces an element of competition into the relationship which now depends much more on sexual exchange and shared values. However if there is differential mobility in the full sense of the term, this will involve the mobile spouse in accepting the values and styles of life of a different occupational group. Hence differential mobility may be seen to destroy the social basis of the marriage since it socially differentiates the spouses (destroys what they share) and it destroys the basis of the exchange relationship. This means that the couple must rely chiefly on sexual differences and personality similarities. This is not to say that it makes the marriage impossible, but it does place it under severe strain.

It must be made quite clear that what is being asserted here is *not* that if women go out to work they will destroy their marriage. What is being asserted is that, if there is considerable differential occupational mobility after marriage, then this will produce grave strains in the marital relationship by diminishing the range of shared values and patterns of behaviour on which the marriage was founded.

DIFFERENTIAL MOBILITY IN THE ELEMENTARY FAMILY

So far we have considered only the case where the wife's mobility gives her a higher position than the husband. Where however the husband's mobility after marriage is so great as to involve his membership of a different status group to that to which husband and wife originally belonged then, although this neither destroys of the complementarity of the relationship nor introduces an element of

[14] To be sharply distinguished from 'the division of sexual labour'.

competition into the relationship, it still destroys the shared values with which the marriage began *unless the wife can change her style of life along with her husband.* This, while not easy, is not as difficult as when both are working, since the unemployed wife does not occupy a position in a group whose status is different from that of her husband. She does not have to perform two different and inconsistent roles at the same time, which would be the case where husband and wife both had different occupational statuses (e.g. female company lawyer and butcher's wife).

The reader will be doubtless quick to spot the fact that the wife does belong to a group which is different from that of her husband if he is mobile after marriage. She belongs to her kin group and at very least that means her elementary family of origin. We have here a nice example of Parsonian 'strain' between the occupational system (demanding the husband's social mobility) and the family. Now with a bit of luck the parents of both wife and husband may be dead before the mobility is great enough to matter. If not, all is not lost. The ties of the nuclear family are the most 'stringent'. Achievement is laudable. 'Your first duty is to your husband and children.' 'We don't want to stand in your way' and (to the son-in-law) 'we're real proud of you son. I never thought I'd live to see the day when a daughter of mine . . .' etc., is what the parents are supposed to say. That is they are supposed to renounce all rights that might interfere with the mobility of the children, thus according primacy to ties within the nuclear family.

This is the orthodox Parsonian 'line'. Parsons' critics, notably Litwak, have argued that differential mobility within the elementary family, though inconsistent with the classical extended family (whose formation is required by the rules governing the family process and where the individual is subordinated to the authority of the group),[15] is not inconsistent with some types of extended family formation (in bilateral systems) which have an egalitarian internal structure. These he calls the 'modified extended family'.

Litwak asserts that arguments that kin groupings wider than the nuclear family are inconsistent with elementary family differential mobility, depend *on two assumptions.*[16] *The first* of these is that

[15] Litwak introduced the term 'classical extended family'. The definition used here is not his. He does not make clear whether nuclear families and individuals are subordinate to the wider group in such a family because of the rules or because of the activities which they undertake. His classical extended family is an empirical and not a theoretical type for which he gives no ethnographic reference. See Litwak, E., 'Occupational Mobility and Extended Family Cohesion', *Amer. Sociol. Rev.* 25, 1960, p. 9.

[16] Litwak, *op cit.* The second assumption is discussed below, p. 133.

'status is achieved by associating with those of equal or greater occupational status'. Against this Litwak wishes to assert that 'status is (also) achieved by being deferentially treated by others'. Now status here means either a social position which confers prestige on its occupant or simply social prestige. Prestige means the ability to evoke deferential behaviour from others. One does not *achieve* prestige by evoking deferential behaviour from others: one is simply *using* it. Nor does one achieve prestige by association with others on terms of equality: this is a sign that one has the prestige which is such as to evoke egalitarian behaviour from the people concerned. Both statements therefore confuse the sign with the thing signified.[17]

There is more to the first statement than this however. 'Social mobility' implies three things: movement from one power/authority category to another, from one style of life category to another and from one social group to another. Occupational mobility therefore is only a part of social mobility. Mobility is only complete when the 'mobile' has acquired the style of life associated with the higher occupational group to which he has moved and been accepted as a member of the group in all respects. The first statement is therefore to be rephrased more precisely. Social mobility is only complete when the 'mobile' *is able* to associate on equal terms with members of the occupational group to which he has moved in all respects.

It does not of course matter that he associates with inferiors on terms of *superiority*. In this respect Litwak is quite correct. The argument concerning the disruptive effect on extended family relationships must therefore have something to do with the special characteristics of the family. Either there must be something about the family which makes the superior-subordinate relationship impossible or, if such relationships can be found between family members, then for some reason these must be different from other relationships of the same kind outside the family in their effect on prestige.

The reader will not be surprised to learn that Parsons' argument centres on these points. In view of the large number of misinterpretations[18] of Parsons it is important to note that his concern with

[17] To say 'X has the same prestige as Y' is to make a dispositional statement that allows us to infer that X will behave in a certain way to Y and vice versa. The statment may be *verified* by getting X and Y to interact. Their interaction on terms of equality however is not instrumental in *creating* the prestige relation between them but is *evidence* of it. Z seeing the interaction of X with someone who is superior to him (that is with Y) may now accord X deference which he would not previously have done, not because X has acquired status, but because he has enabled Z to place him.

[18] See for example, Coult, A. D. and Habenstein, R. W., 'The Study of

universalistic—achievement societies stems from the fact that he sees society as being rooted in the particularistic and ascriptive solidarities of kinship, local community, ethnic group and social class. It is the inconsistency between institutions utilizing ascriptive bases of solidarity and the universalistic-achievement oriented institutions of industrial society that constitutes his focus of interest.

With regard to the family what Parsons says is this: 'The solidarity of the kinship unit is of such a character that if certain facilities and rewards are available to one member, they will have to be 'shared' with other members. In other words the two basic components of the reward system of the society, occupational approval . . . and . . . love and response in the kinship unit must go the same way.'[19]

Parsons is arguing therefore that the prestige of family members is pooled, so that Ego's mobility in prestige terms increases that of his parents while his parents' stability diminishes the amount of mobility that would have been achieved through occupational ascent had Ego not had such parents. Hence there cannot be superordinate-subordinate relationships between kin *based on prestige differences.* Litwak deals with this point,[20] arguing that parents laud the success of the mobile son, who gains the satisfaction of being deferred to by his kin on account of his mobility. This is to make a very elementary confusion between the way a role is performed and its occupancy.[21] Of course parents may be proud of a mobile son—precisely because his prestige increases theirs. Of course the parents hold the son in high esteem—precisely because he is such a 'good' son. Being mobile, in a society that values mobility, is a way of performing the role of son well. The esteem which derives from good *performance* of an existing role (son) Litwak confuses with the deference accorded because of the *occupancy* of a new role (the occupational one). Litwak should try treating his father like he treats the janitor of his apartment and see what sort of reception he gets.

If prestige of family members is pooled, the low prestige of the father diminishes that of the son. One of the functions of the family is supposed to be placement. 'A' places 'B' in terms either of his kin relationship to another known person, or in terms of his ascriptive category membership—*nigger, Welshman, son of* managing director or whatever. We can see now why Parsons regards a social class as

Extended Kinship in Urban Society', *Soc. Quart.* 3, 1962, p. 141. The authors accuse Parsons of asserting that 'particularistic orientations are and must be eliminated' in a universalistic society.

[19] *The Social System,* London, Tavistock, 1952, pp. 160–161.

[20] *Op. cit.*

[21] It is also to confuse Ego's position in the family with his position in society.

having an ascriptive membership. Class membership is kin determined twice over. First the family into which one is born affects one's life chances, i.e. the chance of becoming successful, etc., because of the control over resources commanded by the family and wider kin. Secondly, because family members share prestige, a social relationship with a member of a family group involves an obligation to treat the other members of the group in the same way.

If the elementary family is differentiated through differential occupational mobility, members of the occupational category into which a high-mobile family member has moved will be unwilling to treat him as an equal because so to do might involve treating his kin as equals which, in view of the kin's style of life and lower occupational prestige, they will be unwilling to do. Therefore they must keep their social distance from him, or not permit the approval they accord him because of his job to spill over into diffuse esteem in which members of a ranked social category are held.

If however the occupational position of the 'mobile's' kin are unknown, or the chances of any contact being had are remote because of the distance between them and the 'mobile', then such consideration may have little effect, provided that the ideology of the group concerned does not involve justifying their superior position in terms of superior birth. Litwak is therefore correct to point out that the anonymity of a large city may make it possible for the 'mobile' to segregate kin and his new peers, and that geographical mobility may have the same effect.

We are now ready to turn to *the second assumption* which Litwak alleges underlies the argument that kin groups wider than the elementary family are disrupted by social mobility. This is that there are 'extreme differences in socialization among the various occupational strata'. By this Litwak means that there are differences in what is transmitted. (It is both the differences in life style between strata and their invidious ranking that create the problem. These two aspects need to be kept distinct. The difference in style of life produced by differential socialization is characteristic of all ascriptive groups. Their social ranking is peculiar to styles of life associated with social strata.)

Litwak implies that he accepts that the resocialization of individual members of an elementary family through mobility would constitute a real barrier to extended family communication. He argues as a matter of fact, first that style of life differences are small and narrowing in contemporary American society, and secondly that the degree of occupational mobility found is insufficient to involve crossing status category lines. These views can be questioned both on empirical and theoretical grounds, but to do so here would take us too far out of our way. We may note that he never mentions education in this respect, which would seem to be of some importance, and that he confines his attention to the white Americanized groups so as not to confuse ethnic differences with class differences. In a society where ethnic differences play an important part in determining class position this is an odd line of argument.

His last point however takes us back to ground covered in the previous chapter, namely the frequency with which a high degree of mobility is required by an industrial economy. Here the Parsonian argument may not hold for all stages of industrialization. Our concern here however is not with the amount of mobility *required* but with whether it must disrupt the elementary family *if it occurs*.

It would appear that some types of mobility are possible without disrupting family relationships. Occupational mobility by itself need not be disruptive where it does not lead to social mobility. Where the approval which is accorded to an individual is prevented from spilling over into diffuse esteem, either because of the refusal of the occupational category concerned to accord esteem, or because the job concerned has no clear implications for style of life or group membership, or because the mobile individual refuses to[22] associate with members of the category to which his occupational mobility gives him access (except in the occupational sphere), a disruption of family relationships will not occur. The mobile individual will receive the praises of his family and they will enjoy enhanced prestige within their own category.

Where however the mobility is significant in so far as it involves movement between groups based on different styles of life and/or different economic or political interests, then it is likely to have a disruptive effect. If however the categories concerned do not conceptualize themselves as being differentiated in economic and political terms but in terms of *standard* of living, then there is no reason why mobility should weaken the solidarity of the family group. In such a case the only meaning attached to the term social mobility will be occupational and income mobility, since the society or the area of the stratification system concerned will not be made up of groups or categories but of positions ranked on an income and job-prestige scale.

Where social mobility in terms of group membership is possible however it still may not disrupt family relationships if they can be

[22] This implies a deliberate retention of his old relationships and not their replacement by new ones, i.e. his retention of a position in his old group rather than loss of prestige in his new one.

segregated from other relationships, provided the groups between which the mobile moves are not differentiated in terms of style of life rather than standard of living.

We may accept therefore that industrial society requires occupational mobility, and that where such mobility leads to social mobility in the full sense of the word it will be disruptive of extended family groupings based on solidary ties between members of the elementary family. If different studies[23] appear to provide different conclusions on this point it is because they attempt to base their findings on measures of occupational mobility. As Rosser and Harris have put it 'the discrepancy between occupational achievement and social acceptance by another social group, by slowing down the rate of social mobility of individuals, enables the extended family to accommodate large changes in the occupational status on the part of its members because the consequent changes in social status are much smaller'.[24]

Changes in social status are disruptive because of the way in which, as Parsons penetratingly shows, the ascriptive solidarities of kinship and of social classes and status groups intermesh. Parsons also points out, however, that both are articulated also with the local community since the family is a unit of residence as well as a unit of stratification. It is to a discussion of this relation which we now turn.

THE FAMILY AND GEOGRAPHICAL MOBILITY

Parsons stresses that the family is not only a unit of social mobility but also of geographical mobility because it is not only the basic unit of stratification but also the basic unit of residence. As a consequence family membership determines the membership of territorial groups. This is of course true, but where the 'normal' household's necessary membership is restricted to the nuclear family and no requirement concerning the co-residence of kin is made, the fact that the nuclear family is a household will nevertheless affect the formation of groups wider than the nuclear family since the children will all start off from the same geographical point.

[23] Litwak's study showed that status oriented, non-extended-family oriented mobiles interacted *more* with kin than other categories (Litwak, *op. cit.*). Stuckert found that mobile women interacted and identified *less* with relatives than other categories (Stuckert, R. P., 'Occupational Mobility and Family Relationships', *Soc. For.* 41 (3), Mar. 1963, pp. 301–307). Both measured mobility solely in occupational terms.

[24] Rosser, C. and Harris, C., *Family and Social Change*, London, Routledge 1965.

In societies with advanced transport technologies the individual, once adult, can of course move literally anywhere. Nevertheless it would still be surprising if there was not some relationship between the geographical distribution of the overlapping elementary families, created by the family process, and the point of origin of such a cluster of families. For example one would not expect that, at any given moment, the families of origin of an Aberdonian and his wife, and the families of procreation of their sibs, children and grandchildren, would be no closer to Aberdeen than the same cluster of families of a man who was born at the same time in Penzance. Of course one's expectations might not be fulfilled in any given case, but the chances of two family clusters having widely different points of origin having the same geographical distribution relative to one another's points of origin would certainly be smaller than evens, even though the effect of family ties in restricting mobility was not taken into account.

In other words, just because you have a high transport technology and an absence of rules or residence, it still does not follow that the distribution of family clusters is going to be random. As a result, the individuals who inhabit a given geographical area are likely to be more connected by ties of kinship to other people within the area than they are to people outside it. Where transport is poor or the settlement relatively isolated from other settlements this clustering of kin relationships is likely to be marked.

This is of course true not only of kinship relationships but of other kinds of relationships as well. There is therefore, in every type of society, a tendency to the geographical clustering of relationships whatever the transport is like and whatever the settlement pattern. The transport, the settlement pattern, and the degree of occupationally-induced mobility may affect the size of the areas within which any given degree of clustering takes place, but can never eliminate it. The degree of clustering and the area over which it occurs will determine whether different types of activities involving the individuals in the area can take place. That is to say, it will determine whether the relationships within the area can be used to form groups through which the people concerned can co-operate to carry out different types of activities. That is to say, the degree of clustering will constitute one of the necessary conditions of certain types of group formation. What groups are actually formed will of course depend on the beliefs and attitudes of the people and on the extent to which they vary among them.

All activities however are not dependent upon proximity for their performance. Nevertheless, it is, as we have noted, difficult for group members to act together where they are widely separated. As a consequence, it is unlikely that widely separated individuals will *form* groups for the performance of activities, as opposed to *maintaining* relationships with individuals, or continuing to recognize membership of dispersed groups whose solidarity does not depend on the performance of such activities.

If the members of a locality or an elementary family group are dispersed they may still be members of the territorial or elementary family group but they will not be able to participate in group activities. Nor will members of an elementary family be able to form groups wider than the elementary family for the purpose of carrying out group activities. Members of dispersed groups may however be able to maintain interactive relationships with individuals. Where one member of the group only is physically separated from the rest he may be able to act in concert with the rest of the group. As the proximate group members already act in concert, he has only to co-ordinate his activities with any one of them for the whole group to act together. Hence, if only one of the members of the group is dispersed, this will not prevent the co-action of the whole group unless that particular activity requires proximity.

Now if we keep the preceding argument clearly in our minds a large number of difficulties about the effect of geographical mobility on kin groups disappear. Litwak[25] has argued that modified extended families aid geographical mobility, and that extended family identification is retained in spite of breaks in face to face contact. He substantiates these propositions beyond the possibility of doubt as far as the population he studied is concerned. He is able to show in addition that the extended family oriented are more likely to live further away from kin in the early stages of their career and less likely to be geographically separated from kin towards the end of their career and that the difference between the beginning and end of the career is greater among the higher than among the lower occupational groups. This he explains in terms of the greater requirement of mobility among those in higher status bureaucratic occupations. Mobility is necessary to achieve success, hence when success is achieved it is possible for Ego to move nearer relatives.

What Litwak is saying then is that contact between relatives can be maintained in spite of geographical distance. The existence of an extended family can aid mobility by providing emotional, social and economic aid to its mobile members. There is now ample

[25] Litwak, E., 'Occupational Mobility and Extended Family Cohesion', *Amer. Sociol. Rev.* 25, 1960.

evidence to support the contention that help is exchanged and relationships recognized between widely separated kin who are not members of the same nuclear family. Indeed it is odd that it was ever questioned. The question we have to ask is what Litwak means by an extended family? He offers no evidence of the formation of extended family groups made up of dispersed kin and indeed no evidence of any sort as to what categories of kin his subjects were in touch with. We may assume that the 'relatives' with whom his sample were in touch and who aided mobility were in fact parents. To say that people retain the membership of dispersed elementary family groups and maintain relationships with individuals is not to say that they form extended families in our sense or in Parsons' sense or indeed in any sense which uses the term 'family' to mean 'group'. Once this is understood, Litwak's work loses most of its theoretical importance and becomes instead a straightforward research report of limited generality. The data which he provides are consistent with two hypotheses put forward in this book, namely that the degree of mobility required by the industrial society is related to the level of skill, and that relationships outside the nuclear family are of continued importance in assisting individuals to fulfil the demands made upon them by industrial society.

We may sum up Litwak's contribution to the study of the family as follows. Litwak has not, as he thinks, in any way undermined Parsons' theory. Whereas Parsons' contribution has been to argue that the maintenance of extended family *groups* is inconsistent with the requirements of social and geographical mobility likely to be made in advanced industrial societies, Litwak has shown that the existence of extra-nuclear family *relationships* can in fact be important in aiding this mobility.

It may be argued however that even the existence of extended family *groups* may be of assistance in providing some types of mobility. One of the reasons why it was at one time thought that urban society was characterized by the existence of nuclear families geographically isolated from all kin was that in a period of swift URBANIZATION, that is to say when people were leaving the countryside for the towns, the towns must be full of nuclear families who had left their wider kin behind. We may note that this does not mean that URBAN SOCIETY must necessarily be characterized by such a family type unless towns are only maintained in being by migration to them of a rural surplus population in each generation.

Even in the stage of urbanization it does not follow however that urban nuclear families are necessarily isolated from wider kin. Both common sense and later research suggests that kin ties may play an important part in determining the patterns of migration. For example, Brown[26] has shown in a fascinating article the way in which the migrants from a poor rural area in the Appalachian mountains tend to cluster in certain urban neighbourhoods. The inhabitants from this area, Beech Creek, live in families of a conjugal type but use the family process to form extended family groups. These family groups are ranked into strata and are endogamous within the strata, and hence tend to be interconnected within strata by marriage. In consequence the ascriptive solidarities of 'class', locality and kinship overlap, though there are breaks in the local network of relationships at the boundaries of each stratum. This pattern is reflected in their migration pattern, members of both family groups and strata tending to cluster in the same urban area.

Brown then relates this pattern to the notion of the 'stem family' of Le Play. According to Le Play the advantage of the stem family is that it permits the migration of non-inheriting children without depriving them of the support of parents and sibs in times of difficulty. The maintenance of links with parents and sibs through parents, however tenuous they may appear at the moment at which they are observed, are important because they make possible the retention of a place of safety, as one of Brown's informants put it, 'should things get rough out there'. To Le Play's characterization Brown wishes to add that sibling ties between the non-inheriting children aid migration by facilitating the adjustment of the migrant to the urban community and provide support and assistance in the initial phases of adjustment. The existence in modern industrial society of unemployment relief and other bureaucratic forms of aid precluded the necessity of actually returning to the area of the stem family when things get rough, but the knowledge that one has a place to go to and an ascriptive identity independent of that provided by one's achieved status is of considerable significance to the migrant.

Schwarzweller[27] has followed up this notion with a study of migrants and non migrants in the urban area to which the Beech Creekers move. He is concerned to examine the other side of Brown's argument. If migrants retain an identification with their family of origin, and hence their place of origin, while this may be important in supporting immigrants in the initial phase of their

[26] Brown, J. S. *et al.*, 'Kentucky Mountain Migration and the Stem Family', *Rev. Soc.* 28, 1963, p. 48. See also *ibid*, 'The Conjugal Family and the Extended Family Group', *Amer. Sociol. Rev.* 17, 1952, p. 297.

[27] Schwazweller, H. K., 'Parental Family Ties and Social Integration of Rural-urban Migrants', *Jour. Marr. Fam.* 26, 1964, p. 410.

residence in the city, it is likely to preclude their developing a sense of belonging to the locality to which they move because a large and important number of their ascriptive relationships will not cluster within their new locality. In other words the retention of family ties with another locality will assist their *migration* but not their *assimilation,* either by the group to which they have moved or of the values and attitudes of urban industrial society. He finds no evidence that the maintenance of ties 'with the folks back home' militates against the establishment of non-kin relationships in the new locality or retards upward occupational mobility but finds that the feeling of residential stability is inversely related to frequency of interaction with the parental family. He is unable to say whether the people, who are dissatisfied with their urban situation and want to move, associate more with their stem family because they are dissatisfied, or are dissatisfied because they associate with their stem family.

Our chief concern here is less with the effect of the family on mobility than on the effect of mobility on the family. Brown and Schwarzweller's data seem to indicate that, by aiding migration, the maintenance of extended kin relationships remains of significance to migrants despite geographical separation, and Brown suggests that the process of migration may lead to the establishment of extended family groupings in the urban environment.

Although we have so far dealt separately with social and geographical mobility it is important to recognize that they are usually explicitly related. The Beech Creek migrants are at least economically as well as geographically mobile. If the migrant belongs to a family group 'back home' then, since the family group tends to pool its possessions whether of prestige or of economic resources, the migrant will feel it incumbent upon him to share his new prosperity with family members. There are two ways in which this can be done: either he can send money home or he can save to bring the other members of the family over to him. The existence of strong extended family groups in the migrants' area of origin may therefore stimulate rather than retard *migration*. That is not to say that it will facilitate *individual* mobility, economic or geographical.

Thus we find, among the migrant populations of urban America and increasingly in Britain, that strong extended family ties tend to facilitate migration and lead to the formation of ethnic communities in the host country whose strong ascriptive ties of kinship and locality in their country of origin are recreated in the host country, to which are then added the other ascriptive ties of ethnic and 'class' membership, thus creating highly solidary communities which prevent assimilation into the host society.[28] The way in which extended family ties facilitate migration is vividly illustrated by the way in which attempts by the British government to control immigration have run into difficulty over the attempt to restrict entry to the dependents of existing immigrants. To the British, 'dependents' mean nuclear family members but, to migrants from solidary local communities made up of clusters of extended families, patterns of dependency and economic obligation are infinitely more complex than anything ever dreamed of by either the British legislature or the average immigration officer.

It would appear therefore that the existence of extended family groups affects individual mobility, but individual mobility must adversely affect the assimilation of immigrants. We still have no really adequate data on whether the existence of extended family groups affects individual mobility but individual mobility must destroy such groups where their existence depends on the performance of an activity which depends on co-residence. The maintenance of extended kin relationships can aid mobility by providing services at a distance—money, information, advice—while high levels of mobility may produce a geographically dispersed extended kin network which may be supportive of the person who is highly mobile by providing 'instant' relationships in the various places where he spends his short periods of residence.[29]

THE FAMILY AND THE LOCAL COMMUNITY

In our discussion of the Beech Creek migrants we noted that they retained a feeling of identity not only with their family but also with their locality of origin. It is not the place here to engage in a discussion of the different meanings that have been attached to the term community.[30] It will be sufficient for our purposes to note that the idea of community involves the notion of a plurality of people who hold certain things in common, which things distinguish them from

[28] See for example, Rex, J. and Moore, R., *Race, Community and Conflict*, London, O.U.P. for I.R.R., 1967, pp. 84–132 (esp. 117–120).

For a short survey of immigrants to Britain see Oakley, R. (Ed.), *New Backgrounds*, London, O.U.P. for I.R.R., 1968.

[29] The more mobility destroys local groups the more important kinship relations may become. See Greer, S., 'Urbanism Reconsidered', *Amer. Sociol. Rev.* 21, 1956, p. 25. See also Key, W. H., 'Rural-Urban Differences and the Family', *Soc. Quart.*, 2, 1961.

[30] See Hillery, G. A., 'Definitions of Community: Areas of Agreement', *Rur. Soc.* 20, 1955. See also Morris, R. N. and Mogey, J., *The Sociology of Housing*, London, Routledge, 1965, esp. Ch. 3.

other people. People who live in an area, conceived by them and by other people to be an entity, may be said to live in the *same* place and therefore to constitute a community of residence; that is to say they share residence in the same *locality*.

The difficult question we have to answer is this: what determines which particular cluster of spatial points is conceived of as a whole—as a distinct locality? It may be suggested that there are three broad types of answer to this question. First a locality may be defined as such because it is constituted by a relatively bounded settlement; secondly because it is inhabited by persons belonging to a distinctive social category; and thirdly because the area concerned is populated by people whose social relationships cluster within it.[31]

In the first case nothing else follows from the settlement characteristic: that is to say there is no reason why the inhabitants of a particular settlement should share anything but residence in the same locality. If however the settlement is relatively isolated, relationships are likely to cluster within it—if the population is stable enough for such relationships to be formed. The formation of such relationships will obviously be facilitated the more homogeneous the settlement is, that is to say where the inhabitants conceive of themselves as being the same in some way other than by sharing residence in the same locality.

In the second case nothing necessarily follows from homogeneity except that it will facilitate the establishment of relationships, provided that people seek the formation of relationships within the locality which they will have to do if the locality is a settlement and relatively isolated.

The third case may be seen to be the result of past conditions favouring the establishment of intra-locality relationships, but is independent of those conditions in the sense that such clustering may persist after the conditions which gave rise to it have disappeared and may constitute a condition of future clustering of the same kind.

Now whether or not the population of a locality may be said to form a group, the more relationships an individual has with other people in the locality and the greater the proportion of his relationships which cluster within it, the more likely he is to identify himself with the locality. Similarly the greater the extent to which he regards the other inhabitants as the same as himself the more he will identify with the locality. However all relationships are not of the same kind. Of particular importance in determining identity with the locality will be the ascriptive relationships of kinship, class and ethnic group.

[31] Political boundaries may on occasions also be of importance.

That is to say that the greater is the extent to which the inhabitants are linked by ties of kinship and the same class and ethnic group memberships, the more solidary the locality will be and the more distinctive it will be *vis à vis* other localities.

Mobility will affect this situation in six ways. First the more mobile the population is the shorter time they will have to establish relationships and the less likely it will be that a large proportion of their relationships will cluster within the locality. Secondly the more mobile the people are the less chance there will be of their being connected by a network of kin ties. Thirdly, the more they are mobile the less will be the likelihood of an individual's identifying his family of origin with a locality. Fourthly the more mobile they are the less possible will it be for claims to prestige and social position to be made on particularistic grounds since the particular people, relationships to whom provide the basis of claims to status, will not be known to the other inhabitants, and class categorization will therefore be made on the basis of placement in universalitic categories on the grounds of achievement. Fifth, high mobility will mean that *the locality* will be made up of nuclear families, whether or not they retain ties with extended kin, who retain elementary and extended family memberships. Lastly, a highly mobile population will have a very loosely interconnected locality network and in consequence communication between inhabitants will be poor and dependent on formal means.

Mobility therefore will vitally effect both the family and the locality, and the locality through the family. It should not be assumed however that any of the ascriptive solidarities we have mentioned necessarily enhance locality solidarity. To categorize people as the same is to imply the categorization of others as different. To distinguish a category to whom one has obligations is at the same time to distinguish a residual category to whom one has no obligations. What has been pointed out so far is that, where locality membership and membership of kin categories and class and ethnic group categories *over-lap*, these different types of ascriptive solidarities re-enforce one another. The locality may however be characterized by the existence of different categories *within* it, non-recognition of relationship between whom can be destructive of the solidarity of the locality. In such a case the greater the stress on solidarity within categories the weaker may be the solidarity between them.

This may best be illustrated by a vivid anthropological anecdote told by Freeman.[32] A man recounts how he has just seen a woman

[32] Freeman, J. D., 'On the Concept of the Kindred', *Jour. Roy. Anthrop. Inst.* 91, 1962.

with a child on her back swimming in a river he has just crossed, and remarks that she is sure to drown. When asked why he did not help her he replies: 'She was not of my kindred.' Particularistic solidarities can be as divisive as universalistic ones, and it is fundamentally mistaken to suppose that conflict is characteristic of cold impersonal universalistic societies and not of nice warm friendly particularistic societies and groups.

Campbell[33] for example describes how, among the Sarakatsani shepherds of northern Greece, hostility exists between unrelated families. This hostility exists because the different extended family groups are competing for scarce resources, pasture, and in consequence believe that what is to the advantage of one must be to the disadvantage of another. At the same time however the hostility between unrelated families is intimately related to the rights and obligations inside the elementary family, to the members of which a man owns supreme loyalty. This fact, and the fact that there is no social group within the community that can commit a man to any duty towards persons with whom he is not related by kinship, mean that any relationship with an unrelated person is regarded as a betrayal.

Perhaps the most celebrated, recent description of the divisive effect of kin loyalties in European society is Edward Banfield's study of a town in southern Italy.[34] This society, which is characterized by poverty and apathy towards any communal activity, is also characterized by what Banfield calls 'amoral familism'. By this Banfield means that loyalty to kin, combined with a belief that life is unpredictable and dangerous, leads the inhabitants to recognize obligations to kin only and to justify any action *vis à vis* non-kin which favours the kin group. Hence extrafamilial relations are 'amoral' and not governed by notions of rightness and duty, which notions apply exclusively to members of the family. Using almost the same words as Campbell he writes: 'In the Montegrano mind any advantage that may be given to another is necessarily at the expense of one's own family . . . all those outside the family are at least potential competitors and therefore also potential enemies . . . one cannot afford the luxury of charity or even of justice.'[35] The Montegrano family is nuclear in form, and even relations between mature members of the

[33] Campbell, J. K., *Family, Honour and Patronage*, London, O.U.P., 1964, p. 203.

[34] Banfield, E. C., *The Moral Basis of a Backward Society*, London, Collier-Mac: Free Press, 1958.

[35] *Op. cit.*, p. 110–111.

elementary family are characterized by conflict since they already see each other as rivals.

The consequence of this divisive and over-riding loyalty to the nuclear family is that any community life is almost impossible. The inhabitants do not see themselves as sharing any common interests and the behaviour of individuals who occupy official positions is interpreted solely in terms of the advantage to their nuclear families. Since furtherance of nuclear family interests is the overriding duty of all Montegranesi, it is inconceivable that anyone who should get his hands on an official position should not use it for his own advantage. Hence no community activity is possible since support would mean support of the interests of the organizers.

Banfield seeks the origin of these notions first in the conditions of action. The poor material conditions under which the inhabitants live make life precarious and create a conflict of interests between families. However, the family type means that the individual cannot count on support from kin outside the elementary family which makes the struggle the more desperate. In what terms can the family type be explained?

Banfield once again turns to the material conditions. Because of the increasing division of land due to population growth, few holdings can support more than a nuclear family. Secondly he refers to the permissive manner of child training, which does not make any attempt to instill moral notions into the child.

Banfield's account is highly deficient in that it does not make clear how land is transmitted and what effects this has on the aggregation of holdings, nor is there any detailed examination of the kinship system and the ideas which underlie it. His account does clearly show the way in which family loyalty may be antagonistic to community loyalties when the interests of the families are conceptualized as conflicting. We may note here that interests are likely to be so seen when the success or failure of groups is clearly related to access to scarce resources. In the case of the Sarakatsani the scarce resource is pasture, and, in the case of Montegranesi, land. In industrial societies where the scarce resource is jobs and the total pool of jobs is not clearly recognized, scarcity of employment does not so frequently lead to conflict because loss of employment is often seen in purely individual terms.

It appears that in both the cases we have considered there was one sense in which the inhabitants of the locality were a community—they recognized that the inhabitants of a locality shared access to the same resources.[36] Such recognition, however, leads to conflict where those resources are either absolutely inadequate or inadequate in relation to the expectations of the inhabitants. Conflict in such a situation, because of the sharing of the economic resources between family members, must be between families. Where there is an economic advantage to be gained the various elementary families concerned will group together to improve their chances *vis à vis* other extended families, as among the Sarakatsani. Whether it *is* to their advantage will depend on the material conditions in which they are placed.

This situation is of course one that is familiar to students of primitive societies. In such societies marriage alliances between exogamous descent groups serve to bind otherwise antagonistic kin groupings together with ties of kinship and affinity in each generation. In a bilateral system of recognition, though the units may be nuclear families or *ad hoc* extended families, the web of kin relationships built by the endogamy may very well produce the same effect. Among the Sarakatsani, however, as among Montegranesi, the competition served to curtail the range of recognition of relationship which carried economic obligation. It would appear therefore that, when the inhabitants of a locality come, by their shared residence, to have access to the same pool of scarce resources, this affects the way in which they conceptualize their economic success or failure and that this in turn has effects on the structure of the family which in turn affects the possibility of the development of communal institutions. It should be noted however that this is a very much an hypothesis, which *a priori* seems inadequate because it gives little independent place to the role of culture in the determination of behaviour. This discussion has however been undertaken here because it does provide an interesting example of the way in which kin structure and the bases of community interaffect one another.

Moreover these themes are capable of extension to urban societies. The competition between nuclear families for prestige on new housing estates is of course competition for limited resources. Unlike the rural examples we have seen, however, there is nothing which the population of an urban locality shares except co-residence. Under conditions of high mobility there is no necessary reason for people to be concerned with prestige *vis à vis their neighbours*. In order for

[36] Moss in his study of a similar Italian village is explicit about the existence of a locality orientation (*campanilismo*) while confirming Banfield's general conclusions.

See Moss, L. W. and Cappannari, S. C., 'Patterns of Kinship, Comparaggio and Community in a South Italian Village', *Anthrop. Quart.* 33, 1960, p. 24.

this competition to come about therefore there must be some sense in which the inhabitants are oriented to the neighbourhood population. The existence of local organizations which facilitate the making of relationships in the new area at the same time make possible the community orientation which is a necessary condition of competition. Mobility entails the absence of kin ties and hence of the basis of any solidary ascriptive identification with other families, which can minimize this competition.[37]

In poor localities however shortage of resources tends to create solidary relationships between the inhabitants and thus favours the wider recognition of kinship relationships which seem to be characteristic of this type of community. Such clustering of kin relationships further intensifies the solidarity of the inhabitants who may eventually exhibit many of the characteristics of a group.

Solidary relations with kin and members of the same locality may in some cases be alternatives, as we suggested in the preliminaries to this book. Andrée Vieille has described the way in which the inhabitants of the same *hôtel meublé* in a Parisian working class area utilize neighbours rather than kin to provide domestic services.[38] Here proximity of residence helps to create a system of exchange of aid between neighbours, while the mobility of the population prevents neighbourhood relationships being also kin relationships. In her study of housing in Bristol, Jennings[39] describes how extended kin ties became of importance when the rehousing of the population of a locality disrupted neighbouring relationships on which the inhabitants had previously relied for the exchange of domestic services.

In both these cases the disruption of one set of relationships leads to the utilization of another. In the first case mobility prevents the utilization of kin ties, while in the second migration increases their importance. Explanation in terms purely of mobility and migration is inadequate however. In the French case neighbour relationships are clearly ascribed on the basis of co-residence, irrespective of particular characteristics of individuals and therefore are a universalistic type of relationship; in the Bristol case such relationships are clearly defined particularistically. In the French case mobility makes exchange of domestic services between kin *difficult* in the Bristol case migration makes such exchange with new neighbours *undesirable*.

[37] For a discussion of some of these issues see Mowrer, E. R., 'Sequential and Class Variables of the Family in an Urban Area', *Soc. For.* 40, 1961, p. 107.

[38] Vieille, A., 'Relations parentales et relations de voisinage chez les ménages ouvriers de la Seine', *Cah. Int. de Soc.* 17, 1954, p. 140.

[39] Jennings, H., *Societies in the Making*, London, Routledge, 1962.

In this section we have seen how kin relationships can promote solidarity between inhabitants of a locality, be destructive of such solidarity or be an alternative to it. The exact relation between these two types of ascriptive solidarities in any given case is not therefore predictable until we understand the activities which the inhabitants share and the conditions necessary for their successful performance and the meaning attached to them by the culture concerned.

PART III FAMILY PROCESS AND FAMILY STRUCTURE

6

The Nuclear Family

CENTRAL to our discussion of the family in Chapter Three was the notion of the family process. This notion has been characterized recently as typifying a distinctive approach to the study of the family.[1] The unique characteristic of the type of social group which we call the family is that it arises out of the performance of biological activities. Because such activities involve procreation and maturation it is obvious that any biological group must go through a sequence of stages related to the stages in the maturation of the children and the changing abilities and activities of the spouses. This developmental sequence is an aspect or dimension of the family group upon which some students may concentrate but which none can ignore. No general statements about the structure of the family are possible unless they refer either to the way it changes or to a particular stage in the process of change.

A central preliminary to the study of the family is to construct *general* stages in the process of development, and no study of the family in any *particular* society can avoid explicitly or implicitly elaborating the points in that development at which changes in family structure occur.

What stages one defines depends to a large extent on the use to which you wish your definitions to be put. If you are concerned with the relation of biological development to family structure—with the changing *biological* conditions of action—then one would wish to make a distinction between families on the grounds of the physical maturity of the children. If one is concerned with the *social* condi-

[1] See for example Nye, F. I. and Berardo, F. M., *Emerging Conceptual Frameworks in Family Analysis*, London, Macmillan, 1966; Christensen, H. I., *Handbook of Marriage and the Family*, Chicago, Rand McNally, 1964.

tions of action, one would instead differentiate on the basis of the children's ability to be independent of the nuclear family, which involves—but is not the same as—their physical maturity. If one is concerned with the *process of family formation* it will be the marriage of the children which will constitute the salient point of change. This usually involves both their physical maturity and social independence but need not involve either. If one is concerned with the development of the *household* then one will wish to draw a line at the point at which the children leave home; if with the family as a *residential group* at the point where they move away; if with the family as a productive *economic* group at the point at which the shared means of production are divided—and so on.

In other words the stages distinguished will depend on the interest of the student and that will partly depend, in turn, on the activities of family groups which are significant to the people in the society studied. The only feature common to all societies will be the process of maturation in the children and of aging among parents, and the process of nuclear family formation usually through marriage.

It is not therefore surprising that there have been many different attempts to define stages of family development, and that they are all different. There is a further complicating factor however. The size of the nuclear family varies and its size can be increased at any time until the wife becomes infertile. As a result the movement of the family to any stage in the process may suddenly be reversed by the birth of another child. It is for this reason that the term 'phase' is probably preferable to that of 'stage'.

Most phase definitions depend on the birth and maturation of the children for the definition of the early phases of the cycle. It is the later stages which provide the most variety, different students having used economic self-support, household membership and marriage as distinguishing criteria.

The most elaborate of these definitions is that made by Rodgers[2] whose most important contribution was to base his phases on four positions: father, mother, youngest child and oldest child. Basically what Rodgers does is to follow the career of the eldest child through the stages of infant, pre-school, teenage, young adult until he leaves home ('launching'), and then to subdivide each of these stages by the stage reached by the youngest child. (The family may of course jump straight from 'teenage' or 'school' to 'launching'.) Apart from

[2] Rodgers, R. H., *Improvements in the Construction of Family Life Cycle Categories*, Kalamazoo, Western Michigan University, 1962. See also Rodgers, R. H., 'Towards a Theory of Family Development', *Jour. of Marr. and Fam.* 26, 1964, p. 262.

its limitation to Western societies the utility of such a general and complex approach is by no means clear.

Where the household is restricted to members of the nuclear family, and children go to school, the *parental role* undergoes a sharp change when the youngest child reaches school age. When the first child becomes economically independent of the family there is a shift in the *power structure* of the family. When the first child marries there is a change in his *relationships* with his parents and sibs, but this does not necessarily affect the structure of *relationships within the household.*

To attempt to identify points of change in this way reveals that we are of course concerned with a large number of different things. We are concerned with changes in particular roles, we are concerned with changes in household composition, we are concerned with changes in relationships, and we are concerned with the changing pattern of relationships both within the household and between members of the elementary family. None of these can be predetermined even in a particular culture.

What can be done is to elaborate phases in the life cycle of the *married couple,* or to elaborate stages in the process of family formation. It would not appear to be possible to elaborate in advance the phases in the development of the family group. The parents go through phases of marriage, procreation and rearing followed by a loss of any determinate parental activity on the marriage of their children. The family group goes through a similar process of nuclear family formation, reproduction, new nuclear family formation, death of the original parental generation and so on.

Those who wish to claim that there is a distinctive developmental approach to the family are referring to attempts to establish *a priori* phases in the structure of the family as a group which are related to the process of family formation and the phases of the life cycles of those who compose it. While we cannot ever ignore the developmental aspects of the family, it does not follow that we can therefore construct some sort of developmental theory which is of general application. We have already seen the variety of uses to which the family process can be put under varying material and social conditions. It would not seem useful to seek general patterns of development which are not determined by universal conditions of social action.

This and the following chapter are organized around the notion of the family cycle, Chapter 6 dealing with courtship, mate selection and procreation, that is to say the formation of nuclear families and their characteristic activities, while Chapter 7 deals with relationships between members of the elementary family in the later phases of the family cycle when the children are adult and members of their own nuclear families.

MATE SELECTION: SOCIAL FACTORS

In those societies where mate selection is 'closed', that is to say is governed by rules specifying categories of people who are eligible, or where the choice of mate is made by the parents or kin group of the couple, explanations of the regularities in mate selection must be couched in terms of the fit of the rules governing marriage to other social rules governing kinship behaviour and in terms of the effects of different types of marriage choice on the activities of kinship groups. Where however the marriage system is 'open', the choice of mate depending, formally, on the personal choice of individuals, regularities in choice of mate must be explained in other terms. They must be explained, it might be thought, either in terms of the limitations placed on choice by different types of conditions, or in terms of psychological processes.

Unfortunately it is not quite as simple as this. The difficulty lies in deciding exactly what one means by 'open' and in determining the significance of the absence of beliefs which legitimize the interference of parents in the choice of marriage partner. While it is true to say that in Western society there are no rules prescribing whom one must marry, nor giving parents the right to determine the choice of mate, it does not follow that different groups within the population do not hold beliefs about the desirability of marriage within certain categories, leading to the existence of valued expectations (norms) referring to group membership, which govern choice of mate and which the authority of the parents may be influential in supporting. In consequence the regularities in mate selection which can be empirically observed in Western society cannot be explained by reference to rules governing behaviour, but are understandable only in terms of a complexity of factors: norms *governing* choice of mate, norms *affecting* the choice of mate,[3] parental influence, psychological processes and different types of conditions of action.[4]

[3] A belief that one ought not to marry outside one's group may be said to *govern* choice of mate. Aesthetic or moral norms may vitally *affect* the individual's behaviour and may reinforce norms of endogamy or exogamy but do of course apply much more widely.

[4] The necessity of the distinction between norms and conditions has been explicitly recognized by Kerckhoff. See Kerckhoff, A. C., 'Patterns of Homogamy and the Field of Eligibles', *Social Forces* 42, 1963–1964, p. 297.

The empirical work which has been undertaken on this subject is largely American,[5] is extremely extensive and has led to conclusions which sometimes appear to be somewhat banal. The reader should bear in mind however that the problem with which the American students of this subject have had to deal is not so much the identification of the factors which are operative, as the parcelling out between factors of the responsibility for producing the observed regularities.

Norms

The first problem is the identification of the groups within the population which are significant in that their members share norms which either govern or affect the choice of marriage partner—that is to say have valued expectations that members of the group will marry within it, or share values relevant to this type of choice. Ethnic groups, religious groups, and status groups are the most obvious candidates here. Broadly speaking the data shows that ethnic groups which are regarded by the society as 'racial' groups have the lowest rates of inter-group marriage while other ethnic groups also show a strong tendency to marry within the group though this is less marked than between 'racial' groups. Jewish, Protestant and Catholic marriages also show a high proportion where both partners come from the same faith. Most of the data on marriage between strata are not concerned with marriage between *status groups* but between *occupational categories* and is therefore impossible to interpret.[6] We say that group norms are operative here, but the question is how far they are important when compared with various conditions restricting choice which are also associated with occupational category membership.

This difficulty is relevant also to much of the data on ethnic and religious groups. Membership of a Catholic family will increase the probability of membership of a Catholic Church and Catholic organizations, of Catholic schools and of a Catholic neighbourhood and of a predominantly Catholic ethnic group. Do Catholics marry Catholics more frequently than non-Catholics because they meet more Catholics than non-Catholics or because their church frowns on inter-church marriages or because Irishmen prefer to marry Irish girls and Poles Polish girls? These factors are all probably operative:

[5] For a masterly brief theoretical summary of work in this field see Jacobson, P. and Mathery, A., 'Mate Selection in Open Marriage Systems', *Int. Jour. Comp. Soc.* 3, 1962, p. 98.

For French work on this topic see Michel, A., 'Mate Selection in Various Ethnic groups in France', *Acta. Sociol.* 8, 1965, p. 163.

[6] We may note that a strong tendency to choose mates of the same educational level has been observed.

the question is which, if any, is of the most significance in determining the observed degree of Catholic endogamy.[7]

Age

Age is a factor which must be treated separately since patterns of age at marriage may be seen to be determined both by social norms with regard to the age at marriage of each sex and with regard to the difference in age between the spouses and by other norms regarding marriage and various related conditions of action.

Since women are fertile only in the earlier part of their lives[8] and since their sexual attractiveness is greatest when young, the age at marriage of women is likely to be relatively low. The age at marriage of men will depend on their being able to perform the various activities required by the definition of the role of husband in the society concerned. If they are required to support a wife and this can only be done after a long training or upon inheritance of their patrimony, the age at marriage is likely to be late. Where the definition of the role of husband and the conditions which determine a man's ability to perform it do not determine that the male age at marriage will be late, it does not necessarily mean that it will be early. This will depend on beliefs that the society or groups within the society have about the 'best' age at marriage and the 'proper' limits on the difference between the ages of the spouses.

Since the ability to provide economically for a family is likely to be related to age, either through the progression through a career cycle or by the accumulation of wealth or both, older men will be relatively better able to provide for a wife than younger men. Hence where there is a marked difference between the ages of spouses, the man is usually the senior partner. Older women will be relatively unattractive to younger men, hence once they have passed the normal age at marriage they will find few willing mates since they will be too old for those that are single and most men of the same age will be married. Their chief opportunities must therefore be found among widowers and divorced men. Men who are older than the prevailing age at marriage may be able to persuade young women of marriageable age to marry them by out-bidding their young competitors in material provision, provided that such a marriage does not violate norms governing the permitted difference in age between spouses.

Differences in age at marriage between groups can therefore be related to different definitions in marital roles and different conditions under which the ability to perform them are achieved, as well

[7] See Kerckhoff, A. C., *op. cit.*

[8] That is until their late forties or early fifties.

as to normative differences between groups which are themselves related to those conditions. Hence we would expect to find differences between occupational categories in age at marriage related to patterns of inheritance and length of occupational training, the age at marriage of males in the higher occupational groups being higher than that in lower occupational groups.[9]

Social conditions

It is an obvious but important condition of marriage in any open system of selection that the spouses should know each other before marriage. Factors determining whom one knows will therefore determine the size and characteristics of the field within which one's choice is made. Contacts with other individuals may come about either directly through the performance of activities which involve interaction or through the agency of others. Both the activities which an individual performs and the set of relationships which he has at any given time will be affected by his family membership. This will determine the locality in which he resides, influence the interests he has and the activities he undertakes, and the social groups to which he belongs, while the set of relationships of his parents and sibs will form part of, and influence the development of, his own set of relationships.[10] While it will not be the case that all an individual's relationships will be with the members of the ethnic, religious, locality and status group or category into which he was born, nevertheless he is likely to know more people who are members of the same ascriptive group as his parents than would be expected by chance. Hence he is more likely to marry someone of the same ascriptive groups as those into which he is born, quite apart from any expectations that members of the groups ought to marry within them, or any pressure exerted by others.

Others will however attempt to influence choice of mate by influencing the social contacts which a child has. Selection of neighbourhood, school, and the vetting of friends from an early age may have this effect. The characteristics of friends are important in themselves since norms governing sexual behaviour are acquired, in universalistic societies, not from the family alone, but through

[9] For empirical support of some of these hypotheses see Bowerman, C. E., 'Age Relationships at Marriage', *Marr. and Fam. Liv.* 18, 1956, p. 231.

[10] We are really speaking here of Ego's position in a *network*. Kin relationships and occupational relationships constitute important classes of links which go to make it up. Little attention has been paid to the systematic relation of successive marriages in creating a homogeneous network whose characteristics influence future marriages.

primary groups of age peers (PEER GROUPS).[11] By controlling the child's peer group membership parents can attempt to ensure that the norms transmitted by the family are supported and not contradicted by those of the peer group.

The extent of the parental attempt at influence will depend on the importance to the parents of an endogamous marriage, which itself will depend on the purposes for which the family process is used. Parental attempts at influence will also be affected by the degree of segregation of the groups to which they belong from other groups within the society.

Material conditions

Sustained contact with other individuals depends on proximity. Hence the field from which an individual chooses a mate is going to be limited by the degree of population density and mate selection is likely to be related to residential propinquity.[12] Moreover where courtship patterns require the expenditure of money there will be a tendency for courtship to occur within economic categories, since cross-'class' courtship will lead either to the financial ruin of one partner or to the dissatisfaction of the other. Where however, the burden of expense falls on the man, he will be able to operate at advantage in lower strata, combining both economy and superior bargaining power to obtain the consort of his choice. Hence we would expect to find that cross-class courtship patterns were dominated by associations of high men and low women.

Theoretically we must separate out the influence of material and social conditions and of different types of norms; empirically of course they all operate together and re-enforce one another. Different religious, ethnic and status groups overlap one another, and cluster in the same localities. Consequently the expectations as to group endogamy and the material and social conditions which favour it tend to be found together. It is partly for this reason that

[11] On the function of peer groups in universalistic societies see Eisenstadt, S. N., *From Generation to Generation*, Free Press. On the relation of parents and peer groups see Rosen, B. C., 'Conflicting Group Membership: a Study of Parent-Peer Group Cross-pressures', *Amer. Sociol. Rev.* 30, 1955, p. 155.

[12] See Koller, M. R., 'Residential and Occupational Propinquity', *Amer. Sociol. Rev.* 13, 1948, p. 613.

It should be noted that there is some evidence of norms of locality endogamy. It would seem however that these merely summate other endogamous norms in homogeneous localities where class, religious and ethnic groups overlap. Patterns of local endogamy appear to break down when the population becomes more mobile. See Haavio-Mannila, E., 'Local endogamy in Finland', *Acta Sociol.* 8, 1965, p. 155; Rosser, C. and Harris, C., *Family and Social Change*, London, Routledge, 1965.

parental control is of minor importance. The control required to ensure intergenerational family continuity is minimal. Nevertheless the system is theoretically an open one and though through the social processes we have described most children make the 'right' choice, the power of the parents to enforce their wishes *at the point at which the choice is made* is small.

We may now construct a model of the situation of the single individual under conditions of open marriage. Ego may be seen as having to make choices among a range of social contacts whose distribution of social characteristics is not random but skewed in the direction of the social characteristics of Ego and his family of orientation. Within this field is a sub-category, 'the field of eligibles', which contains those social contacts of Ego which are normatively defined either negatively or positively as possible future mates. These norms which Ego has acquired by his family and peer group memberships are supported by sanctions of approval and disapproval exercised by family and peer group members. The smaller the field of eligibles, both absolutely and in relation to the field of social contacts of the opposite sex, the greater will be the likelihood of Ego going outside it.[13]

The smaller the group concerned, the narrower the 'field of eligibles' will be, and the harder it will be to segregate group members from out-group contacts. Since the control over choice of mate is most important where property and style of life are involved, and since, in highly inegalitarian societies like Britain and America, the people to whom such considerations are the most important constitute the smallest sections of the population, it follows that in the higher social strata the controls over children's behaviour are stronger and the whole process of their marriage fraught with parental anxiety. The groups who are perhaps the most vulnerable in this respect are status groups or categories who do not possess a great deal of economic power and cannot therefore apply economic sanctions to their children, and whose only distinguishing characteristic is their style of life.

The whole subject of inter-class marriage is a fascinating one. Since the male plays the occupational role and the female the domestic one, in societies where class membership is dependent upon occupational position it is possible for the woman to marry up and the man to marry down, since the woman is accorded the same class membership as her husband. Where however we are dealing with a status category or group within a class the position is reversed. The

[13] It may be very small indeed—see Wallace, K., 'Factors Hindering Mate Selection', *Soc. and Soc. Res.* 44, 5, p. 317.

maintenance of a style of life depends to a large extent on the way the family's home is run and in this the wife plays a predominant part. We should therefore expect that marriages between two status groups within a class to be characterized by the man marrying up and the woman marrying down. Though studies of mate selection still operate with an extremely primitive set of stratification concepts and no confirmation of this hypothesis can be obtained from that source, the marriage of the second generation industrial upper class into the ranks of the landed aristocracy in the nineteenth century England would appear to be characterized by this type of arrangement.[14]

MATE SELECTION: PSYCHOLOGICAL FACTORS

Having described the situation of a typical Ego in an open marriage system, it is now necessary to elaborate the process whereby a particular marriage within the field of eligibles is made. The theory which fulfills this requirement has been called the theory of 'complementary needs'.[15] Since it is quite properly a psychological theory, a detailed discussion of it and of the brisk controversy which has followed its formulation is out of place in a sociological work. It is sufficient to note here that its authors adopt a similar starting point to that we have reached, and then argue that what determines the marriage of Ego to a particular eligible is the ability of the couple to satisfy each other's psychological needs. These needs depend on differences between the couple. For example if the man needs the sort of care and protection provided by a mother and the woman needs to dominate and 'mother' other people then their different psychological needs fit one another—that is are complementary.[16]

The process by which a fit between the needs of Ego and Alter are obtained is one of trial and error, eligibles with non-complementary needs being rejected not as a result of conscious process[17] of selection but as a result of feelings of dissatisfaction with the relationship, which does not blossom into 'love'; that is to say does not evoke from the

[14] For a discussion of the relation between sex roles and *hypergamy* (the woman's marrying up) see Littlejohn, J., *Westrigg*, London, Routledge, 1963, Ch. 7.

[15] Winch, R. F., Ktsanes, T. and Ktsanes, V., 'The Theory of Complementary Needs in Mate Selection', *Amer. Sociol. Rev.* 19, 1954, 241.

[16] This is a very crude example used purely for illustrative purposes.

[17] On the process see Kerckhoff, A. C. and Davies, K. E., 'Value Concensus and Need Complementarity in Mate Selection', *Amer. Sociol. Rev.* 27, 1962, p. 295.

individuals that emotional response towards one another based on their mutual ability to gratify one another's needs.

These theories are far from being fully accepted, largely because of the difficulties in defining and measuring psychological needs and because variation of the field of eligibles between individuals is always a confounding factor.

HOMOGAMY, COMPLEMENTARITY AND THE MARITAL RELATIONSHIP

It has been customary to refer to the fact that individuals sharing the same social characteristics marry each other, by saying that mate-selection is governed by the principle of homogamy. This is a fundamentally misleading way of stating the position since it describes as 'a principle', a regularity which is the outcome of a whole set of social processes[18] most of which have nothing to do with mate selection. To say that people tend to marry mates with the same social characteristics and different personality needs is merely a useful mnemonic.

Taken together there is however something rather seductive and familiar about the principle of homogamy and the theory of complementary needs. This is so because it echoes very closely Durkheim's theory of social solidarity which he specifically applied to the marriage relationship.[19] There are two chief types of solidarity said Durkheim, 'organic' solidarity and 'mechanical' solidarity. Mechanical solidarity derives from the *similarity* of persons who act in the *same* way under the *same* social and material conditions. Organic solidarity arises from the interdependence of individuals who are *different* because they act in *different* ways under *different* social and material conditions. Marriage is characterized by both types of solidarity. There is a division of sexual labour based on biological differences and a further social division of labour based on the first division. At the same time the married couple share common residence and standard of life, and the same children.

[18] Kerckhoff (*op. cit.*), has pointed out that homogamy studies have been more concerned with *outcome* than *process*. A French student has made a similar point. See Michel, A., *op. cit.*

[19] 'Without doubt, sexual attraction does not come about except between individuals of the same type, and love generally asks a certain harmony of thought and sentiment. It is not less true that what gives to this relationship its peculiar character and what causes its particular energy, is not the resemblance but the difference in natures which it unites . . . . Only those differences which require each other for their mutual fruition have this quality . . . the sexual division of labour is the source of conjugal solidarity.' Durkheim, E., *The Division of Labour* (1893), Free Press, 1933, p. 56.

In a system which is open and where spouses are expected to act together, the sharing of common values which can determine the choices between alternative courses of action is a necesaary condition of a minimally successful marital relationship. Where the society is a *plural* society, that is to say where it is composed of different groups having different values, this condition can only be fulfilled by mating which is homogamous with respect to the values of the mates.

In a society where norms governing the performance of marital roles differ widely between groups within it, a marital relationship has little chance of success unless the spouses share similar expectations about marital behaviour, whether or not husband and wife are expected to act together.

The marital relationship, like all other social relationships, is therefore based on shared expectations. It is maintained however by *exchange* between the partners, and has therefore within it elements of a contractual relationship. Exchange is only possible on the basis of *differences*. Each partner has different things to offer in exchange and other eligibles or ex-eligibles offer or would have offered a different bundle of goods in exchange for Ego's bundle. How advantageous to each party are the terms on which an actual exchange is arranged will depend upon the power of Ego in the market. The actual terms of the exchange result from process of bargaining.

The distinction between open and closed systems is less that one is based on a love complex[20] and the other on an exchange between groups, than that both are systems of bargaining in a market, the market in an open system being open and in a closed system closed. Where there are no restrictions placed by groups on an individual's choice of partner, the bargaining takes place between individuals. The conclusion of the bargain has however to be legitimized. It cannot be legitimized in terms of agreement between groups, therefore it has to be legitimized either in terms of ideas referring to the fit between the attributes of the individuals, that is in terms of love, or in terms of societal norms governing selection.[21] In practice it is legitimized in terms of both.[22]

After marriage, exchange continues. The spouses acquire rights in

[20] This is Goode's term. By 'love complex' Goode refers to a set of beliefs which make love a condition of marriage. See 'The Theoretical Importance of Love', *Amer. Sociol. Rev.* 24, 1959, p. 38.

[21] These norms may of course vary between groups within the society. Norms peculiar to a group need not have any reference to a group membership and should be distinguished from norms of endogamy or exogamy.

[22] For example to be 'head over heels in love' with a woman 40 years one's junior would probably not fully legitimize a marriage.

each other by marriage: a relationship is established. Given that relationship, however, the actual way in which the marital roles are further defined will depend on a process of bargaining which will continue through the marriage and whose outcome will depend on the relative power of the spouses, which is determined not by their position in a market but by the various material and social conditions under which they act. It is to a discussion of marital roles therefore that we now turn.

DETERMINANTS AND ANALYSIS OF MARITAL ROLES

Given a prior definition of roles in the society as a whole, variation between couples in the conditions under which they act will affect the way in which their roles are performed, and will thus affect the way the roles come to be defined in the family concerned. Where a plurality of families exists under the same conditions, similarities between families in the way in which they define the roles will be observed and may come to be institutionalized within the plurality. Where changes in conditions are so great as to be incompatible with the definitions shared by the members of the society as a whole, the societal definitions of roles may also undergo change.[23] Since each marital role involves the occupant in the performance of different activities, there will be a variation between the sexes in the conditions which affect role performance.

We need therefore to attempt to elaborate the way in which conditions affect the performance of each marital role separately, before we can see how the differing performance of one role affects the other and hence how the marital relationship changes as a result of the changed conditions of performance. We shall not, however, be able to relate changed conditions directly to changes in the relationship since the relationship also partly depends on the societal definition of roles. The difficulty here is that the societal definition will partly determine the activities which performance of the role involves, and hence it is extremely difficult to make general statements which list what activities are involved and hence to specify in general what conditions vitally affect their definition within the family.

Material conditions

In all societies the role of wife is likely to involve the bearing and raising of children and some domestic duties. The performance of the

[23] This formed the subject of part of our discussion of the relation between industrialism and the family. (See above Ch. 4.)

role will therefore be affected by the age at marriage of the wife, the number and spacing of the children, the level of domestic technology in the society, the degree of access to that technology possessed by any given wife, and the degree of access to domestic assistance.

In all societies the husband is concerned with the economic provision for the other members of his nuclear family, however this is arranged. Hence the type of economic production, the way in which it is organized in the society as a whole and the position occupied in the productive system by any given husband, will constitute the crucial conditions affecting his performance.

It must be stressed that this list is composed of minimum conditions only. In addition, where the role definitions and material conditions permit it, the role performance of the wife will be affected by the availability of female employment, her access to it, the type of employment and her position within the productive process.

Social conditions

The social conditions affecting the performance of marital roles will be the pattern of relationships and group memberships the spouses each have outside the nuclear family at any given time. These relationships will affect the marital role performance in the following ways.

First, where the society is composed of different groups each having different expectations with regard to marital behaviour, and where the spouses come from different groups, the ability of any given spouse to maintain their role interpretation over and against that of the other spouse will depend on the support provided by other people. Hence the maintenance of close relationships with such groups is likely to vitally affect the nature of the eventual compromise between the spouses which constitutes the basis of their relationship.

Secondly, where a spouse or the spouses retain membership of a primary group outside the family which is single sex, this membership will affect the marital relationship by making the spouses relatively independent of each other (except in the domestic and sexual spheres) by providing a source of primary group satisfaction outside the nuclear family *to which both spouses cannot belong*.

Thirdly, the existence of relationships outside the nuclear family may be important in providing help and support in the performance of activities integral to the marital role. Since these activities are different for each sex, the member of the supportive set of each spouse is likely to be of the same sex as the spouse supported.

The analysis of marital roles

Marital roles have been analyzed in terms of two main dimensions: authority and activities. Different types of family have been distinguished with regard to the extent to which one spouse exercises authority over or makes family decisions on behalf of the other and with regard to the degree of authority held by parents over children. Different types of family have also been distinguished with regard to the extent to which different areas of activity are shared.

Wolfe[24] for example has distinguished four types of authority within the family, by viewing authority as having two dimensions: relative authority and shared authority. Where the relative authority (the authority of one spouse over another) is at its maximum, there can be little shared authority. Hence there are two polar types where the husband or the wife is DOMINANT. Where the relative authority of one over the other lies between these extremes and the amount of shared authority is high, he describes the distribution of authority as SYNCRATIC. That is, each spouse has relatively few activities in which they are the boss, and control of most activities is shared. Where the amount of relative authority is intermediate but the degree of shared authority is low, he describes the distribution as AUTONOMIC. That is to say that the spouses split up family activities into two sets, the wife having authority over the husband in one set of activities and the husband over the wife in the other.

Bott,[25] in her celebrated study of families in London, abandoned an attempt to classify activities in terms of whether they were governed by the authority of one or other or both partners and attempted instead to classify the activities of each spouse according to whether they were performed *together* with the other spouse or *separately* and according to whether the activity of husband and wife were 'different . . . or the same'. (It is difficult to see exactly what this means. If we take an activity performed by a given spouse which is never performed by the other spouse then it would presumably be classed as 'different'. If on the other hand it was performed by both spouses it would be 'the same'.)

This gave Bott six[26] possible types of activity, but she found the resulting classifications 'exceedingly cumbersome to apply'. In the

[24] Wolfe, D. M., 'Power and Authority in the Family' in Winch, R. F., McGinnis, R. and Barringer, H. R., *Selected Studies in Marriage and the Family*, London, Holt Rinehart, 1962, p. 582. See also Herbst, P. G., 'The Measurement of Family Relationships', *Hum. Rel.* 5, 1952, p. 3.

[25] Bott, E., *Family and Social Network*, London, Tavistock, 1957, Appendix B.

[26] She subdivided 'different' into two further categories.

end she simply classified all the activities performed together plus the same activity where performed separately as 'joint activities' and classified different separate activities as 'independent'. We end up therefore with a simple classification into *joint* and *independent*.[27]

We shall be referring to Bott's study later in this section. Before leaving this particular aspect of her work it will be useful to note her reasons for abandoning a classification in terms of authority. She records that differences between families as to who made the decisions appeared to be more a matter of personality characteristics than of role expectation. Informants could not describe how decision were made—it just happened. Most conflicts between husband and wife were considered to be clashes of personality and people could not describe any general rules about the way in which conflicts were resolved.

It would seem that what we are dealing with in the case of Bott's informants is a situation in which conflicts are resolved or decisions made as the result of a balance of *power* between husband and wife rather than with any reference to any rules either general in the society or which have been developed by the husband and wife themselves.[28]

Power is one of the most elusive sociological concepts of which various definitions have been put forward. For our purposes here an individual may be said to have power when he is able to affect the behaviour of others in the way he desires. Authority may be seen as a special type of power, which depends on Ego's having a *right* to affect the behaviour of others. We may therefore put forward another way of classifying marital roles, that is in terms of the distribution of power between husband and wife.[29]

When a relationship is based on complementary needs,[30] Alter's need and Ego's ability to supply it will mean that Ego has power over Alter. Supplying a need is an activity, and all activities require resources for their performance. In the marital situation the resources commanded by each spouse are of course the goods for which the marriage bargain was made. However these resources can be withheld from Alter by Ego and this ability to withhold some-

[27] This is virtually a division in terms of manner of performance: together/separately. Bott makes it clear that her difficulties arise from trying to distinguish activities as 'the same' or 'different'. It appears that respondents classified activities in different ways and that the manner of classification was not independent of the type of relationship.

[28] It is important to note that Bott's families all were in the early phase of the family cycle and hence had had relatively little time to develop family norms.

[29] For a discussion of power and authority in the family see Wolfe *op. cit.*

[30] That is an exchange relationship.

thing that Alter wants constitutes a source of Ego's power. If Alter can find *other* sources than Ego for the gratification of his needs, the power of Ego over Alter will thereby be diminished.

The resources available to the marriage partners may be regarded as internal (the physical and psychological characteristics of the spouses) or external. External resources are resources to which the spouses have access by virtue of their participation in relationships outside the marital relationship, and are therefore determined by the material and social conditions under which the partners act.

The marital relationship therefore will be determined by a process of bargaining within the marriage whose outcome will depend on the differing resources of the spouses which will be determined partly by the marriage bargain and partly by their social and material conditions of action.

Ideas and conditions

Conditions rarely if ever completely determine the outcome of social interaction. Their effects on behaviour depend on the ideas and beliefs of the actors. Simply because spouses do not follow explicit rules, which reflect the ideas and beliefs they have, this does not mean that ideas are not important in determining the nature of the relationship. General notions about the position of women and men in society, about differences in sexuality, and unspoken assumptions about family life, will effectively limit the exercise of power within any marital relationship, even if they could not be described as a cluster of normative expectations which are sufficiently precise to be described as a role.

These general expectations will themselves be related to the general conditions of action of marital couples in the society as a whole and to the collective beliefs and attitudes shared by the society's members. In considering variations between *individual* families we have to take the *general* conditions and beliefs as given.

THE DETERMINATION OF ROLE PERFORMANCE

The peculiar beauty and agony of sociological work, as the reader is by this time probably aware, is that it is difficult not to mention any one element in a situation without mentioning all the others, nor to identify factors which determine other factors, because they all interaffect one another. Worse than this is the fact that the very factors change their nature depending on the point of view from which they are regarded. The existence of a certain number of children is clearly a factor which places limits on the way a woman performs her role at any given time. However, the number of children she has is of course the result of the bargaining process between husband and wife, the social definition of marital roles and access to resources such as contraceptive knowledge and means. Hence the number of children is therefore a factor external or internal to the marital relationship, depending upon the point in the cycle which you take. We are after all dealing with a process, and actions taken at one point in time have results which are the conditions of the performance of the next set of actions.

In order to understand the interrelation of the various factors determining marital roles, we have therefore to see this as a process through which the exact configuration is determined. This is perhaps best illustrated by means of an example. The illustration used is not a description of the process in an actual family but is created by drawing together elements from a number of British studies dealing with a certain type of working class family life.[31]

The future spouses grow up in a locality which is relatively closed, that is to say in which the inhabitants spend most of their social life, there being little movement outside the locality even to work or shop, and in which there is little movement of residence which crosses locality boundaries. The men work in the same industry and have similar occupational status. Work is usually heavy manual labour, wages are relatively low, housing standards poor with considerable over-crowding. At adolescence the children's play groups split into single-sex groups. Sex roles are sharply differentiated, the man being expected to be forceful and rough, and softness, tenderness and consideration are regarded as feminine traits. These roles are learnt within the single-sex peer groups especially among the boys, where gang warfare and petty crime are considered evidences of toughness and masculinity. Sexuality is considered dirty or disgusting but is frequently discussed between members of the same sex, but never between the sexes or between family members.

Most people leave school at the age of fifteen and the level of education and the understanding of sexual matters is low. As a result the family size tends to be high. Women are not generally thought to derive much pleasure from sex (at any rate in marriage) and a good husband is thought to be one who 'doesn't bother you'. Since interaction is confined to the locality, the field of eligibles is small and the scope for bargaining limited. Most girls spend their working adoles-

[31] This example is *not* a description of contemporary working class life in Britain, but of a small, rather old fashioned segment of it. The illustration is based on the studies summarized in Klein, J., *Samples from English Cultures*, London, Routledge, 1965, Vol. 1, Section 1. Some of the characteristics have been reported for other working class areas, notably Bethnal Green, Oxford, parts of Swansea and Liverpool.

cence in trying to obtain the best bargain possible by improving their appearance on which a large part of their earnings is spent.

The persistence over a period of time of the beliefs, attitudes and social and material conditions described, have resulted in the existence of certain expectations with regard to marital roles. Marriage is seen as an arrangement whereby a man obtains sexual and domestic services from a woman in return for economic provision. Large family size and poor domestic conditions on the one hand, and long hours of work on the other, preclude joint activities of husband and wife outside the domestic sphere and limit co-operation within it. The fact that the men share work relationships and that work occupies the main part of their lives and energies, means that the solidarity of the peer group is carried over in to the work situation, and dominates the whole social life of the men. The women, on the other hand, confined to the house and street by their children, vulnerable to financial and other domestic crises such as sickness and child birth, are dependent upon what help they can get from each other, and the ability and duty to provide help are the chief criteria in determining the establishment of relationships with persons outside the domestic group who are categorized as neighbours and relatives rather than as friends. Hence little is expected of marriage, and the criteria that are applied in evaluating a husband are that he should be a good provider, not knock the kids about, not spend too much time or money drinking with his mates, and not 'bother you', while a good wife is a 'good manager', who lets you 'bother her', always has a hot meal ready when you come home, generally organizes the household to suit your conveniences and doesn't nag.

These expectations are realistic rather than normative. There are normative elements among them however. The man is expected to exercise authority in the household: a henpecked husband is regarded with contempt among both men and women. The activities of the spouses are expected to be different. Women are not expected to work after marriage, nor husbands to help in the house—'I don't want a great clumsy man in my kitchen'.

Faced with this initial situation our future spouses are going to do the best they can for themselves in choosing a mate and the match will be evaluated in that light. 'She done very well for herself I must say'. Because of the fact that the society of which the locality is a part is dominated by a 'love-complex', while everybody else's match is evaluated in terms of bargaining, one's own mate selection is regarded as something of a mystery. 'We just seemed to belong together'.[32] One does not—or at least the woman does not—lightly shed the ideals of romantic love which informed her adolescent reading. While she does not believe for a moment that 'one day her prince will come'

[32] See Slater, E. and Woodside, M., *Patterns of Marriage*, London, Cassell, 1951, p. 119.

and certainly doesn't think her Fred is a prince, she nevertheless insists on legitimizing her choice in terms of some mysterious love process.

Once married there will be further attempts at bargaining. 'When I saw other girls get married and start a baby straight off I swore I wasn't going to get caught, but I'd only been married three months when I fell.' Since birth control techniques are poorly understood the woman's ability to resist the consequences of her husband's legitimate demands for intercourse are slender. She relies on the husband to 'take precautions' or 'be careful'.[33] In consequence of her lack of resources she fails, thus determining the conditions under which she will perform her marital role at another time. Early conception also has the consequence that there will be little time for the married couple to develop and define shared patterns of activity before the birth of the first child which, in a situation where independent activities are expected, is a precondition of shifting the definition of the marital role.

Let us suppose that the wife does succeed in controlling the family size and spacing of children, perhaps because she has been able to marry a man who is more considerate or who takes more sophisticated precautions. A joint pattern of activities may begin to develop. Such a pattern will militate against the man's participation in peer group activities. Pressure will be exerted upon him to resume his role. If he should attempt to do so the wife will have no redress. Not only will her demands that he does so not be legitimated in terms of shared expectations in the locality ('*other* wives don't expect . . . '), but any exercise of power on her part—refusing to sleep with him, withdrawing household services, nagging him—are only likely to force him into the companionship of the peer group or his family of origin, both of whom will support him against her.

Conversely the man who finds that his work prevents him from spending as much time with his wife as he likes, and wishes to escape the pressures exerted by peer group and local community, will find that any attempt to move away will be resisted by a 'normal' wife who is frightened of losing the support of a family or neighbours on which she relies, even if she would prefer a more joint pattern of activity. Inability to leave the area will inhibit the man's ability to improve his occupational status and thus the material conditions which make the wife's reliance on kin important.'

For the purposes of illustration we have taken a very extreme case. The material and social conditions, the beliefs and attitudes of the people concerned, and the definition of marital roles general in the group to which they belong, all combine to force the spouses into actions which in turn have consequences which tend to support

[33] Male 'precautions' (sheath) or 'care', i.e. with withdrawal, are still the most popular means of contraception in contemporary Britain, cf. Pierce, R. M. and Rowntree, G., 'Birth Control in Britain', *Pop. Stud.* 15, 1961–1962, p. 127.

the predominant pattern. If any one of the factors here listed is absent however, there will be much more scope for the couple to manoeuvre.

CONJUGAL ROLES AND SOCIAL NETWORKS

A great deal of the preceding discussion has been made possible because of the attention which has been given to the whole topic of the relationship between the character of conjugal roles and the social environment of the spouses as a result of the study of a small number of London families by Bott.[34] Bott as we have seen was concerned with the degree to which the activities of the spouses were shared or independent or, in her terminology, the degree to which the roles were *segregated.* (Bott does not distinguish terminologically between 'role'—what is normatively expected—and 'role performance'—what actually happens.) Bott suggested that there was a relationship between the performance of conjugal roles and the type of locality in which the family lived, the services exchanged between spouses and people outside the household, their mobility, and the occupational status of the husband. These factors she saw not as affecting the family directly however but through the social network of the spouses. She put forward the hypotheses that *the degree of segregation in the role relationship of the husband and wife varies directly with the connectedness of the family's network* (p. 60).

Now stimulating and seminal as Bott's study is, it is not remarkable for its conceptual clarity. As Turner[35] has pointed out Bott does not make it clear whether she is referring to the networks of each spouse separately or of both together or of all the adults in her respondents' households. We may add an additional point here. It is not clear what 'varies directly' implies. Does it mean that all families with segregated roles will have close-knit networks and those with joint roles loose-knit networks? Or does it mean that the proportion with segregated roles should increase as the connectedness of the network increases?

If the degree of interconnectedness is a condition of the spouses' action, then we should not expect a 'one-one' correspondence between network type and role type, since conditions limit human action but rarely uniquely determine it. If on the other hand the network type determines the marital relationship, this must be through some non-social mechanism which must be specified. Roles and networks cannot be related through the fit of ideas since a net-

[34] Bott, *op. cit.*, to which page numbers throughout this section refer.
[35] Turner, C., 'Conjugal Roles and Social Networks,' *Hum. Rel.* 20, 1967.

work is not a pattern of action understandable in terms of ideas governing it, but is the result of all sorts of processes and activities.

Bott of course discusses the way in which one affects the other. The explanations which she suggests are:

1. Availability of alternative sources of emotional satisfaction make the spouses less dependent on the marital relationship where the spouses have close-knit networks prior to marriage.

2. Loose-knit networks mean that social control will be less effective.

3. Loose-knit networks mean that mutual assistance will be more fragmented and less consistent.

4. Members of a close-knit network tend to reach consensus on norms (unspecified).[36]

All but the last of these explanations refer explicitly to the conditions of action. Each of the first three explanations contains three terms. The first, for example, links network type with sources of emotional satisfaction with conjugal role. In no case does the existence of the condition connoted by the middle term depend on the network type. I may find emotional satisfaction among the members of a primary group without my whole social network being close-knit or even the members of the group constituting a close-knit network.[37] It is possible to conceive of situations in which a loose-knit network would make social control less effective but it does not follow that it therefore must be less effective. Nor does it follow that aid to Ego will be less consistent and more fragmented, though it must logically reduce the degree of possible exchange to aid between *all* the members of the network.[38]

Why then does Bott put up such easily refutable propositions? The answer is to be found in the last explanation. This doesn't refer to marital roles at all but to conditions favouring group formation. The more interconnected the network, the greater chance its members have of developing common norms, and the better will they be able to act together, because both these processes require effective communication of which a close-knit network is the structural prerequisite.

Bott's explanatory hypotheses imply therefore that interconnected networks are a necessary condition of good communication, and good communication of group formation, and that where Ego is a member of such a group before marriage he will be forced to retain an active

[36] These are rephrased as propositions for clarity of presentation.

[37] The links between the points in Bott's use of the term network are interactions not relationships. Bott, p. 59, Note 1.

[38] This is of course only meaningful if the network is relatively bounded.

membership of such a group after marriage and this will affect the performance of his marital role.

As an anthropologist, Bott was concerned with the way in which the nuclear family group was not, in western urban society, 'encapsulated' in wider social groups. The families she studied were not components of extended family groups nor members of cohesive locality groups. The spouses nevertheless had a wide range of relationships outside the nuclear family. Of the greatest importance were kinship relationships, neighbour relationships, friends, and relationships in the occupational sphere. Being unable to explain nuclear family roles in terms of the activities of a wider *social group or groups* of which the nuclear family constitutes a part, she sought to explain the way in which marital roles were performed in terms of *an encapsulating network* (p. 99).

We have just said however that Bott's argument depends on the spouses being members of different 'groups'. Therefore the whole problem depends on the use of the term 'group'. Bott defines two senses of the term group: first as a plurality of persons sharing the same attribute—that is to say a logical class; secondly, as a plurality whose members have distinctive interdependent relationships with one another. She says that she uses the term 'organized group' in the latter sense (p. 58, note 1).[39]

It is immediately evident that Bott's definition of an organized group is also a definition of a network composed of relationships of the same kind.[40] For example, an extended kin network and an extended kin group would both have these characteristics. Now it does not of course matter that the definitions make it possible for entities which are groups, also to be networks, but it does matter that Bott does not distinguish between them in her definition, since the problem, as she sees it, is precisely that the spouses are encapsulated in a network but not in groups. She must have some distinction in her mind. It may be suggested that the clue is to be found in her use of the term 'organized'. While not implying that by 'group' she means 'corporate group', the notion of organization

[39] In fact in some places she seems to use 'group' to mean a plurality *all* of whom *interact* in contrast to a close knit network, *most* but not all of whose members interact. (p. 213). Bott is both a social psychologist and an anthropologist. From social psychology we get a definition of group in terms of interaction and from anthropology a concern with the structure of relationships. Bott's definition is therefore in terms of a group as an interactive structure. Norms are rightly seen as the result of these conditions but excluded from the definition of 'group' itself. It is from this exclusion that most of the confusion arises.

[40] i.e. of occupational or kinship or neighbour links.

does suggest that the relationships referred to in her definition are of such a nature and constitute such a pattern that it is possible for the members to act together. If they are to act together they must share values in terms of which decisions to act can be made, and they must be able to interact in such a way as to make co-action possible.

This interpretation fits in nicely both with her explanatory hypotheses and with the approach that we have so far adopted. Ego is not born into encapsulating groups, but he does acquire a set of relationships over time. Depending on the characteristics of the members of the set and their interconnectedness and the nature of the traffic along the links, the members of the sets of the members of Ego's set may, together with Ego, come to constitute a group—that is to say come to share valued ways of acting (norms) and a capacity for acting together. Where this happens, each spouse will have an interconnected network of relationships of the same kind, have outside sources of gratification through membership of a primary group, be able to mobilize resources through his group membership and be subjected to considerable pressure to conform to group norms. Where in addition different group memberships overlap[41] and where the different groups share the same norms, the effectiveness of social control will be even greater, because Ego will be more completely encapsulated, and hence unable to draw on resources from outside the complex of overlapping groups. The more different group memberships overlap, the more interconnected Ego's network will be.

We have already noted however that access to outside resources (explanations 1 and 3) does not require, though it is provided by, the existence of either interconnected networks or groups of which the spouses are members. Equally, effective social control is not dependent on these conditions. All that is required is the existence of primary relationships between Ego and others. Now Bott, once again comparing the London situation with that of families in primitive societies, stresses that in an urban community families are highly *individuated,* that is to say 'separated off, differentiated out as a distinct, and to some extent autonomous social group . . . families with close-knit networks are less individuated than those with loose-knit networks . . . Husband and wife are able within broad limits to perform their roles in accordance with their own personal needs. These broad limits are laid down by the norms of the nation as a whole' (p. 101).

Because of this individuation it will not be likely that the set of

[41] As in the case of her only family with a close network and a segregated marital relationship (The Newbolts).

persons with whom Ego has relationships will share the same norms unless they form part of an interconnected network. If we look at the situation of the spouses at any given point of time there need be no association of connectedness with the type of marital relationship. At any given point what affects the relationship is the sharing, between members of Ego's set, of norms governing marital interaction. And that is dependent on *prior* interconnectedness without which the norms could not have been formed.

Bott was therefore onto something very important but failed to state its precise nature. Nothing follows from the interconnectedness of the networks of the spouses taken singly or together. Network interconnectedness of an Ego is a condition of group formation, and of a high degree of social control of Ego once the group has been formed. Where each spouse belongs to a separate group, each will have resources external to the marital relationship and be less dependent on the other spouse. This will make possible conjugal role performances which are relatively independent, but will *not determine* such performance. Where the spouses do not have external resources they will *have* to adopt a more joint pattern of relationships. There is no need for different kinds of network to interlock for the Egos to have group resources outside the marriage, however, and when both spouses share the same group membership outside marriage it is hard to see why this should not lead to *joint* activities on the part of the spouses,[42] though it will diminish the ability of either spouse to violate group norms within the family, since by so doing the deviant spouse will both lose support of the other and of groups outside the marriage.

The existence of a shared group memberships will of course not be possible if the groups are single-sex groups, nor will shared group memberships result in joint conjugal roles if the norms of the group specify the propriety of segregated roles. Even if, therefore, we substitute the notion of 'group membership' for 'network', and differentiate sharply between the membership of each spouse, we cannot assume that the spouses' membership of such groups necessarily increases the degree of role segregation, unless we specify the content of the norms which the groups share, and the affects of group activities on marital activities.

Where each spouse belongs to a *mono-sex group*, however, one feels intuitively that marital roles are more likely to be segregated. Now there are only two ways in which different actions can be related: logically through the rules governing the activity, or empirically by

[42] See Fallding, H., 'The Family and the Idea of a Cardinal Role', *Hum. Rel.* 14, 1961, p. 342.

the activities constituting conditions of each other's performance. Mono-sex groups are likely to be formed where the sex roles are themselves rigorously differentiated. Since marital roles are parts of sex roles there is likely to be a fit between mono-sex group membership and role segregation at the logical level. Where spouses are unable to perform their distinctive activities except with help from others, the groups which they form to perform these activities must be single-sex.

It is not quite as simple as this however. The definitions of sex roles must be related to the conditions under which they are performed. Notions about men, women and their place in society make sense of an empirical situation in which people find themselves. Hence not only do the conditions under which activities take place determine the need for extra-familial supportive relations, and the ideas about sexual roles determine both the characteristics of both peer group structure and the marital relationship, but the conditions under which the activities are performed affect the definitions of the roles.

It would therefore appear that, given certain conditions of marital role performance, we are likely to get both a definition of marital roles as segregated and the involvement of the spouses in mono-sex groups.[43]

We may conclude therefore that in the absence of social relationships outside the family which can provide resources which lessen the spouses' dependence on one another, spouses will be forced into a more joint relationship. Where such relationships exist *and* are characterized by activities which require the independent action of the spouses, *or* are used to enforce norms of marital role segregation *or* both, then the existence of such relationships will be associated with marital role segregation.

Such relationships will exist where the spouses are members prior to their marriage of such social groups as are able to provide these resources. Control over the spouses will be facilitated by a close-knit network. The formation of norms and groups will be facilitated by the existence of a close-knit network. Where such groups or sets of relationships are mono-sex, their members are likely also to share norms of marital role segregation which derive both from the fit of ideas and from the conditions under which marital roles are performed. If the roles are defined as segregated and cannot be performed without resources provided by external relationships, then those relationships will be between persons of the same sex. Hence we

[43] As was the case with Bott's only family with segregated roles and close knit network, the Newbolts, as Fallding (*op. cit.*, p. 342) has pointed out.

should expect to find an irregular relationship between network interconnectedness and role segregation, but a strong relationship between membership of mono-sex networks and marital role segregation. This is what the only satisfactory attempt to verify Bott's hypothesis found.[44]

Perhaps the really lasting significance of Bott's study is that she has made impossible the proliferation of studies of the internal structure of the family which take no account of its social environment. She explicitly recognizes the implications of Parsons' description of the nuclear family—its segregation *qua* family from wider groups and the autonomy of the spouses as a couple—while recognizing that this does not imply that the family is isolated in the sense that its members, *individually,* are isolated. This is of course obvious *once it has been said.* Before it was said it was easy to slip into confusing the segregation of the group with segregation of individual members and hence to assume that what went on outside the family had no bearing on what went on inside it. It is to be hoped that the reader finds it very difficult to understand how this mistake could ever have been made, since the whole of this book is constructed in an attempt to prevent him from making just this error.

MARITAL AUTHORITY

Marital authority is used here to refer to the authority of one spouse over the other. As we have already seen, degree of authority of one spouse over the other must not be confused with the segregation of roles.[45] Authority can be autonomic or syncratic in its distribution, without either spouse having an *overall* superordinate position. Indeed it may be argued that a segregation of activities is antipathetic to the *pre-dominance* of one spouse over another, since it provides for each spouse a clearly demarcated area of activity and control in which the other spouse has not the expertise to interfere.[46] There would seem to be an association of norms providing for authority of men over women with the segregation of activities of the spouses which gives back to the woman in bargaining power what she loses in authority. The factor linking the two is probably the material conditions. The poorer the material conditions in the society as a whole the more likely is it that differences between the sexes will

[44] Turner, *op. cit.*

[45] Bott stresses this point: *op. cit.*, p. 64.

[46] For a racy and amusing overview of the position of women in primitive societies which makes this point see, Linton, R., 'Women in the Family' in Sussman, M., *A Source Book in Marriage and the Family,* Boston, Houghton Mifflin, 1962.

bar the woman from effective participation in the tasks of economic provision and the more she will be tied to domestic duties by poor living conditions and large family size. Hence in such a society a low economic level entails male authority and segregated marital roles. 'All the weight of tradition reinforces the position of husband as the lord of the family, of the house, and of everything that belongs to both spouses. The woman must obey and serve her husband... But in fact these are the public aspects of this relationship: they are only in force outside the front door. Within the house we find that practice is not the daughter of theory.'

In his study of a Spanish town from which this quotation is taken, Lisón-Tolsana[47] goes on to describe what goes on behind the front door. 'The thoughts of the husband being intent on superior matters', he does not concern himself with 'small cares and household chores'. As a result 'the house is the undisputed realm of the woman'. The man is entirely unfamiliar with his own house; he cannot change his shirt if his wife has not put one ready—he does not know where she keeps them and anyway she keeps the key to all the cupboards. He cannot cook, his wife buys all his clothes, she controls all the money—she collects the wages of her husband and sons herself.

The power of the wife is widely recognized in societies where normatively the man is the autocrat. The Spanish say, 'The husband commands in his house—when his wife is not at home'. The Germans who traditionally have invested the husband with supreme authority say, 'Der Mann denkt, die Frau lenkt' (Man proposes; woman disposes).[48]

The typical Spanish family which Tolsana describes is by implication by no means poor. The worse the material conditions of family life become the greater is the dependence of the man on the woman, since she determines how far the meagre family income goes; but the more meagre it becomes the less room for manoeuvre the woman has. Hence among the very poor one finds an ideology of male dominance and a segregation of roles which does not compensate for the wife's lack of authority with an increase in her power proportionate to the degree of role segregation.[49] The poorer the family the greater the need for extra-familial resources and the

[47] Lisón-Tolsana, C., *Belmonte de los Caballeros*, London, O.U.P., 1966, pp. 147–151. This whole paragraph is adapted from his account.

[48] It is odd that so perceptive a student as Goode should think this saying inconsistent with 'a woman should learn to serve'. One refers to authority *de jure* and the other to authority *de facto* as Lisón Tólsana puts it (*op. cit.* p. 149), or one refers to a norm and the other to an actual balance of power. Cf. Goode, W. J., *World Revolution and Family Patterns*, London, Collier-Mac: Free Press, 1963, p. 67.

greater the segregation of sex roles across the network, the greater the dissatisfaction by each partner with role performance and the greater therefore the hostility between the sexes maintained by their membership of single-sex networks and groups.

At the other end of the economic scale the possession by each spouse of independent means and the lack of interdependence of a domestic nature may equally lead to a relative powerlessness of one spouse over the other. The power of the woman is therefore greatest in the middle of the economic range and where roles are segregated.

The authority of the male will also be affected by his familial and kinship activities as well as by his activities in the society as a whole. We have already noted (see above pp. 80–1) that parental authority will be affected by the economic activities of the family. Where the family constitutes a proprietary or productive economic group or substantial wealth is transmitted through kinship ties and property is controlled by males, this cannot but enhance their power which is likely to be legitimized and hence come to constitute authority. Hence one would expect to find that male authority is highest at the top of the economic scale in societies where males control wealth, as well as high among families at the bottom of the economic scale or in societies existing under poor material conditions.

Women in families at the top of the economic range will not however be necessarily tied to a domestic role. It would not therefore appear to follow that, among the rich, conjugal roles must necessarily be segregated. If we now split the population up into three categories ranked in order of their material circumstances, we can say that the lowest category is likely to have a high degree of segregation and male authority, and that the highest is likely to have a high degree of male authority. One can say nothing at all about the middle category. In terms of relative power one can say nothing either, except to reiterate the point about the compensatory effect of segregation.

If we now turn to the empirical findings we are at once confronted with difficulty, since the concepts used are all different and refer usually not to power and authority but to decision-making. Now decision-making studies usually deal with the end result of a process in which both power and authority are involved. Komarovsky[50] in reviewing some of the literature argues that the

[49] The division of labour is 'forced' in Durkheim's terms; see his *The Division of Labour*, Free Press, 1933, pp. 374–388. It is forced however not because one party enforces a division on the other but because the material conditions enforced a particular bargain.

[50] Komarovsky, M., 'Class Differences in Family Decision-making on

evidence from American studies shows that joint decision-making is highest in the middle category and lowest in the others. We do not know whether the carrying out of the decisions (activities) was independent or joint and we do not know in the other two categories whether joint decision-making did not occur because the authority distribution was wife dominant, husband dominant, or autonomic. We know only that it was not syncratic.

Komarovsky does produce some evidence which suggests that autonomic decision-making is higher in the lowest and highest economic categories. Since the data mainly concerns purchases this suggests that segregation also follows this pattern.

Wolfe's[51] data suggest that male authority is highest in the high social status categories. They also show that the wife has greatest control over money in the autonomic family type.

Goode[52] reports the findings of two surveys in France and Germany which report substantial control over family expenditures by the wife in France (except in the highest occupational category) but a much more joint pattern in Germany. The German data show however that control by the wife is highest in the lowest income groups, that joint control is highest in the middle groups and control by the husband highest in the highest income groups.

There have been no recent sociological studies of this problem in Britain. The evidence from community studies seems to suggest, among the working classes, an association of male authority with role segregation leading to an autonomic authority pattern whose exact details are subject to regional variation, but with a more syncratic type of authority associated with joint activities in the middle class. So far no British sociologist has dared to try to study the domestic habits of the upper class.

It is to be hoped that in the near future we shall see some conceptually rigorous empirical studies conducted in this field.

Before concluding this section however, mention must be made of two important factors affecting marital authority. The first concerns the effect of women working. Wolfe[53] has shown that the wife working is negatively related to the dominance of the husband; Blood and Hamblin[54] have shown that more activities are shared and decision-

Expenditures' in Sussman, M., *Source book in Marriage and the Family*, Boston, Houghton Mifflin, 1963, p. 261.

[51] *Op. cit.*

[52] *Op. cit.*, p. 69.

[53] *Op. cit.*

[54] Blood, R. O. and Hamblin, R. L., 'The Effect of the Wife's Employment on the Family Power Structure', *Soc. For.* 36, 1958, p, 347.

making becomes more joint when the wife works. This study also shows that this shift comes about through a change in expectations about the distribution of authority on the part of both spouses which the authors interpret as normative. Hoffman's study lead her to draw similar conclusions.[55]

The second concerns the effect of family size. Heer[56] in a study of the effect of wives working which confirms the results of the studies mentioned above, came up with the unexpected finding that family size is positively related to the husband's power in decision-making. Larger family size is likely to lead to greater segregation with a complementary shift to autonomic decision-making, but it does not imply the husband's dominance. It seems possible therefore that dominance of the male in decision-making may affect family size.[57]

PARENTAL AUTHORITY AND PARENT-CHILD RELATIONS[58]

The nuclear family may not be encapsulated in a wider group but the child is completely encapsulated in the nuclear family. At birth he is completely in the power of his parents. As he grows, however, he acquires power largely through an increasing ability to interfere with and disrupt his parents' activities. This power the child increasingly uses to achieve his own ends in the face of opposition from his parents. The parents are however fighting with one hand tied behind their backs, since their response is limited by notions of parental duty.

Parent-child relationships are therefore rooted in conflict. As the power of the child grows it becomes increasingly necessary to equalize the conditions of conflict by limiting the action of the child by the inculcation of moral notions of comparable force to those which restrain the parent. Two types of moral notion may be distinguished here: those which limit the pursuit of individual ends

[55] Hoffman, L. W., 'Effects of Employment of Mothers on Parental Power Relations and the Division of Household Tasks', in Farber, B., *Family and Kinship Organisation*, London, Wiley, 1966, p. 316.

[56] Heer, D. M., 'Dominance and the Working Wife', *Soc. For.* 36, 1958, p. 341.

[57] For a discussion of the relation between female emancipation and family size see, Banks, J. A. and O., *Feminism and Family Planning in Victorian England*, Liverpool Univ. Press, 1964, Ch. 9.

[58] This section is informed by the following articles: Warren, R. W., 'Social Disorganisation and the Interrelationship of Cultural Roles'; Davis, K., 'The Sociology of Parent-Youth Conflict', both reprinted in Stein, H. D. and Cloward, R. A. (Eds.), *Social Perspectives on Behaviour*, London, Collier-Mac: Free Press, 1958, pp. 186 and 35 respectively. Eisenstadt, S. N., *From Generation to Generation*, Free Press, 1956, esp. Ch. I.

without regard to the consequences for others in the society in general, and those which define the duties and obligations of a child as opposed to an adult. Both types of moral rule or norm will involve initially modification of behaviour to the parents from whom those norms are acquired. Both types of norm will improve the position of the parent. Initially therefore both types of norm are not distinguished, and the internalization of both types serves to legitimate the power of the parent. The meaning of authority and its moral source of legitimation originate therefore in the notion of parental authority. It is from this fact that the future problems of both family and society arise.

It will be immediately obvious that where the authority distribution between spouses is autonomic, the child will soon distinguish different areas of authority which are sex-linked, thus stressing from an early age the differentiation between sex roles. Where the child has siblings he will learn to distinguish earlier between parental authority and general moral constraints. Where the number of children is large he will learn to distinguish an age-related difference in the distribution of authority. Patterns of behaviour will therefore be associated in all families with the ascribed characteristics of age and sex.

Where most social roles are allocated on the basis of kinship, there will be no sharp transition to be made when the child's sphere of interaction extends beyond the nuclear family. Where however this is not the case the child will be confronted with sources of authority which rival the authority of the family itself. The more plural the society and the more individuated the family, the greater the chance of the values transmitted by that authority being inconsistent with those of the family. This fact immediately provides the child with greater scope for the manoeuvre and hence limits the effectiveness of the authority both within the family, and outside it.

At the same time participation in non-family activities exposes the child to new and different experiences through which he becomes a person whose knowledge, attitudes and values differ in many ways from those of his parents. Hence no sooner has the child internalized norms which serve to legitimate parental authority than this is itself challenged. Where however the locality in which the child lives is relatively homogeneous with regard to beliefs, values and patterns of family life, the child at school will be thrown into company with a group of peers whose family-derived attitudes tend to reinforce one another. In this situation, though the child may use the authority of the school against the authority of the parents for his own ends, it is unlikely that values transmitted by the school will be internalized by the child since both his primary groups will exert pressures in the opposite direction.

The process of physical and psychological maturation in the child is accompanied by successive redefinitions of his social role both in the family and in the society. In many primitive societies some of these transitions are marked by rituals which ceremonially confer a new status on the child whose duties and obligations are quite clearly defined. Even where this is not the case, homogeneity of the society will mean that most children are brought up in families of a similar type and under similar conditions. This combined with the publicness of family life in such societies leads to the existence of fairly explicit expectations of what age-related roles involve, even where these cannot be said to be governed by explicit rules.

In Western society the individuation of families, combined with the private nature of much family living, makes the transition between age-related roles much more vague, and hence subject to much more parent-child bargaining. Confusion about the rights and duties attaching to the status of child at different ages is of critical importance during the period which the inhabitants of such societies describe as adolescence. This period is defined largely in terms of sexual maturation and personality development. The internal strains and stresses to which the family is subjected at this time are largely seen as results of emotional disturbances in the children associated with these processes.

While not in anyway denying the stresses involved in a profound psychological transition from child to adult, it is necessary to recognize that such transitions are changes in the 'self' and that the 'self' is socially defined. The definition of social roles which determine the patterns of social interaction through which the self is created cannot but have a vital effect upon this psychological process. This fact has led some writers to say that the storms of adolescence are a cultural artifact of the social definition of roles. It is certainly true that in many primitive societies pubescent children do not appear to go through anything like the same amount of 'disturbance' that characterizes this period in Western society. These considerations have led Hollingshead to define adolescence as 'the period in life of a person when the society in which he functions ceases to regard him as a child and does not accord to him full adult status or functions'.[59]

It is certainly true that Western culture does not define any clear sequence of statuses through which the child passes on route to adulthood. This problem of transition from child to adult status has

[59] Hollingshead, A. B., *Elmtowns Youth*, London, Wiley, 1949, p. 7.

been variously dealt with by defining children as small adults or defining mature individuals as children. Where the individual is under the authority of a family group wider than the nuclear family, it is of course possible to define a child as adult, since adults as well as children are not autonomous in many respects, but under some other adult authority.

When this is the case the adult role is less onerous. We have already noted that where an individual retains membership of a wider group, marriage does not require the performance of marital roles unaided or the demands of those roles are not severe.[60] In such a situation there is no need to postpone marriage until the man is economically capable of earning an independent living and the woman capable of raising children and running a household alone. In such a situation, it may be possible (depending on the type of productive property involved, and type of inheritance) for young people to marry when they are sexually mature. Where however this is not possible or where the family is restricted to the nuclear family, the young person will have to remain under the domestic authority of his parents long after his physical maturation.

There is of course no reason why a household of adults should not have an egalitarian authority structure. However, in the case of a family, the accordance of equal status to mature adults would create difficulties since it would involve the relative deprivation of authority of the parents, and because the whole notion of familial authority is age-related. In this situation there is a strong tendency to define 'adolescence' as 'childhood' thus preserving a consistency between age and authority distributions. The difficulty of this is that the power distribution within the family no longer corresponds to this situation. The adolescent children may be earning and be financially independent even if they cannot support a nuclear family of their own. As a result adolescence is characterized by acute parent-child conflict and personality difficulties arising from the inconsistent roles that the adolescent is forced to play.

The achievement of sexual maturity before the socially required degree of economic independence also creates problems in a society where premarital sexuality is forbidden. The upper-class Victorian solution to this problem was, as we have seen, to lock up their daughters (which was pretty easy since they were women and women had no adult legal status anyway) and provide brothels for the men staffed by women who, being working class, didn't count. This was unsatisfactory at the level of ideas, since it involved coupling a doctrine of the sinfulness of premarital sex with that practice on

[60] See above p. 77.

the part of men, which was legitimized by the unspoken belief that it only applied to intra-class sexuality. The Victorians were by no means unaware of this problem. It really became acute however with the development of more egalitarian notions and the slow recategorization of the working classes as people.

To speak of egalitarian notions is of course to refer to beliefs about authority, and authority is first learnt within the family. Industrialization had of course brought about not only a reduction in parental power in many families, it has also led to the formation of social classes and the partial success of attempts to use the power of combination to improve the terms of the bargain between the classes in favour of the workers. The reduction of the power of those in authority demanded legitimation in terms of egalitarian doctrines which in turn affected other social institutions associated with the upper classes, especially the churches who were the main agents for the re-enforcement of beliefs concerning sexual morality. The decline of these authorities produced and made possible an extension of the practice of premarital sexual relations (which had always been found among the mass of the population) to the middle class.

Changes in the distribution of power in society therefore affected changes in the distribution of power and then authority in the family, and also attacked the sources of legitimation for sexual norms which were becoming increasingly difficult to apply because of the tensions which, in an industrial society with a nuclear family form, they produced. It is not surprising therefore that there has been a close association between notions relating to authority and those concerning family life.[61] Those in authority saw changes in family life as a rejection of that authority. They were of course quite right since the undermining of parental authority cut off an important source of legitimation of authority in society as a whole, while the same shifts in the balance of power affected both. Since those in authority were so quick to see the connection, it is not surprising that those under authority eventually saw the connection as well, and freedom to love and freedom from other types of authority have recently come to be associated.[62]

[61] In recent years we have heard a great deal about sexual 'delinquency', as if this was in some way connected with juvenile delinquency, and deviation from the sexual norms of those in authority was itself a crime.

[62] The position of universities is of particular interest in this respect. Since students are under twenty-one, the university is *in loco parentis*. Hence the university is placed in even more difficulty than the parents. It cannot treat students individually as adult, since they are minors; it cannot act as a parent (a) because it is impossible to control the intimate lives of thousands of young adults, (b) because there is no consensus as to what parents should require of

To attempt simultaneously to use authority to restrict or prohibit sexual outlets to adults, while at the same time reducing the basis of power of that authority is to ask for some kind of explosion both in the family and in society.

Relations of parents and 'children' are particularly subject to conflict in industrial society for yet another reason, that is the speed of social change. Where change is great, then the parent will transmit the content of his experiences, beliefs and values which are already different from those of the society in which the child will have to live. This irrelevance of what is transmitted, not only produces conflict between child and parent but undermines the authority of the latter. Educational mobility of the children has a similar effect.

CONCLUSION

The reader has probably found it odd that the themes of marriage and parent-child relationships have been dealt with in terms of resources, power, authority, conflict, bargaining—terms which are more in place in a text on industrial than on family sociology. It is not really odd at all. If these concepts are applicable to social relationships in industry they must be applicable to family relationships since these are social relationships too. Contrariwise, if the concepts of loyalty, love, affection and duty are applicable to the family, they are also applicable to industry.

The basic idea we have used which links these two sets of concepts is that of a division of labour, creating interdependence and exchange between two or more parties. Husband and wife, parent and child, like management and worker, constitute two such parties. Their interdependence can lead either to solidarity through their mutual gratification or to conflict over the terms of the exchange. The ability to gratify the other, created by the other's love, is just as much a source of power as the ability to gratify by raising wages or productivity. If the reader finds this hard to accept he might consider the old saying that love and hatred are but different sides of the same coin.

children any way, (c) because the students have the power to resist such control. It cannot however do nothing because it is held responsible for the conduct of the minors in its care and will be blamed for any action on their part which conflicts with the norms of one or other social groups outside it. It is in the university that the parent-youth conflict becomes 'class' conflict since it makes possible the combined action of the 'children'.

7

Adult Relationships in the Elementary Family

DEMOGRAPHIC FACTORS AND THE FAMILY CYCLE

IN the previous chapter we have considered certain aspects of nuclear family formation and the activities which characterize it. These phases of the family cycle, marriage, procreation and rearing, may vary in their duration according to the number and spacing of the children. Except where the age of marriage is extremely late or the age of death extremely early or both, there will, as we have already noted, be a period towards the end of their life cycle when the married couple have all their children married. This is sometimes referred to as the 'post-parental' stage in the life-cycle of the married couple. It is not necessarily the same as 'old age'.

What 'old age' means exactly is by no means clear. Like 'adolescence' it may be defined either in terms of physical or psychological changes associated, in this case, with advancing years, or it may be defined in terms of the stage in the sequence of age-related social roles which has been reached. These three types of factors are quite distinct but they are also interrelated. The changed definition of the roles people are required to play will affect their personalities, while changing ability to perform various types of physical activity will partly determine the roles they perform. Changing physiological characteristics will affect cognition and perception, but the extent and rate of this change will also be affected by the extent to which the roles they play make demands on these faculties. Physiological and psychological and social types of aging, while logically distinct, are therefore empirically interdependent.

Neither physiological nor social factors are tied to age in the sense that they are determined by it. The living conditions of the population and the type of diet will determine the expectation of life and hence the timing of the onset of physiological aging and the decline in cognitive faculties which are physiologically based. From this it follows that variation in life expectation determines not only whether there will be any post-parental life but also its quality.

Where the ability to perform roles is diminished by non-social aging there will be some 'role loss' on the part of elderly people. Where this involves loss of an economically active role, then in those societies where the majority of families do not possess property, this must entail that the parents experience a period of economic dependency towards the end of their life cycles. Depending on the shape of the cycle, this period of economic dependency may occur during the early phases of the children's family cycles, when the children themselves are in most need of help from outside their nuclear families, or it may occur later in the children's cycles when their own children are already independent.

To speak of the *family* cycle is to speak of the way in which the *life* cycles of successive generations of parents and children interlock. The family cycle refers to the time dimension of the family process. It is more than a dimension however, since the way in which the different cycles interlock, that is the speed with which the generations follow one another, will determine who is alive at the same time, and who needs what sort of help when. 'Time' is more than a dimension or aspect of the family process therefore, since the temporal sequence of family formation will affect family structure. To speak of time is of course to speak of the temporal pattern produced by the actions of individuals in different generations which are systematically interrelated. Marrying 'late' not only affects *Ego's* life cycle—it will mean less time in the post-parental phase and more overlap between that phase and physiological old age; it also affects the *children's* life cycles. It may mean that the children have to care for and support their parents at the same time as their own children are young. It may force a child to postpone marriage in order to look after aged parents, thus reproducing the late marriage pattern in the next generation.

Industrialization involves, as we have seen, the concentration of property so that the family ceases to be a proprietary group. It also lowers the age at marriage. We may now note another related effect. Historically, industrialization has brought about a long run improvement in living standards leading to an increased expectation of life. We have to be a little careful here. Expectation of life can be calculated at different ages. It is broadly true to say that the most dramatic effect of higher living standards on life expectancy has not been to increase the life expectancy of those well advanced in years, but to increase the expectation of life of the younger age groups. To put this another way: it means that if you are so fortunate as to reach the age of sixty you cannot expect to live all that much longer than your grandfather could. But your chances at birth, or even at the age of twenty, of surviving until the age of sixty have increased considerably. What is different about advanced industrial societies is not that some people survive to ages greater than those to which people lived in pre-industrial societies. What distinguishes modern society is that *more* people live to an advanced age.

If we now put these three consequences of industrialization together it will be seen that they have the effect of changing the shape of the family cycle by extending the post-parental phase of the life cycle, and ensuring that some part of it is a period of economic dependency. Now it is of course true that if there had been considerable increase in the length of the period of child-bearing, this could have wiped out the 'gains' from the other factors. Two points should be noted here. First, one element in the increased expectation of life at birth has been the decrease in infant mortality. We might say that reproduction is more efficient today in that the wastage rate has been reduced, enabling the achievement of the same amount of production in a much shorter space of time. Secondly, there has been a sharp decrease in the achieved number of children in Western countries in the last hundred years. This is not the place to discuss the arguments which attempt to relate 'family size' and industrialization. We simply note that as a matter of fact there has been a reduction in 'family size'.[1] The effect of reduced 'family size' could have been cancelled out by the wider spacing of children which improved contraceptive methods make more possible. Two factors operate against wide spacing. First, higher educational standards and increased opportunities for married women to work make some women 'bunch' their children in order to ensure a period in the life cycle when they can resume their career. Second, the possibility of increasing earnings by both spouses working is an important factor at lower educational levels which has the same effect.

We may now reformulate our proposition concerning the effect of industrialization on the life-cycle. Loss of property, lower age at marriage, longer life expectancy, lower infant mortality, smaller family size, and 'bunching' of the births of the children, together have the effect of increasing the length of the post-parental phase of the life cycle. In consequence the family cycle has changed its shape. It is no longer characterized by a flow of services from parents to

[1] i.e. the number of children.

children (while the children are immature) and the flow of services to the married children in the *early* stages of their cycles, followed by the death of the original parents. It is now characterized by a flow of services from parents to married children in the *early* stage of their cycles, followed by a flow of services from children to parents in a *later* stage of their cycles, followed by the death of the original parents.[2]

It must be recognized of course that such broad statements as are made above describe only general trends based on shifts in *average*[3] ages. Whatever the average or typical pattern, there will be, within the society for which it holds good, considerable variation based on the differing conditions under which different families act and upon their memberships of different groups sharing different norms and characterized by the performance by the family of different activities.

There will moreover be considerable variation within any given cluster of overlapping elementary families in the shape of the family cycle seen from the point of view of *each* of them. The first child of a given set of parents to be born and married may experience a very different pattern of relationships with its parents from the fifth. When the former marries the parents will still be caring for their remaining immature children. When the latter marries the parents may be already retired.

Relationships between parents and children depend on the stages reached in their respective life cycles. The cycle of the elementary family is therefore made up of the overlapping life cycles of each of its members, and relationships between parents and children can never be understood by merely elaborating the stage in the life cycle reached by either party, nor by noting a stage reached by the parents which specifies only the marriage of the children. It is vital to know the point reached in the life cycles of *all* the children if the parents position is to be adequately assessed.

It is then important to recognize that substantial proportions of families will exhibit family cycles markedly different from the 'average'. Table 1 shows the shape of the women's life cycle in the United States for the generations born in the 1880s and 1930s. The table indicates that, for the 1930 generation, one parent dies about the same time as the birth of the first great grandchild. These figures suggest that the family is typically three generational, and that the

[2] It may be noted that this relieves the 'children' of responsibility for car of both aged parents and their own immature children at the same time.

[3] Average is used here in its popular sense. More strictly the point that is being made is that care must be taken in the use of numerical models based on measures of a central tendency—mean, mode or median.

TABLE 1. Life cycle of women born 1880–1889 and 1930–1939 in US

Stage of family	*Median age* 1880–1889	*Median age* 1930–1939
First marriage	21·6	19·9
Birth of first child	22·9	21·5
Birth of last child	32·9	30–31
First marriage of last child	56·2	51·5–52·5
Death of one spouse	57·0	64·4

Source: Glick, P. C. and Parke, R., 'New Approaches in Studying the Life Cycle of the Family', *Demography*, 2, 1965.[4]

parental generation will not probably be in need of services from its children until the children's children are already adolescent or about to marry. The 1880 generation appear to die when the children's children are still quite young. Neither set of figures suggest that a large proportion of families in the US today are four generational. In fact 39 per cent of all *old people,* sixty-five and over, in the US have great grandchildren and are therefore members of four generational families. (The British figure is 22 per cent.[5])

It is equally true however that a substantial number of families in societies exhibiting average parental life cycles similar to those shown for the US may diverge from this pattern in the opposite direction by being only two generational or being characterized by the overlap of the period of parental dependency with the early phases of the children's life cycles. It would appear however that divergences in this direction are less common, only 7 per cent of old people with children in the US and 12 per cent in Britain being members of two generational families.[6]

In spite of these drawbacks, the use of average measures to describe the changing life cycles of individuals are of great value in tracing changes over time in the 'shape' of the family process and the study of such demograpically based changes is indispensable for our understanding of behaviour, especially in the post-parental phase of the individual's life cycle. This account has stressed two main types of need: the economic need of parents after the cessation of their

[4] For a discussion of the changing shape of the life cycle see Glick, P. C., 'The Life Cycle of the Family', in Winch, R. F. *et al.*, '*Selected Studies in Marriage and the Family*', London, Holt Rinehart, 1962, p. 59.

[5] Shanas, E., Townsend, P. *et al.*, *Old People in Three Industrial Societies*, London, Routledge, 1968, p. 143.

It would not of course be true that such a large proportion of the generations concerned *survived* to form members of four generation families. The proportions concerned are proportions of survivors, not of the original generation.

[6] *Ibid*, *op. cit.*

economic activities and the need of help by children during child-bearing and rearing, and has focused on the effect of demographic changes in determining the way these are phased. We need now to examine the nature of services exchanged between families and the implications which these exchanges have for family relationships.

PREPARATION FOR CHANGE IN FAMILIAL ROLE

Even where the family size is small, the bearing and rearing of children is a relatively lengthy business. While exasperated parents may console themselves with the thought that 'the great thing about children is that they grow up', the process is remarkably long drawn out. The modern mother with a nicely spaced[7] family of three cannot expect to spend less than ten years with pre-school children at home, nor less than eleven years with at least one child at school and no pre-school children. Even with the low prevailing age at marriage, and even assuming the children all get married at the statistically 'correct' age, she cannot expect to get rid of the youngest by marriage until some twenty-five years after she became pregnant with the first.

It is important to remember of course that if the mother married at twenty-one, she will only be forty-six at the marriage of her last child and hence have fourteen years of working and fifteen years of retired post-parental life in front of her. But it is equally important to remember that twenty-five years is a very long time and, if the mother survives it, she will inevitably have evolved certain standard patterns of thought and activity based on the fact that in one way or another she is required to minister to the needs of her children. The loss of the last child through marriage therefore constitutes a major point of change in the role of mother which is paralleled only by the role change of the man at retirement. Although being a house-wife and mother is not regarded by the British Registrar General as 'an occupation', it is of course the major activity in adult life for the majority of women.

A priori then we may say that this is the greatest transition that the mother has to face. *In practice* this may not be the case. Where the children continue to reside in the same dwelling or locality after marriage the mother may still be involved in the raising and rearing of children—in this case her grandchildren. If the post-parental role is defined in this way, the very term 'post-parental' becomes a misnomer—'grandparental' would be more apposite. The loss of

[7] i.e. two years between the births of each of the children.

domestic occupation may be gradual, beginning when the first child marries and only becoming complete when the last of the youngest grandchildren go to school. Even then the mother may still be able to render all kinds of domestic services and baby-sit for married children until well into her old age.

Where parents and married children do not form extended family groups of this kind and are widely separated by distance, even though the mother may continue to perform domestic services for them, the change in her role will be much more sharp. Hence we would expect to find that the role transition is more abrupt in the more mobile groups in the population and more abrupt among the higher occupational categories (who are more mobile) than among the lower.

The ease with which this transition is effected will depend on the extent to which the mother is prepared for the changes which she experiences. Now in all societies, people pass through a succession of age-related roles. This transition is achieved relatively smoothly because people have role models derived from the observed behaviour and recounted experiences of those older than themselves. Of obvious importance here is the mother's knowledge of *her own* mother's experience. We have already noted, in discussing the parent-youth conflict in the last chapter, that when a society is changing fast the knowledge and experience of one generation is discounted by the next. However where the experience is less obviously related to a changing situation, the irrelevancy of that experience may be less easily perceived. While the mother's methods of housework may be regarded by a daughter as obviously old fashioned, her mother's changing familial role may well affect the expectations of the daughter as to what her life holds in store, although her mother's role is no more consonant with the daughter's situation than the skills of starching and bleaching in a drip-dry age.

There is another complicating factor here. The expectation of the way familial roles are to be played involves *moral* notions. A role is composed of normative expectations about the way in which one ought, or should, behave to other people. Moral notions are regarded as absolute and consequently such expectations are much more slow to change than expectations of behaviour which are more clearly related to achieving an end in a given situation. The disapproval of the young by the old is not merely *a mistake* like thinking you starch the collars of drip-dry shirts. The reciprocal patterns of behaviour of old and young expected by the old, are valued by them intrinsically as right, although they are in part only relevant in a particular situation. Where normative expectations of the mother are based on the experiences of her own mother in a very different situation, the fact that her own post-parental life does not approximate to her expectations may make her feel betrayed by her children, or lead her to attempt to coerce them into performing roles reciprocal to the post-parental role of *her* mother which are impossible, given the conditions of action of the families concerned. Even where this is not the case, the role transition involved is a major one, and its successful accomplishment will depend to some degree on the extent to which the parents have successfully visualized its implications in advance.

In a fascinating article, Deutscher[8] has shown how American middle-class parents, by experiencing situations which are analogous to the post-parental situation *before they 'lose' the children through marriage,* are prepared for the adoption of the post-parental role. High school, university, youth camps, and military service all provide opportunities of rehearsing at any rate new *domestic* roles, and accustom the parents to the notion of the child's independence.

THE STRUCTURE OF POST-PARENTAL RELATIONSHIPS

In this connection, Deutscher makes a further point of interest. He suggests that the existence of what he calls 'the mother-in-law myth' may help to prevent the parent from failing to recognize the necessity for honouring the sovereignty of the newly independent child. By laughing at jokes about interfering mothers-in-law, the parent is made aware of the dangers of carrying over the role of mother, unadapted, to the mother-married child situation. Certainly no anthropologist studying the strange customs and beliefs of the natives of the West could fail to note the prevalence of this 'myth' in widely differing cultures or fail to observe that it was still a source of humour even where 'interfering mothers-in-law' were the exception rather than the rule. Faced with this behaviour he might well suspect that there was some *structural* explanation.

Now in our discussion of marriage throughout this book we have followed the traditional anthropological pattern of stressing the antinomy between the conjugal bond and the sibling tie. When we look at the family in Western society we find again and again that what is stressed is not this antinomy but that between husband and wife on the one hand, and parent and child on the other. To stress the first of these two contrasts is however really to stress the contrast between ties of filiation and ties of marriage. The unity of the sibling

[8] Deutscher, I., 'Socialisation for Post Parental Life' in Rose, A. M., *Human Behaviour and Social Process*, London, Routledge, 1962, p. 506.

group derives of course from the fact that siblings share the same ties of filiation, either to common parents or to common ancestors. The unity of the sibling group is therefore correlative to the stress on the importance of ties of filiation.

The interfering mother-in-law situation is not therefore to be explained (as it might appear) in terms of the stress on parental as opposed to sibling ties. In order to understand it we have to refer to a third characteristic of kinship structure in primitive society, that of the separation of generations. Primitive society is an age-graded society. It is impossible to 'catch up' and 'overtake' your seniors. In Western society this is exactly what happens. The post-parental phase involves the catching up of parents by their erstwhile children, since there are only two clearly demarcated age statuses in our society—child and adult. The interfering mother-in-law is an example of the way in which the parent-youth conflict is carried over into post-parental life. She is resisting her demotion relative to her children.

We have already had cause to note that the provision of services, because it requires resources, involves the possession of power. The man does not provide domestic services. He provides money, but he cannot control the behaviour of those to whom he provides it except in the most general way. The continued presence of the woman in the home places her in a much stronger position. Since marriage involves the removal of her children from her territory and in the case of her *son* invests another with her power, she suffers a sharp deprivation quite unlike anything experienced by a woman living in a patrilineal joint household, where the son's new wife comes under her authority, or in a matrilineal household where her daughters remain under her control.

Even in an age-graded society, however, it is still true that parent and child relations undergo a sharp transition with the attainment of adult status by the children. This situation is frequently dealt with by customs of avoidance which serve to reduce contact between the generations and structure interaction between them. In such a society however tensions between generations do not arise because of the *interference* of the parents, since the nuclear family is not autonomous but forms part of a wider kin group. The problem with which the myth of the interfering mother-in-law deals is therefore the result of three factors. First, the lack, in our society, of any clearly defined age grades other than those of child and adult. Second, the stress on the conjugal tie over and against ties of filiation. Third, the absence of any norms governing interaction between generations (such as avoidance) which serve to structure and control the relationship. One might also add a fourth factor which does not arise from the structure of the family system but from the nature of the society. In a plural and fast changing society the chances of there being a normative conflict between parents and children and children-in-law is much greater than in relatively homogeneous societies with slower rates of social change.[9]

What Deutscher is saying, therefore, is that the mother-in-law myth acts as a prescription for a type of avoidance, and serves to prepare parents for this avoidance in advance of their children's marriage. There is however yet another type of avoidance which is practised on the part of the children. Both in Britian and America studies have shown the widespread belief that parents and children should live near—but not too near. Living *not too near* implies living far enough away to be able to control the frequency of contact with parents.

This is of course not universal. To explain differences it is necessary to refer once again to the degree of power possessed by the parties which derives from the provision of services. Where the viability of the children's nuclear families is maintained only by the support received from parents and that support is domestic and requires co-residence in dwelling or locality, the parental tie may come to be stressed over and against the conjugal tie.

It is necessary to recognize that the stressing of matrilateral[10] ties in the working class which has been noted in this country or the stressing of patrilateral ties among the upper classes, is quite different in kind from the stressing of ties of filiation in primitive societies. The stress on ties through one parent is not, in Western society, based on any ideology of descent and does not lead to any correlative solidarity between siblings. Where sibling solidarity is found it is the result of interaction which derives from common dependence on the parent. In other words the stress on parental ties and any resultant sibling solidarity depends on the activities of the families concerned, and it is not the case that the activities depend on the stress on ties of filiation and upon the solidarity of the sibling group. Thus it is that when, through rehousing for example, the conditions of the performance of activities linking a cluster of elementary families are removed, sibling interaction is sharply

[9] It has been found that, of all the role conflicts with which the wife is involved, those with parents and in-laws are the most persistent and most marked. See Taylor, P. H., 'Role and role conflicts in a group of middle class wives and mothers', *Soc. Rev.* 12, 1964, p. 317.

[10] This is strictly a misnomer. What is stressed is ties *to* the mother rather than ties through her.

reduced. Ties are maintained chiefly between parents and children.

How then do we explain the maintenance of intergenerational ties? We were not saying that the *recognition* of relationship was dependent upon the activities of the individuals concerned. We were saying that the *relative stress* could be thus explained. Relationship between sibs and parents and children are still recognized. Removal and the cessation of provision of services leaves the children with an obligation towards their parents who were the principle source of aid, and, in cases where extended family formation is a result of maternal dominance inhibiting the child from adequate independent performance of her adult roles, there may be a psychological dependence as well.

We are then dealing with a situation in which stress is placed simultaneously on two ties—parent-child and husband-wife. Somehow a balance has to be maintained between these types of relationship. In fact of course it is more complicated than this, there being two sets of parents involved in each marriage. It is not therefore a case of balancing the parental relationship against the conjugal but of balancing the conjugal relationship against two sets of parental relationships since in a bilateral system each are of equal importance.

We are dealing with three *marriages*. The pattern of relations which are possible may be related to the types of marital relationship of the parents. Where the significant parent from the child's point of view is the mother the key relationships will be

hu.mo.—hu.—wi.—wi.mo. Mother dominant

Where the significant parent is the father the pattern will be

hu.fa.—hu.—wi.—wi.fa. Father dominant

Where the nuclear family exhibits a segregated sex role pattern

hu.fa.—hu.—wi.—wi.mo. Segregated

Where the significant parent is of the opposite sex

hu.mo.—hu.—wi.—wi.fa. Œdipal

There is one logical possibility left (apart of course from the various permutations involved in intermarriage). This is the joint type:

hu.fa. and mo.—hu.—wi.—wi.fa. and mo. Joint.

Now it is all very well to elaborate the logical possibilities. The question is what do we mean by the *key* relationship or the *significant* parent? Since we are involved in discussing the autonomy of the child's nuclear family we are concerned with evaluating relationships in terms of the way in which they affect the solidarity of the marital ties. This as we have noticed depends both on normative concensus between the parties and on exchange between them. We noted in the previous chapter that the interdependence of the spouses will be reduced by the existence of other exchange relationships between them and persons outside the nuclear family. In that chapter we stressed the effect of such relationships in affecting the power of the spouses. Here our purpose is to point to the consequences of such relationships in determining which parent is of importance to the married child. When in the post-parental phase of the parents and in the early phases of their children's cycle, there is a flow of domestic services to the children, it is obvious that relations between women are going to be of great importance. Hence we find authors of the Bethnal Green studies[11] writing that the 'the great triangle of adult life is Mum-wife-husband'. Rosser and Harris dealing with a much more varied sample in Swansea[12] stress 'the four cornered relationship of hu.mo.—hu.—wi.—wi.mo. Bell[13] studying a more extreme section of the middle class in Swansea, while refraining from identifying any set of key relationships stresses the importance of the fa.—so. and da.hu—wi.fa. relationships.

The reasons for these discrepancies is clear. Both Young and Willmott and Rosser and Harris see the family system as composed of *mothers and children*. Because of the exchange of domestic services in Bethnal Green, Young and Willmott stress the *mother-daughter* tie. Because of the flow of male-mediated financial aid among the middle class, Bell stresses the ties *between males*. Rosser and Harris though stressing the ties between women nevertheless include the son-mother tie, thus asserting that the Swansea family is typically of the mother dominant type. The authors of the Swansea study therefore imply that the pattern of life within the family leads to the establishment of a strong bond between mother and children which is carried over into interfamily relations even where not reinforced by an exchange of services. They go on to stress the problems created by the necessity to maintain a balance between the two sides of the family, and point out that neolocal residence ('not too near') has the effect of enabling the spouses to maintain this balance.

We need to distinguish very clearly, therefore, two distinct ways in which relationships can be 'significant': first, in terms of exchange of services; secondly, in terms of the sentiments of the actors deriving from their experiences in the nuclear family of origin. The internal structure of the nuclear family which we discussed in the last chapter will therefore partly determine the structure of post-parental

[11] Young, M. and Willmott, P., *Family and Kinship in East London*, London, Routledge, 1957, p. 46.

[12] Rosser, C. and Harris, C., *The Family and Social Change*, London, Routledge, 1965, p. 238.

[13] Bell, C., 'Mobility and the Middle Class Extended Family', *Sociology*, 2, 1968, p. 182.

relationships. We need therefore to look at the content of marital roles from the point of view of the effect that it has on the children as well as to relate it to the type of relationships the spouses have with parents. As far as the present author is aware, this has never been attempted in an empirical study, the effect of intergenerational relations on the marriage being considered, and not the effect of the marriage on intergenerational relations.

If we look at the mother-in-law myth a little more closely we recognize that it is always the wife's mother who is most frequently referred to and not the husband's. There would appear to be a cultural presupposition that the husband will be dragged into the ambit of his wife's family rather than drag his wife into his own. This appears to be a frequent pattern. The young couple most often share accomodation with the wife's parents.[14] Where husband and wife come from different localities they tend to live nearer the wife's than the husband's parents. Now this cannot be explained by, and must not be confused with, the importance of the exchange of services between women as opposed to men. Hu.mo. and so.wi. can exchange services just as easily as mo. and da.

To seek an explanation of this pattern we have to return once again to the role sequence of the mother. The loss of the children entails the relative deprivation of authority on the part of the mother and the loss of a large part of her domestic occupation. Co-residence with a married daughter preserves to the mother a domestic occupation and prevents a loss of authority. Given that the daughter needs support in her domestic role, and given the fact that she is likely to be a stranger to *her* mother-in-law, it is therefore highly likely that the husband will end up seeing a good deal of *his* mother-in-law, either through co-residence or through residence in the same locality. The explanation involves therefore *both* the role sequence of the mother *and* the stress on the exchange of domestic services between families. These together combine to produce the stress on the importance of uxori-lateral as opposed to viri-lateral ties.[15]

It has been argued that this stress on uxori-laterality both is, and must be, characteristic of industrial society. Thus Sweetzer has written that 'intergenerational solidarity follows the line of male succession in instrumental tasks; when the latter disappears, matri-lateral solidarity between generations becomes the rule'.[16] In other

[14] See Sweetzer, D. A., 'Asymmetry in Intergenerational Family Relationships', *Social Forces* 41, 1962–1963, p. 347.

[15] That is to say, ties traced through the wife rather than through the husband.

[16] Sweetzer, D. A., 'The Effect of Industrialisation in Intergenerational Solidarity', *Rur. Soc.* 31, 1966, p. 169.

words, because the family is no longer an economic group, the activities of a son are unaffected by the father. The father cannot offer a job or property to the son. At the same time father and son never act together in the way that mother and daughter do. In consequence the tie between father and son is not based on sentiment deriving from shared activities within the elementary family, nor reinforced by the exchange of services. This leaves us with only two parent-child ties undamaged and for reasons stated above the mo.-da. tie will be favoured as against the hu.mo.—so.wi. relationship.

In their study of the middle class London Borough of Woodford, Willmott and Young found a similar tendency towards uxori-locality and say that the mother-daughter tie, though less strong than in working class Bethnal Green, was still stressed. They too argue that the stressing of the mother-daughter tie is a universal phenomenon in industrial society.[17]

As we have seen these arguments are based on both the structure of the nuclear family and on the nature of the exchange of services between parents and adult children. As regards the nuclear family it is beyond dispute that in a conjugal family system in an industrial society the only joint activities that are necessarily undertaken by members of different generations are domestic and recreational. This must entail that only the women at any time share the performance of their main adult roles.

With regards to the exchange of services it does not follow that because son and father do not share instrumental activities in the economic sphere that therefore males *cannot* exchange services. What does follow is that such services as financial help and advice which fathers can and do provide do not require proximity. *Of course* one would expect *co-residence* to be weighted in favour of the wife's parents. Similarly it is no surprise to learn that in Woodford it is the married daughter that cares for her parents. We may accept the weighting of the balance between the two sides of the family in favour of the wife's parents, *with regard to domestic services.* Domestic services require proximity. If husband and wife come from different areas they will naturally be drawn into the wife's family circle. This does not mean that the tie between sons and their parents is not equally important. Given that sons are likely to be separated from their parents, we have to examine the extent to which services *not* dependent on proximity are maintained.

[17] Willmott, P. and Young, M., *Family and Class in a London suburb*, London, Routledge, 1960, p. 127.

We would expect that the higher the economic level the less was the need for the exchange of domestic services, and that the greater was the ability of fathers to aid their sons. It is simply not possible to assert that throughout industrial society there is a stress on ties through the wife rather than through the husband until we have more studies which investigate the exchange of services other than those of a domestic nature. What little evidence we have with regard to Britain suggests that ties between fathers and sons are of importance in the higher economic categories. All the American material stresses the extent of the provision of services which do not require proximity, but does not distinguish the sex of the child to whom it is provided.

It would be mistaken to suppose that these considerations show Sweetzer to be wrong. Sweetzer is explicit that any regularities we perceive are the outcome of many factors, and that there is considerable variation between families and different areas of society. Broadly speaking we may accept that the nuclear form, in which domestic activities predominate, leads to greater intergenerational solidarity between women both through the participation in shared activities and through an exchange of services.

PARENTAL AID TO MARRIED CHILDREN

Perhaps the most fascinating thing about the American material is that it elaborates the way in which aid from parents may be seen as being reconciled with norms stressing the autonomy of the nuclear families of the children. Sussman's early article on this topic is of particular interest.[18] Concern with not seeming to usurp the responsibilities of the husband is a recurrent theme of Sussman's parental respondents. It is 'not right' to give money to married children 'all the time'. Anyhow 'they wouldn't accept it'. The children will only accept help to complete a project once they had started it themselves and had got into difficulties. Since however they would not ask for help the parents had 'to work through their *daughters* to get the inside information'.

'I found out from my daughter that he (da.hu.) became quite upset over my offer to pay the bill (for hospital expenses in connection with da.'s confinement). He and Mary had planned for this baby, down to every conceivable cost, and here I blundered (in) trying to

[18] Sussman, M., 'The Help Pattern in the Middle Class Family', *Amer. Sociol. Rev.* 18, 1953, pp. 22–28.

take a father's privilege and responsibility. Later on there was... only appreciation when I offered to buy a carriage for the grandchild.'

'(My husband) said to me "now that we have spent $50,000 on our children's education let's leave them alone; we have done our part now it's up to them" I never took him seriously... we have more money than we can use and they now need our help...'

These quotations are of great interest. (It is to be deplored that so few American articles present and analyze material of this kind.) First, not only do they show how both sides retain norms concerning nuclear family autonomy but they illustrate the way in which it is thought to be necessary to preserve the autonomy of the husband, and his financial independence of kin. There could be no better illustration of the structural isolation of the nuclear family.

Secondly, these quotations show how adherence to these norms may favour the mother-daughter tie as against that between father and son. Mother-daughter aid does not interfere with the independence of the daughter, since financial provision is not one of the components of her marital role. She therefore can be relatively frank with her mother about financial difficulties. The husband cannot be frank with his father without appearing to imply that he is not really independent of his father economically. Given that parents cannot give indiscriminate aid to children and that the aid has to be specific or in kind, then the flow of aid between parents and children is dependent on the provision of gifts that are needed. This requires information as to current difficulties and wants and this cannot flow between the husband and a parent. Hence it must flow between a wife and a parent. Since the wife is likely to have a closer relationship with her own parents than her husband's, it will therefore flow between wife and wife's parents.

The flow of financial aid cannot however be considered in isolation from other types of aid. Domestic help it would appear is acceptable in crisis situations—illness, childbirth, moving house—and is not regarded as reflectiving adversely on the daughter's ability to perform her marital role properly. A gift of household equipment may be conceptualized as domestic aid or financial aid according to context and such ambiguities open the way for the tactful improvement by the parents of the living standards of—in particular—their married daughters.

It is of course true that even in America all families do not follow the nuclear pattern. That is to say the families of the children are not conceptualized as independent entities, and the question of aid undermining that independence does not therefore arise. The overlap of elementary families and the consequent ambiguity of the concept in everyday speech makes possible the simultaneous holding of norms of independence and the acceptance of aid. Where the son follows a father's occupation, help in getting the son started is usually accepted. This help doesn't suddenly become illegitimate the moment the son gets married. Where the son enters the father's business his very salary is a type of parental aid, or could be so seen. If it is tolerated this is because the autonomy of the nuclear family is interpreted in terms of the autonomy of the nuclear family *household* rather than the severance of ties of dependency with the elementary family of origin. The son therefore belongs to two separate but overlapping groups: the male members of his elementary family with whom he shares economic activities, and the members of his nuclear family household which is segregated from the households of other kin. Provided the authority of the father *at work* does not interfere with his son's authority *in the household* no problem arises.

As Kerckhoff[19] has rightly pointed out, the isolation of the nuclear family refers to a lack of any normative prescription governing obligations between overlapping nuclear families rather than their prohibition. Parental aid to married children is 'non-norm' rather than 'counter-norm' behaviour. You don't *have* to do it but you don't have *not* to do it either. The norm of nuclear family independence is really a norm of the independent performance of adult roles. Provided therefore that aid does not question the ability of the young spouses adequately to perform their roles or create obligations which they do not wish to fulfil, it is perfectly acceptable. Bell reports an incident which illustrates this point very well.[20]

'I wanted to buy into a practice as a partner. But I wanted a couple of hundred more than I had. I went to the local with my father-in-law (his father is dead) and told him that I was considering changing my job like I said. I didn't ask but to tell the truth I hoped . . . Eventually he gave it me, called it a loan but said I needn't pay it back. But I am, though, so I don't feel obligated to him.'

To ask would imply dependence on the father-in-law and hence his inability to perform in the economic sphere without help. How-

[19] Kerckhoff, A. C., 'Nuclear and Extended Family Relationships: a Normative and Behavioural Analysis', in Shanas, E. and Streib, G. F. (Eds.), *Social Structure and the Family*, London, Prentice-Hall, 1965, p. 93.

[20] Bell, C., 'Mobility and the Middle Class Extended Family', *Sociol.*, 2, 1968, p. 173.

ever the question of his ability *to support a family* does not arise. His father-in-law calls it a loan—thus recognizing that a gift is not acceptable. The son-in-law accepts but insists on repayment fearing an unknown obligation. The concept of the autonomy and independence of *families* does not enter the minds of the actors.

There are cases however where the membership of a wider family group explicitly does have this implication. To quote one of Sussman's cases again: 'My husband feels that they ought to have a good start and not struggle as we had to. He said to me recently, "How would it look for a sales promotion manager of . . . Company to have his children living in the worst section of town or going around like wrecks?" '

This comment recalls our discussion of the family and social stratification in Chapter 5. This remark depends on the families living in the same town, but it may serve to recall that irrespective of residence the nuclear family shares its resources, whether material or symbolic. The adult elementary family is made up of the same individuals. These relationships cannot be severed or transformed simply by marriage of the children. There is therefore a tendency for the patterns of nuclear family life to persist after the marriage of the children. The resources shared will of course differ between families and between strata. Most of the illustrations in this section have been taken from the middle class, because of the relative stress on working class families in the British literature and the concern with domestic services.

Whatever the nature of the services it is necessary to recognize that to speak of norms of nuclear family independence is only a convenient way of referring to norms constituting family roles which regulate family relationships. Once it is clearly recognized that we can only explain behaviour in terms of relationships—however helpful it is to break them down further into roles—a lot of the confusion created by talking of the coexistence of parental aid to married children with the norms of nuclear family independence disappear. The crucial norms concern the independent performance of marital roles. Independence refers to independence of parental authority and control. What constitutes independence will depend on the nature of the parent-child relationships which pre-existed the marriage which founded the new nuclear family. Once again we are dealing with a sequence of roles through which, not the parents but, in this case, the married children pass. The meaning of behaviour of the actors at any given time will be determined by its position in the sequence and its relation to other elements in the total relationship of which it forms a part.

AID TO ELDERLY PARENTS

The recognition that we can only understand role performance in relation to the actor's position in a role sequence, prepares the way for an understanding of the position of elderly parents *vis à vis* their married children. Studies of this phase of the family cycle have shown the widespread preference of elderly people for what Rosenmayr and Köckeis[21] have called 'intimacy at a distance', that is to say, that old people in Western industrial societies prefer to live near but not too near their children. So far as the present author is aware this has not led anyone to talk about norms of denuded elementary family independence and this of course is not the point. To be on the receiving end of help in old age would amount to an abrupt reversal of the parental role which as we have seen is carried over, as far as provision of help is concerned, into the post-parental phase of the parents' life cycle. It is therefore important that the parent appears to remain independent of the child, even though the child may have contracted obligations to support the parent in old age through the receipt of help from the parent at an earlier stage.

This transition from provider to recipient of help, which is based on poorer economic circumstances related to retirement and upon changing health, would seem to constitute a major reversal of parental role and to be fraught with difficulty.[22] In fact this is by no means always the case. In the first place, retirement does not mean the sudden economic dependency upon children. Middle class parents are normally able to make provision for their old age. In many countries social security benefits prevent *total* dependence. Secondly, where extended families characterized by an exchange of domestic services exist, and especially where co-residence with married children is common, the extent to which the change from provider to recipient is perceived as such may be small. The contribution of the older woman in terms of household services is slowly reduced as her health fails but the pattern of co-operative domestic activity remains. Where there are many daughters who co-operate together with 'Mum', the extent of her dependency may not be explicitly recognized by any of the parties. Thirdly where the period of parental dependency overlaps with the period of need for domestic support on the part of the children, there will be an exchange of services

[21] Rosenmayr, L. and Köckeis, E., 'Propositions for a Sociological Theory of Ageing and the Family', *Int. Soc. Sci. Jour.* 15, 1963, p. 418.

[22] See Glasser, P. H. and L. N., 'Role Reversal and conflict between aged parents and their children', *Marr. and Fam.* 24, 1962, p. 46.

between mother and daughters which is consistent with their equality and may even be interpreted by the old person as constituting a retention of her role as provider. Once again ambiguity can ease a situation which is potentially conflict laden. Whereas the daughter sees her visits as 'keeping an eye on Mum', Mum may see the visits as the daughter turning to her for help and advice. Where, however, the shape of the cycle is such that the parents' period of dependency occurs *after* the period of greatest need on the part of the child, the dependent parent may be forced into the unequivocal position of recipient, less because she cannot *provide* services than because the children do not *require* them.

The transition from provider to recipient is therefore potentially fraught with difficulty. These tensions can be accommodated however under certain circumstances. The preference for 'intimacy at a distance' may be seen to be a means whereby such tensions are accommodated. Similarly the fact that even in old age there is relatively little financial aid from parents to children is a further indication, not of the children's unwillingness to support their parents, but of the latter's unwillingness to accept help.

The type of 'aid' that elderly parents appear to want from their children most of all is usually reported as 'affection'.[23] They prize visits from children, want to live near to make such visits possible and so on. Most studies which can be drawn on, unfortunately do not distinguish the exact phase of the family cycle reached by their aged respondents and the results of studies of the old are not always easy to interpret from the point of view of the student of the family. We do not know what proportion of those expressing a wish to be near children are in fact wanting to be near children so that they can participate in the early phases of the rearing of the grandchildren, what proportion wish for proximity to ensure help for themselves, whether the affection that they want is compounded of *respect* or a need to be useful. Is it perhaps gratitude and appreciation rather than simply affection that they seek?

What the studies of the old do however show beyond doubt is that old people with children are not isolated from them, that a vast majority see them frequently, and that, in spite of the alleged high degree of mobility of American society which is supposed to render the clustering of kin impossible, the differences in the degree of old people's proximity to children in America is not greatly different

[23] See for example Streib, G. F., 'Family Patterns in Retirement' in Sussman, M., *Source Book in Marriage and the Family*, Boston, Houghton Mifflin, 1963, p. 410. and Streib, G. F., 'Intergenerational Relations: Perspectives of the Two Generations on the Older Parent', *Jour. Marr. and Fam.* 27, 1965, p. 469.

from that of other supposedly more stable European countries.[24] If we are to understand the relationships between parents and children it is vital to know how the observed proximity comes about. Where there is proximity because the child has not yet moved away, the parent-child relationship is very different from cases in which the child has postponed mobility or actually returned to care for an elderly parent. The observed proximity is in fact the result of a large number of factors: the nature of norms determining duties of children to parents, the willingness of children to disregard such norms, the degree of mobility required by the economic system, and the shape of the family cycle, the number of children available, and their age, sex and marital state. Before we can evaluate such findings from a theoretical viewpoint we need to investigate in far more detail than has been so far possible the details of the process whereby care and proximity come about, and estimate the extent to which each of the above factors are operative. In spite of the large amount of work which has been done on the situation of the old in Western society, the theoretical issues involved in the study of the dependency period of the post-parental phase in the older three generational or four generational family is only just beginning to be made clear.

[24] See Shanas and Townsend, *op. cit.*

8

Conclusion

MANY of the statements made in this book about the family may, taken singly, appear to the reader obvious or even banal. As we proceeded, however, it became increasingly necessary to refer back to previous statements, either implicitly or explicitly. The 'position of women' had to be discussed before we could proceed to the consideration of the effects of social mobility on the family; this itself could not be understood without reference to the effect of industrialization on female employment, and so on. To speak of the actions of individuals as family members, as of the actions of members of other types of group, involves the elaboration of the relations between a large number of apparently simple statements constituting a total set of statements whose interrelationships are extremely complex. These statements have served to relate explicitly the structure of the family to that society in which it is set. Thus it is that our discussion has taken us out of the 'domestic domain', not because family relationships in Western society have, individually, political or economic significance in the society as a whole, but because family and other types of activities vitally affect each other.

There is another sense in which the study of the family is concerned with very much more than merely domestic matters. The same intellectual problems and difficulties which have been encountered in the study of the family are also encountered in the study of any social group, and so we have frequently found ourselves struggling with seminal theoretical issues. Moreover the 'big' issues of sociology, of power and authority and individual freedom, of conflict and consensus are found within the familial as within all other kinds of social group; and the conceptual tools we have used in the discussion have been those which have been devised for the study of social relationships as a whole.

This book has been only an introduction to the family. We have not been able to examine various types of family 'breakdown' such as divorce, nor to consider the family in relation to many other types of social institution with which it comes into contact—with the social services, political and religious institutions and so on. Nor has there been space to examine explicitly the range and recognition of kinship in Western society and its significance. We have however made a beginning, and it is to be hoped that the reader by means of this introduction may have been stimulated to read more widely in a field which is not only of great fascination but of considerable social importance.

FURTHER READING

Bell, N. W. & Vogel, E. F., *The Family*. Free Press, Revised Edition, 1969.
Winch, R. F., McGinnis, R. & Barringer, H. R., *Selected Studies in Marriage and the Family*. Holt Rinehard, Second Edition, 1962.
Blood, R. & Wolfe, D. M., *Husbands and Wives*. Free Press, 1960.
Christensen, H. T., *Handbook on Marriage and the Family*. Rand MacNally, 1964.
Farber, B., *Kinship and Family Organization*. Wiley, 1966.

The following studies of local communities in Britain contain useful information concerning the family.

Littlejohn, J., *Westrigg*. Routledge, 1964.
Williams, W. M., *A West Country Village: Ashworthy*. Routledge, 1963.
Dennis, N., Henriques, F. & Slaughter, C., *Coal is our Life*. Eyre & Spottiswoode, 1957.
Stacey, M., *Tradition and Change*. Oxford University Press, 1960.
Willmott, P. & Young, M., *Family and Class in a London Suburb*. Routledge, 1963.
Mogey, J., *Family and Neighbourhood*. Oxford University Press, 1956.
Willmott, P., *The Evolution of a Community*. Routledge, 1963.
Rosser, C. & Harris, C. C., *The Family and Social Change*, Routledge, 1965.
Young, M. & Willmott, P., *Family and Kinship in East London*. Routledge, 1957.
Morris, P., *Widows and their Families*. Routledge, 1958.
Townsend, P., *The Family Life of Old People*. Routledge, 1957.
Jackson, P. & Marsden, D., *Education and the Working Class*. Routledge, 1962.
Kerr, M., *The People of Ship Street*. Routledge, 1958.

The reader's attention is drawn to the following British studies published after the completion of the book.

Firth, R. *et al.*, *Families and their Relatives*. Routledge, 1969.
Goody, J., *Comparative Studies in Kinship*. Routledge.

And the following forthcoming volume:
Harris, C. C. (Ed.), *Readings in Urban Kinship*. Pergamon.

INDEX OF AUTHORS

INDEX OF SUBJECTS

(References to the definition of terms are indicated by the letter 'd'.)